Getting Started With RM/COBOL-85

Second Edition

Nancy Stern
Hofstra University

James Janossy
DePaul University

Robert A. Stern
Nassau Community College

D0082123

John Wiley & Sons, Inc.
New York/Chichester/Brisbane/Toronto/Singapore

This book is dedicated to the memory of
Grace Murray Hopper (1906-1992)

ab uno disce omnes

Recognizing the importance of preserving what has been
written, it is a policy of John Wiley & Sons, Inc. to have
books of enduring value published in the United States
printed on acid-free paper, and we exert our best efforts to
that end.

Copyright 1994 by John Wiley & Sons, Inc.

All rights reserved. Published simultaneously in Canada.

Reproduction or translation of any part of this work beyond
that permitted by Sections 107 and 108 of the 1976 United
States Copyright Act without permission of the copyright
owner is unlawful. Requests for permission or further
information should be addressed to the Permissions
Department, John Wiley & Sons.

ISBN 0-471-30672-X

Printed in the United States of America

10 9 8

Preface

The RM/COBOL-85 package you receive with this guide includes one of the easiest to use and most capable COBOL compilers made for IBM Personal Computers and compatible machines. RM/COBOL-85, manufactured by Liant Software Corporation of Framingham, Massachusetts, fully supports the ANS COBOL 1985 language standard. Included with the compiler and its runtime system is a program development package called RM/CO* (RM "Co-Star"), which you can use as a text editor and environment for creating programs, and compiling, debugging, and running them.

Liant Software has made available an educational version of RM/COBOL-85. Like most educational versions of software, this one has some limitations, which are discussed in detail in Chapter 1. This educational version of RM/COBOL-85 has a full-screen text editor, and a compiler and runtime system that you can use to learn how to program in COBOL. The educational version is available on a single 3-1/2 inch diskette, which is one of the two diskettes provided with *Getting Started With RM/COBOL-85*.

This guide helps you learn how to use RM/COBOL-85. We focus on the use of RM/CO* for text editing and the RM/COBOL-85 environment for compiling, running, and debugging programs. This guide is far more detailed than most educational software manuals. We provide step-by-step explanations of all concepts discussed along with illustrations and numerous examples.

This guide is not, however, designed to teach COBOL. Our objective here is to show you how to effectively use the RM/COBOL-85 system. We assume that you have a COBOL text for learning COBOL syntax and programming rules. For a proven, comprehensive introduction to COBOL programming, we recommend that you use *Structured COBOL Programming*, 8th edition, by Nancy Stern and Robert A. Stern, published by John Wiley & Sons, Inc. in 1994, as your main text.

You can obtain additional copies of this guide and the RM/COBOL-85 disk by contacting your local Wiley representative or by contacting Debra Riegart, John Wiley & Sons, 605 Third Avenue, New York, NY 10158. The telephone number is 1-800-CALL-WILE. This guide and the accompanying disks can be purchased separately or at a substantial discount if purchased with *Structured COBOL Programming*, 8th edition, by Nancy Stern and Robert A. Stern.

If you purchase the guide and disks along with the text you will have two books that were written to accompany each other. Moreover, one of the disks for *Getting Started With RM/COBOL-85* includes source code, input data, and output for many example programs from the main Stern and Stern text. The examples include programs with commonly made errors that you can use to practice debugging. A READ.ME file on the diskette provides details on how to use these examples with RM/COBOL-85.

You can use any IBM Personal Computer or compatible for creating, compiling, and running RM/COBOL-85 programs, from the slowest original 4.77 Mhz IBM PC to the most modern IBM-compatible computer system. Even the slowest personal computer will execute the RM/COBOL-85 compiler and your compiled programs in a thoroughly acceptable way. RM/COBOL-85 requires only that you use DOS version 2.1 or higher (version 3 and higher recommended) and have a computer system with at least 512K bytes of memory. By today's standards, these are minimal requirements! While you can use a diskette-only PC, a hard disk system is recommended. RM/COBOL-85 will consume less than one megabyte of your hard disk space.

How This Guide Is Constructed

The guide is written in a clear manner using the pedagogic techniques common to our other texts. Screen displays are provided to help you identify what should happen when you enter various commands. Self-tests, with solutions, are included at selected checkpoints to assist you in assessing your understanding of the material.

In **Chapter 1**, we begin with an introduction to the RM/COBOL-85 educational compiler. In **Chapter 2,** we cover procedures for installing the compiler, RM/CO*, and the run-time system. In **Chapter 3**, you'll learn how to use RM/CO* to edit programs, and how to receive on-line help, which is included in RM/CO*. Since Chapter 3 gets you up and running with a sample program that reads data from a file, you'll quickly see how to code the SELECT statement using the ORGANIZATION IS LINE SEQUENTIAL clause, which is required to read most files created with a text editor. Chapter 3 also covers advanced text editing features of RM/CO*, how to compile programs, and how to debug programs.

In **Chapter 4,** we discuss preparing, compiling, and running COBOL programs outside of the RM/CO* environment. Instead of using RM/CO*, you may prefer to use your favorite word processor to prepare COBOL program source code, and DOS commands to execute the RM/COBOL-85 compiler. This is easy to do, since the source code to RM/COBOL-85 need only be standard ASCII files ("DOS" files). Step-by-step debugging is also accessible with direct use of the compiler, and we'll show you how to do it in Chapter 4.

We have provided coverage of disk file handling with RM/COBOL-85 in **Chapter 5.** In this chapter we'll show you more about coding the SELECT statement for sequential, relative, and indexed files and print output. In **Chapter 6** we show you how to use ACCEPT and DISPLAY for interactive programming, and how to define screens, including the use of color.

In **Appendix A,** we have placed material about microcomputer hardware and software concepts, for readers with no prior experience using microcomputers. This appendix covers the PC keyboard, monitor, printer, disk drives, and some elements of DOS usage.

RM/COBOL-85 provides certain extensions to the ANS COBOL 1985 language standards. We cover these concisely in **Appendix B** in case you want to explore them. RM/COBOL-85 also provides several compiler and runtime options, which you can use to request enhancements in your compile listing and program execution. These are summarized and several are demonstrated in **Appendix C.**

You can access the interactive debugger provided with RM/COBOL-85 either through RM/CO* or via DOS directly when you execute a program. Since the debugger commands are the same regardless of how you execute the program, we have grouped documentation about them in **Appendix D**. Manipulation of a program during debugging has become easier with this second edition of *Getting Started With RM/COBOL-85* because you can access fields by data name alone. (In the previous edition, we showed access to data fields by address and data type, a more complicated process.)

Programming in any environment requires having reference materials to look up error codes and messages. **Appendix E** consolidates reference materials for your convenience, including error codes and messages produced by the RM/COBOL-85 compiler, its runtime environment, file status and input/output errors, and sort-merge messages.

Finally, our experience with RM/COBOL-85 over the last few years has allowed us to recognize certain areas in which newcomers are most likely to encounter problems. We have grouped hints about commonly encountered problems in **Appendix F,** at the back of this guide. If you encounter an unusual problem, check Appendix F first.

Questions and Suggestions

If you have any questions about the material in this guide or the programs provided as examples, or would like to make any suggestions, please direct them to us at:

Dr. Nancy Stern
BCIS Dept.
Hofstra University
Hempstead, NY 11550

We can also be reached via Internet at "acsnnn@vaxb.hofstra.edu" and our CompuServe address is 76505,1222.

We would like to express our appreciation to James Janossy of DePaul University (janossy@cs.depaul.edu), who completely revised the first edition of this guide, supplied several new programs, and set the copy for it using Ami Pro and a LaserJet III. Jim has published several books with Wiley that complement our COBOL texts, such as *Practical MVS JCL Examples* (1993), *Advanced MVS/ESA JCL Examples* (1994), *VS COBOL II Highlights and Techniques* (1992), and *VAX COBOL On-Line* (1992). Several people at Liant Software helped in various ways: Jack Funchion and Janet Dunford reviewed the manuscript for the first edition, James Cooper and Marilyn Meyer assisted in the preparation of the program examples, Thomas H. Morrison and Jerry Rowley provided technical assistance, and Barbara Moyer helped in securing updated copies of RM/COBOL-85 software. We would also like to thank Beth Lang Golub and Andrea Bryant, editors at Wiley, for their assistance and support.

Related Publications

RM/COBOL-85 is a product of Liant Software Corporation, 8911 Capital of Texas Highway North, Suite 4300, Austin, Texas 78759, (800) 762-6265. RM/COBOL-85 is available for minicomputers and microcomputer networks as well as single-user microcomputers, and runs under UNIX, OS/2, Windows/NT, and Novell NetWare in addition to DOS and other operating systems. Program source code is portable across all supported machine platforms.

Getting Started With RM/COBOL-85 was developed using information in several manuals supplied by Liant Software Corporation. While this guide is as complete as possible given its purpose as an introduction for students to RM/COBOL-85 and RM/CO*, you may find it useful to consult the original manuals once you become an advanced COBOL programmer. Your school's labs might be able to provide you with access to these original manuals for reference purposes:

RM/COBOL-85 Language Reference Manual, Version 5.2, part number 301535.

RM/COBOL-85 User's Guide, Version 5.2, for DOS, OS/2, and NetWare, part number 301556.

RM/CO, Version 1.0 for DOS,* part number 300632.

Contents

5   File Input and Output: The SELECT Statement   89

6   ACCEPT and DISPLAY for Interactive Processing   99

Appendixes

Chapter 1

An Introduction to RM/COBOL-85 for Microcomputers

1.1 Introduction to the Educational Version of RM/COBOL-85

T his book focuses on Liant Software's COBOL, version 5.24, which is called RM/COBOL-85 and which is designed for PC use (we use the term **PC, microcomputer,** and **micro** interchangeably in this guide). The software for an educational version of this software is included with this book on a 3-1/2 inch diskette. The RM/COBOL-85 software encompasses a program development package called RM/CO* (pronounced RM/CO-STAR) with text editor, a compiler, and a runtime system for running compiled programs. The compiler and runtime system are fully compatible with the ANS COBOL 1985 language standard, and RM/COBOL-85 is as powerful as mainframe versions of COBOL.

We also provide, on a second diskette, sample programs that include solutions along with data for Programming Assignment 1 in each chapter of the Stern and Stern *Structured COBOL Programming*, 8th edition text, published by John Wiley & Sons in 1994. These examples also include programs that contain errors to give you practice in debugging. We assume that you have already learned basic COBOL syntax, using either the Stern and Stern text or some other COBOL text.

1.2 Limitations of This Educational Version

Educational versions of software are basically the same as the standard or full versions except that they have some limitations designed to render them impractical to use in a business environment. These limitations do not detract from the usefulness of the software for students. The main advantage of an educational version of software is that it is usually available at a substantial discount as compared to the full version.

Educational versions of software, as with many full versions, may be copy-protected, which means that attempts to copy the program files will fail. Our RM/COBOL-85 disks are *not* copy-protected. But note that you are free to make only as many copies as you need *for your own personal use* (you do not have the right to copy the software for use by others).

The following limitations exist in the educational version of RM/COBOL-85:

- A program cannot exceed 1000 lines of code.

- Program execution always begins in "debugging" mode. This enables you to step through a program a line at a time or to resume execution in the normal way (see Chapter 3). To turn off debugging mode enter an "e" when you execute the program.

- You may use only one level of a CALL, that is, you can CALL a subprogram, but a subprogram cannot CALL another subprogram. Multiple level calls will produce runtime errors. The full commercial version of RM/COBOL-85 permits nested CALLs.

- The program source code listings produced by the compiler are set for 132-character printouts only. This means that if you have an 80-character printer many lines on your printouts may "wrap around" to the next line. Since your actual COBOL coding uses a maximum of 80 characters per line, this limitation should not significantly affect your ability to read your source code listings. For printed output, we recommend that you use a printer or print mode capable of printing more than 80 characters per line, such as the "compressed" print mode available on many dot matrix and laser printers. Alternatively, you should design your printed output so that it does not exceed 80 print characters per line to avoid line wraparound.

- A program can define a maximum of four files.

- Sequential and relative files are restricted to 1000 records per file with a maximum length of 132 characters per record.

- Indexed files are restricted to 100 records per file with a maximum length of 132 characters per record.

- Indexed files are restricted to a maximum of a primary key and one alternate key.

- RM/COBOL-85 does not support Report Writer.

- While the SORT and MERGE verb are supported, you may need to specify the number of bytes that RM/COBOL-85 should use for work space. You need to include the additional parameter T=*integer* with the compile command where *integer* specifies the number of bytes needed for the sort, such as T=20000. The educational version of RM/COBOL-85 uses a default of 16,000 bytes, which is sufficient, for example, to sort or merge 160 records of 100 bytes length each.

- Some utilities available with the full RM/COBOL-85 package cannot be used with the educational version. These include advanced debugging and analysis utilities generally of little interest to beginning students.

If you compile a program using the educational version of the RM/COBOL-85 compiler, you can only run the program using the educational runtime environment. Compiling a program using the full package and then running it using the educational runtime environment, or vice versa, will cause an error. Also, the educational version of RM/CO* can be used only with the educational version of the compiler.

These limitations are likely to make the educational version unacceptable to commercial programmers who often must operate on a large number of records and files. But the limitations make it possible for us to distribute the educational version at a small fraction of the cost of the full commercial version of the compiler, and they protect Liant Software from "giving away" a product useful for commercial work.

1.3   Why a Separate RM/COBOL-85 Guide?

The RM/COBOL-85 compiler conforms to the ANS COBOL 85 standard, which makes it one of the most up-to-date compilers available and totally compatible with compilers designed for mainframe use. Why, then, do we include an entirely separate guide for this version of the COBOL language? Following are some of the reasons we provide a separate guide to accompany the software.

1.4   Microcomputer and Mainframe Applications Differ

The ways that microcomputers are used for business applications differ from the ways in which mainframes are used. This guide focuses on microcomputer concepts that make PCs best suited for certain types of COBOL applications.

Hardware differences between mainframes and microcomputers or PCs are really differences of degree. Mainframes are technologically similar to microcomputers, but they are larger, process data faster, are more costly, and are designed to be shared by multiple users. A microcomputer tends to be a single-user, stand-alone desktop device that is much cheaper and smaller than a mainframe. Some high-end microcomputers, however, approach the capabilities of minicomputers and mainframes.

Because mainframes are often shared by many users, they are more appropriate for batch processing applications in which large volumes of data are processed all at once. A mainframe is often used to report from or update a file or database using transactions accumulated over a period of time. Batch runs are performed on a regularly scheduled basis, such as daily or weekly. Producing payroll checks, updating a payment file, and producing an accounts receivable report are applications typically run on mainframes in batch mode. Such applications minimize the need for an interface between user and computer. Most COBOL texts focus on batch processing operations.

While microcomputers can also process data in batch mode, many more microcomputer applications tend to be interactive, with users communicating with the computer more often and more directly. A microcomputer is less often used for batch processing and more often used for immediate, interactive, on-line processing where users enter data or transactions using a keyboard. Suppose a company stores an inventory file on a disk. The inventory file could be updated as each order is processed rather than on a regularly scheduled basis. This would be an on-line, interactive application requiring the update program and the inventory file to be available at all times. Using one or more microcomputers in a network to process inventory data as it is transacted, rather than in batches, would be the most up-to-date method of business information processing.

1.5   Methods of Entering Programs Differ between Microcomputers and Mainframes

The methods used for communicating with a computer are determined by the operating system and the support or utility programs available with the computer. Communicating with a mainframe is often different from communicating with a microcomputer. In this guide, we discuss how to use the RM/COBOL-85 compiler with the DOS operating system, and we discuss some features of microcomputers that facilitate the processing of COBOL programs.

In this guide we teach you to use RM/COBOL-85's full screen text editor, which is part of the RM/CO* program development environment. You may use any text editor or word processor to enter an RM/COBOL-85 program, but since Liant Software provides one, we discuss it in detail. Our version of RM/COBOL-85 is relatively unique in its inclusion of this powerful, menu-driven text editor. You can use the text editor to enter or view data files as well as programs.

1.6   RM/COBOL-85 Is Ideally Suited to PC Applications

Liant Software's RM/COBOL-85 includes COBOL enhancements that make it ideal for PC applications. For example, it supports screen display features such as reverse video and color that make interactive processing more user-friendly. These involve the use of the ACCEPT and DISPLAY verbs, which are used extensively in the microcomputer environment. Chapter 6 provides complete examples of interactive use of RM/COBOL-85 adapted from another Wiley textbook, *VAX COBOL On-Line,* by James Janossy (John Wiley & Sons, Inc., 1992).

1.7   You Need to Know Some Microcomputer Concepts

We provide a brief discussion of microcomputer hardware components in Appendix A, for those of you with little or no familiarity with microcomputers. That appendix provides coverage of microcomputer hardware, including the keyboard, monitor, printer, disk drives, and some commands and features of the DOS operating system.

1.8   RM/COBOL-85 Has its Own Interactive Debugger

In the mainframe environment, students often find it difficult to identify errors when a program fails. Because of the batch nature of mainframes, interacting with the COBOL program being executed is difficult, and the only clue to an error is likely to be an obscure message or incorrect output. Students and programmers often need to include extra DISPLAY statements in the program to be able to see data values as the program executes.

An interactive debugger enables a programmer to step through the logic of a program as it is being run, line-by-line or paragraph-by-paragraph, and view the contents of selected data fields during debugging. We show you how to use the RM/COBOL-85 interactive debugger, a tool that makes program testing easier, in Appendix D.

1.9 RM/COBOL-85 Has Its Own Unique Error Messages

Every compiler and runtime environment has its own format for informational, warning, and error messages. IBM mainframes and DEC VAX minicomputers, for example, use widely differing error message formats and codes. RM/COBOL-85, too, has its own set of error messages and diagnostic information. We provide a concise set of error messages in Appendix C, so that you can quickly look up any error code or message produced by the RM/COBOL-85 compiler or runtime environment.

1.10 Incompatibility with Prior Versions

The first edition of this guide, published in 1991, was supplied with RM/COBOL-85 Version 4.10.05. The version with this second edition of the guide is Version 5.24.00. Enhancements exist in the syntax supported by the later version of the compiler, such as controls for color on computer screens, but all programs that compiled successfully under the earlier version should work with the later. You can't, however, mix RM/COBOL-85 software components between versions; for example, you can't compile with the newer compiler and run a program under the old runtime environment. If you already have the earlier version of RM/COBOL-85 installed on your computer, make sure you install the newer version in a different subdirectory, or completely replace your old RM/COBOL-85 software with the newer version. *In particular, make sure you replace the RMCOBOL.OVY overlay file when you install the new version as a replacement for the old, because the overlay files differ!* (The differences are internal, and not visible or apparent, but the old overlay file does not work with the new version of the compiler.)

1.11 How to Use This Guide

Structured COBOL Programming, 8th edition, by Nancy Stern and Robert A. Stern, published by John Wiley & Sons in 1994, covers the COBOL programming language in depth. We recommend that you use that book along with *Getting Started With RM/COBOL-85*, 2nd edition. You may, however, use any COBOL text along with this guide. The text you use will teach you the syntax rules of the COBOL language. *Getting Started With RM/COBOL-85*, 2nd edition, specifically teaches you how to use RM/COBOL-85 and all its features on a microcomputer. This guide is intended as a supplement to a COBOL programming text, not as a replacement for it.

Chapter 2

Installing RM/COBOL-85 On Your Microcomputer

2.1   Equipment You Need to Use RM/COBOL-85

ou can use the RM/COBOL-85 compiler with any microcomputer running DOS version 2.0 or later (version 3 and higher recommended), regardless of whether it uses the original 8088, 8086, 80286, 80386, 80486, or Pentium microprocessor. You will need a keyboard, monitor, and a 3-1/2 inch floppy disk drive to load the software. While a hard disk is not absolutely essential, you will find that it is tedious to use a two-diskette system without a hard disk. The RM/COBOL-85 software will require less than one megabyte of hard disk space. Your computer must have a minimum of 512,000 bytes of memory. In terms of modern equipment, the machine requirements of the RM/COBOL-85 are truly minimal.

You do not need Windows to run RM/COBOL-85 software, and Windows may interfere with RM/COBOL-85 if it is active. If you have Windows installed, you should not activate it when you are using RM/COBOL-85. That is, execute RM/COBOL-85 software directly from DOS rather than accessing it via Windows.

2.2   Diskettes Supplied with This Guide

Two diskettes are supplied with this guide. Diskette 1 is labeled "RM/COBOL-85 Educational Version" and contains the RM/CO* editor, the compiler, and the runtime environment, and several small demonstration programs. The instructions in this chapter explain how to install the software on diskette 1.

Diskette 2 is labeled "Example Programs" and contains programs from *Structured COBOL Programming*, 8th Edition by Nancy Stern and Robert A. Stern. For information on copying the programs on diskette 2 to your computer and accessing them, examine the READ.ME file on diskette 2.

2.3   Files on Diskette 1 (RM/COBOL-85 Educational Version)

The RM/COBOL-85 educational package includes a compiler, a runtime program, the RM/CO* program development text editor, and several COBOL programs. Diskette 1 contains these files:

File name	Approx. Size	Contents
RMCOBOL.EXE	160K	The RM/COBOL-85 compiler
RMCOBOL.OVY	95K	Additional logic for the compiler
RUNCOBOL.EXE	162K	The runtime system that interprets and runs the object file
RMCOSTAR.EXE	97K	Optional text editing and execution environment (RM/CO*)
RMCOSTAR.HLP	57K	A file of help messages for the RM/CO* text editor

File name	Approx. Size	Contents (continued)
FIRST1.CBL	1K	A simple program to test your installation
SAMPLE.CBL	3K	A program that reads records from the DATA4E file and creates a report to be printed (this program is from *Structured COBOL Programming,* 7th edition, by Nancy Stern and Robert A. Stern (John Wiley & Sons, Inc., 1994)
DATA4E.DAT	1K	Data read by the SAMPLE.CBL program
BUGGY1.CBL	2K	A program with syntax errors
COPYIT.CBL	3K	A program demonstrating file access *(*)*
WORKERS.DAT	1K	A data file read by the COPYIT program
ACCEPT1.CBL	1K	The first interactive program on Diskette 1
ACCEPT2.CBL	1K	An enhanced version of the ACCEPT1 program
ACCEPT3.CBL	2K	A final version of the ACCEPT1 program
CALC1.CBL	3K	Demonstration interactive program *(*)*
CALC3.CBL	6K	Enhanced interactive program *(*)*
CALC5.CBL	7K	Interactive program using a SCREEN section
PARTS.DAT	1K	Data to be loaded to an indexed file by the PARTLOAD program
PARTLOAD.CBL	5K	Program to load PARTS.DAT to indexed file PARTS.IXF
UPDATE1.CBL	11K	Program that interactively updates PARTS.IXF
RULER.CBL	1K	Column ruler for word processor use
BOX.CBL	1K	Template for a source code comment box
EJECT.DAT	1K	Page eject to clear your printer (copy to your printer to force ejection of last page of output)
R.EXE	38K	Line number renumbering utility *(*)*
TERMTORM.EXE	44K	Source code conversion program; VAX "terminal" format to RM/COBOL-85 *(*)*

*(*) These programs are provided for your convenience with the permission of the publisher. They are a part of materials supplied with **VAX COBOL On-Line** by James Janossy (John Wiley & Sons, Inc., 1992) and **Practical MVS JCL Examples** by James Janossy (John Wiley & Sons, Inc., 1993).*

2.4   Making a Backup Copy of the RM/COBOL-85 Diskette

Copy-protected software disks are difficult to work with because you are prevented from making backup copies. Your diskette containing the RM/COBOL-85 system is *not* copy protected, so you are able to make backup copies for your own use. Always begin by making working copies of all new software disks you acquire and storing the originals.   In this way, if your working copy becomes unusable, you can always recreate it.

If you have a hard disk, you will make your working copy of the RM/COBOL-85 diskette on the hard disk. If your computer system does not have a hard disk, see Section 2.7. We cover the hard disk environment first, because hard disk systems are now the most common.

2.5 Copying RM/COBOL-85 to Your Hard Disk

Computers with a hard disk drive can be started without a diskette because the DOS operating system is stored on the hard disk drive. The hard disk drive can also be used to permanently store the RM/COBOL-85 compiler, the runtime system, the RM/CO* text editor, and your programs. Once copied onto the hard disk, you will not need to use diskettes at all except if you want to put your personal files on them as a back up. Follow these steps to install RM/COBOL-85 on your hard disk:

1. Start the computer, respond to any prompts, and arrive at the DOS prompt, which is similar to C:>.

2. Make sure you are in the root directory by entering this at the DOS prompt:

    C:> cd\ <Enter>

3. Create a subdirectory named \RMCOB by entering the command:

    C:> md \rmcob <Enter>

4. Change to the \RMCOB subdirectory by entering the command:

    C:> cd \rmcob <Enter>

5. Place the RM/COBOL-85 diskette (Diskette 1) into your 3-1/2 inch floppy diskette drive. If you have a computer system with one diskette drive and hard disk, the diskette drive will most likely be named drive A. Copy all files on Diskette 1 to your \RMCOB subdirectory by entering the command:

    C:> copy a:*.* c:\rmcob <Enter>

You now have all the RM/COBOL-85 files in your \RMCOB subdirectory. We recommend you use the same subdirectory to store your programs and listings, at least until you develop more experience and expertise in DOS commands.

2.6 Testing Your Software Installation

One of the files you have copied from the RM/COBOL-85 diskette to your hard disk is the program FIRST1.CBL. This short program simply displays a welcome message when compiled and executed. Test your installation of the RM/COBOL-85 compiler by taking these final installation steps:

```
C:\RMCOB>type first1.cbl

000100 ID DIVISION.
000200 PROGRAM-ID.  FIRST1.
000300 AUTHOR.  JIM JANOSSY, DEPAUL UNIVERSITY, CHICAGO.
000400
000500******************************************************************
000600*  A simple COBOL program to test your installation of the    *
000700*  RM/COBOL-85 compiler             Jim Janossy, July 1993    *
000800******************************************************************
000900
001000 PROCEDURE DIVISION.
001100 0000-MAINLINE.
001200        DISPLAY '                                        '.
001300        DISPLAY ' Welcome to the world of RM/COBOL-85!   '.
001400        DISPLAY ' Best wishes from Liant Software Corp.   '.
001500        DISPLAY '               John Wiley & Sons, Inc.   '.
001600        DISPLAY '               Nancy and Robert Stern    '.
001700        DISPLAY '               Jim Janossy               '.
001800        DISPLAY '                                        '.
001900        STOP RUN.

C:\RMCOB>
```

Figure 2.1

Source Code for the FIRST1 Program

You can compile and run this small program to confirm that
you successfully installed your RM/COBOL-85 software.

6. Use the DOS TYPE command to look at the source code of the FIRST1 program by
    entering:

    ```
    C:> type first1.cbl  <Enter>
    ```

In response, you should see the screen shown in Figure 2.1.

7. Enter the following command to compile the FIRST1 program. In response, you
    should see lines of messages as illustrated in Figure 2.2:

    ```
    C:> rmcobol first1  <Enter>
    ```

This will create an object file named FIRST1.COB.

8. Initiate execution of the compiled FIRST1 program by entering the following
    command. This will produce the response shown in Figure 2.3:

    ```
    C:> runcobol first1  <Enter>
    ```

9. Enter the letter "e" as shown in Figure 2.3. This entry ends operation of the
    runtime debugging environment and allows the program to execute without
    stopping at each line. You should see a box containing a welcoming message from
    the producers of this guide, as shown in Figure 2.4.

```
c:\RMCOB> rmcobol first1

RM/COBOL-85 Compiler - Version 5.24.00 for DOS 2.00+.
Configured for 001 user.
Educational Version - Restricted Usage
Copyright (c) 1985, 1992 by Liant Software Corp.  All rights reserved.
Registration number: GY-0000-00860-01

Total generated object size:         650 (X"0000028A") bytes

Errors: 0, Warnings: 0, Lines: 19 for program FIRST1.

Compilation complete -- Programs: 1, Errors: 0, Warnings: 0.
```

Figure 2.2

Compiling the FIRST1 Program

Compiling a program with the RM/COBOL-85 compiler simply involves entering the command "rmcobol" **and the** name of the file that contains the source code.

If you cannot successfully complete steps 6 through 9, repeat steps 1 through **5 and try** again.   When you have completed steps 6 through 9, your installation of RM/COBOL-85 on a hard disk system has been accomplished. Each time you want to use the RM/COBOL-85 system, you must start your computer system, and, after reaching the C:> prompt, become current in the \RMCOB subdirectory as in step **4** above.

You can now go on to Section 2.8 to use RM/COBOL-85 with a program from *Structured COBOL Programming*, 8th edition, by Nancy Stern and Robert A. Stern.

2.7 Using a Two-Diskette Computer System (No Hard Disk)

If your computer does not have a hard disk, you can still use the RM/COBOL-85 educational system, but you will find it a slower process. The process described in this section is suitable for these types of computer system configurations:

- Two 720K or 1.44 Mb. 3-1/2 inch diskette drives

- One 720K or 1.44 Mb. 3-1/2 inch diskette drive and a 1.2 Mb. 5-1/4 inch diskette drive

```
C:\RMCOB>runcobol first1

RM/COBOL-85 Runtime - Version 5.24.00 for DOS 2.00+.
Configured for 001 user.
Educational Version - Restricted Usage
Copyright (c) 1985, 1992 by Liant Software Corp.  All rights reserved.
Registration Number: GZ-0000-00860-01




ST 11 FIRST1 C? e
```

Figure 2.3

Running the FIRST1 Program

You will get the debugger prompt when you run a program using the educational version of RM/COBOL-85. Enter the "e" command to end debugger operation and execute the program without debugging.

```
ST 11 FIRST1 C? e

    ┌───────────────────────────────────────────┐
    │ Welcome to the world of RM/COBOL-85!       │
    │ Best wishes from Liant Software Corp.       │
    │               John Wiley & Sons, Inc.      │
    │               Nancy and Robert Stern       │
    │               Jim Janossy                  │
    └───────────────────────────────────────────┘

COBOL STOP RUN  at line 19 in FIRST1 (C:\RMCOB\FIRST1.COB).

C:\RMCOB>
```

Figure 2.4

Output of the FIRST1 Program

You will see this on your computer screen after successfully compiling and running the FIRST1 program. Welcome to COBOL programming on a PC!

If one of your diskette drives is an older, lower capacity 360K 5-1/4 inch diskette drive, you face the need to take special steps to create your RM/COBOL-85 working environment. In such a case, read this section for background but do not attempt to take the actions indicated. Then, adapt the actions as required by your equipment.

You will need to make a working copy of the RM/COBOL-85 diskette and use it for processing. Follow these steps exactly as listed to make your working copy:

1. Put your DOS diskette into the A drive and start the computer. Respond to any prompts, and arrive at the DOS prompt, which is similar to A:>.

2. Create a formatted system diskette by placing a blank diskette (or a disk whose contents you do not mind erasing) in drive B and entering the command

   ```
   A:> format/s b: <Enter>
   ```

   Follow the prompts of the formatting utility. This will create the magnetic tracks divided into sectors that are used to house information on the diskette. *Caution! Do not format your RM/COBOL-85 diskette (Diskette 1)!* Formatting wipes out any information previously recorded on a diskette.

3. Remove the formatted diskette in drive B. Write "RM/COBOL-85 WORKING COPY" on a label and apply it to this diskette. Then put this diskette back into drive B.

4. Remove your DOS diskette from drive A and place your RM/COBOL-85 diskette into drive A.

5. Enter the following command to copy all of the files from the RM/COBOL-85 diskette to your diskette:

   ```
   A:> copy a:*.*  b:*.*  <Enter>
   ```

6. Remove the original RM/COBOL-85 diskette from drive A and store it in a safe place. You will not use it again unless a problem arises with your copy of it.

7. The diskette in drive B is your working copy of RM/COBOL-85 system. Remove the diskette from drive B and place a write-protect tab covering the square notch on its right side if it is a 5-1/4 inch diskette, or slide the write protect tab to a position closest to the edge if your diskette is of the 3-1/2 inch size.

8. Write "COBOL Source Code" on another label and apply it to a blank diskette. Format this diskette without operating system files by entering the following command:

   ```
   A:> format b: <Enter>
   ```

To test your installation of RM/COBOL-85, complete steps 9 through 13 below:

9. Put your working copy of RM/COBOL-85 in drive A, and your COBOL source code diskette in drive B. Enter the following command to copy the source code on your RM/COBOL-85 working copy diskette to your source code diskette:

   ```
   A:> copy  *.cbl  b:*.*  <Enter>
   ```

10. View the source code of the FIRST1 program by entering the DOS TYPE command:

```
A:> type b:first1.cbl <Enter>
```

This should produce a screen that looks like Figure 2.1.

11. Enter the following command to compile the FIRST1 program:

```
A:> rmcobol b:first1 <Enter>
```

This will create an object file named FIRST1.COB on the diskette in drive B. You will see lines of messages similar to those shown in Figure 2.2.

12. Initiate execution of the compiled FIRST1 program by entering the following command. This will produce the response shown in Figure 2.3:

```
A:> runcobol b:first1 <Enter>
```

13. Enter the letter "e" as shown in Figure 2.3. This entry tells the runtime debugging environment to execute the program without stopping at each line. You should see a box containing a welcoming message from the producers of the book you are reading, as shown in Figure 2.4.

If you cannot successfully complete steps 9 through 13, repeat steps 1 through 8 and try again. When you have completed steps 9 through 13, your installation of RM/COBOL-85 on a two-diskette computer system with no hard disk is accomplished. Each time you want to use the RM/COBOL-85 system, you must start your computer system with your DOS diskette in drive A, and after reaching the A:> prompt, remove the DOS diskette and put your working copy of RM/COBOL-85 in drive A. Your commands to compile and run programs must be prefaced by "b:" so that the compiler and runtime environment access files on the diskette in drive B. When you are creating programs using your own word processor, your word processor diskette must be in drive A, and your COBOL program source code diskette must be in drive B.

2.8   Hands-On Assignment

At this point you might want to gain some experience with the RM/COBOL-85 system. On your Examples Disk (Diskette 2) there is a program called C0401.CBL, which is the solution to Programming Assignment 1 of Chapter 4 of *Structured COBOL Programming*, 8th edition. The input data file for this assignment, C0401.DAT, is on Diskette 2 as well. Copy the contents of Diskette 2 to your \RMCOB subdirectory by repeating steps 4 and 5 in section 2.5. Then, to view the program on the screen, enter this command:

```
C:\RMCOB> type c0401.cbl <Enter>
```

To print this program, use the command:

```
C:\RMCOB> copy c0401.cbl lpt1 <Enter>
```

You can display or print the input file by entering:

```
C:\RMCOB> type c0401.dat  <Enter>
```

To compile this program enter:

```
C:\RMCOB> rmcobol c0401  <Enter>
```

You need not specify the extension .CBL on your source code file name because RM/COBOL-85 assumes it. This program should compile without any errors since it has already been tested. To see the names of the files created by the compiler on your default drive enter:

```
C:\RMCOB> dir  <Enter>
```

See if you can find the object file created by the compiler for program C0401. It will be named C0401.COB. To run this program, enter:

```
C:\RMCOB> runcobol c0401  <Enter>
```

The .COB extension is assumed by the runtime system, RUNCOBOL. When this program runs, it creates an output file named C0401.RPT. To see it, enter:

```
C:> type c0401.rpt  <Enter>
```

In this case you do have to enter the file name extension because the DOS TYPE command can't assume any particular extension for the name of the file you want to bring to the screen.

2.9   An Overview of SELECT Statements

The ASSIGN clause of the SELECT statement is one of the few places in COBOL where the implementor of a compiler determines how a statement should be coded. This means that the ASSIGN clause is coded differently for IBM mainframe COBOL, VAX COBOL, RM/COBOL-85, and MicroFocus COBOL. In this guide, we cover the SELECT statement for RM/COBOL-85 programs in Chapter 5. We provide a brief example of an RM/COBOL-85 SELECT statement for disk files here, in case you want to get started working with existing programs immediately.

Example (reading a file from a floppy diskette):

```
SELECT  IN-FILE  ASSIGN TO  DISK "A:EX1.DAT"
     ORGANIZATION IS LINE SEQUENTIAL.
```

In this example EX1.DAT is the actual file name of an input file on the diskette in the A drive. In DOS terminology, the "EX1" part of this file name is sometimes referred to as the "filename" and the ".DAT" part is called the "extension." Your SELECT statement for data files must have an A: prefix as shown if these files are on the separate "Example Programs" diskette in your A drive. If you have copied your example programs and data to your hard disk in the \RMCOB subdirectory, you can optionally code C: here, but you need not. Without a prefix such as A: for an output file name, the computer will write your output data files to drive C if you have a hard drive. You can code a path name in the SELECT statement. For example, this is a SELECT statement to read data from a file named EX1.DAT in subdirectory \COBDATA:

Example (reading a file from a different directory):

```
SELECT  IN-FILE  ASSIGN TO  DISK "\COBDATA\EX1.DAT"
    ORGANIZATION IS LINE SEQUENTIAL.
```

The SELECT statement clause ORGANIZATION IS LINE SEQUENTIAL is required when you read sequential disk files that have one record per line. Files created with a text editor, where the *<Enter>* or *<Return>* key is used to end a record, require this clause. Sequential disk files you output from a program (where you WRITE records to the file instead of reading them) can be created with or without ORGANIZATION IS LINE SEQUENTIAL, *but we recommend that you always use this clause for sequential files.* If you omit this clause from the SELECT statement, RM/COBOL-85 will not put a line feed/carriage return at the end of each record. If you intend to examine an output file using a text editor, you should include the ORGANIZATION IS LINE SEQUENTIAL clause.

Example (outputting printlines to a disk file):

```
SELECT REPORT-FILE ASSIGN TO PRINTER "REPORT1.DAT".
```

This SELECT statement writes output lines to a disk file and automatically puts a line feed/carriage return at the end of each line. You can view a file created as is REPORT1.DAT by using the TYPE command, your text editor, or by copying it to your printer:

Example (copying a file to the printer):

```
C:> copy report1.dat lpt1  <Enter>
```

2.10 A Special Note on Printing Files

You may have to press a "form feed" button on your printer or send one blank page to the printer to force it to eject the last page of print when you copy a file such as REPORT1.DAT to it. Alternatively, you can copy the file named EJECT.DAT (provided on the RM/COBOL-85 diskette, Diskette #1, and now in your \RMCOB subdirectory) to the printer.

Example (forcing the printer to eject a page):

```
C:> copy eject.dat lpt1  <Enter>
```

EJECT.DAT contains a form feed character to cause the printer to eject a final, partial page of print should you need to force this action. Copying this file to the printer may be handier for you than physically pressing the "form feed" button on the printer.

Use this page for notes about your local computer lab facilities

Chapter 3

Using RM/COBOL-85 With RM/CO*

3.1   What Is a Text Editor?

A text editor is interactive software that allows you to manipulate information in memory, store it on disk, and retrieve it to change it. The most common form of text editor is a word processor.

The RM/COBOL-85 package provides the RM/CO* ("RM/CO-star") program environment, which includes a text editor for your convenience. In this chapter we focus on RM/CO* and show you how to use it. You need not use RM/CO* to develop, run, test, and debug your programs. You can use any text editor you wish to prepare an RM/COBOL-85 program, such as the DOS editor or a word processor you may already be familiar with, so long as the program is prepared as an ASCII text file (a "DOS" file). In fact, you need not use RM/CO* at all for entering text, compiling, or debugging programs, although it is a powerful programming tool. If you prefer learning RM/CO* later, skip this chapter and go on to Chapter 4, which describes how you can compile and run RM/COBOL-85 programs directly from the DOS prompt.

3.2   What Is RM/CO*?

RM/CO* is a programming environment that includes a text editor that has been specially integrated with the RM/COBOL-85 compiler and debugger. Using RM/CO* you can compose a program from scratch or work on an existing program and modify it. An advantage of using RM/CO* for COBOL programming is that COBOL's A margin (columns 8-12) and B margin (columns 12-72) are preset as the default. In addition, it automatically supplies the file extension of .CBL for your programs. You can also use the RM/CO* text editor to prepare sequential files of test data, which you should designate with a suffix of .DAT. For test data files, RM/CO* gives you full access to records, beginning with column 1 instead of 7.

Because RM/CO* is designed for programmer use, rather than as a general purpose text editor, it is "connected" to the RM/COBOL-85 compiler and runtime system. Without leaving RM/CO*, you can syntax check a program, and if errors are found, directly correct them. In other words, you can view the source code listing ordinarily directed to the printer, and can correct your programming errors directly on the screen. This is a tremendous advantage! You need not await print to be able to clean up your program errors, and RM/CO* actually helps you speed your search for and location of errors. When you achieve a "clean" compile of a program, you can execute it, view the output, and even run the program again, interactively step-by-step, to debug it. With RM/CO*'s interactive debugger, you can set breakpoints to stop the program and view the contents of data names within it.

RM/CO* is typical of the modern, productive programming environments gaining prominence in the computing industry. By learning how to use it, you not only gain a tool that can help you be productive in your coursework, you gain skills that apply across various software products on-the-job.

3.3 DOS Files and RM/CO* File Naming Conventions

File names consist of one to eight characters followed by a period, and three more characters called an "extension." The first eight characters can be any name you desire. To create file names, you can use letters or numbers, and symbols such as !, @, #, $, %, _, ^, &, -, and the twiddle, ˜. When you use RM/COBOL-85 you will create two basic types of files:

- Files of COBOL source code, which contain the COBOL instructions for processing data. Files containing COBOL source code will be named with the extension .CBL.

- Data files, named with the extension .DAT.

RM/COBOL-85 and RM/CO* create additional files named with various extensions. You should avoid using these extensions for files that you create:

.COB Object file
.CPJ Project file
.C*nn* "History" file (*nn* are two digits)

In addition, if you use indexed files in support of interactive programs, as illustrated in Chapter 6, you will find it desirable to use a consistent file extension for them. We suggest the use of .RLF as the file extension for relative files and .IXF as the file extension for indexed files.

3.4 Learning RM/CO* By Using It

The best way to learn how to use RM/CO* is simply to begin running it. The sections that follow are arranged as a self-pacing series of brief tutorials. Each tutorial guides you through a series of actions to achieve specific tasks. The tutorials show you what you should see on your computer screen, so you can confirm that your actions are correct.

3.5 RM/CO* Tutorial 1: Creating a Project and Adding Members

In this first session we'll create a project and add three programs to it. Before you begin, make sure that you have completed installing your copy of RM/COBOL-85 from diskette #1, as described in Chapter 2. This step-by-step guide will help you rapidly gain familiarity with RM/CO*. We suggest you begin with step 1 and check off your actions as you complete them in your first tutorial session.

1. Start RM/CO* (Figure 3.1)
To begin using RM/CO*, move into your \RMCOB subdirectory and enter the word RMCOSTAR:

```
C:> rmcostar
```

The initial RM/CO* "greeting" screen appears as in Figure 3.1. Press any key to reach a menu, as specified on the last line of the display.

2. Select NEW Project (Figure 3.2)

The RM/CO* "menu" shown in Figure 3.2 will appear blank because this screen is intended as a listing of projects and you have not yet created a project. You establish one or more projects to serve as a library of programs. Think of a project as a filing drawer, and every folder within the drawer as a different program or file of data. Each program or data file is called a "member" in RM/CO*. Choose to define a project at this time by pressing the <*Enter*> key. (Note: RM/CO* consistently allows you to most easily select a function, such as "New" here, which is completely shown in reverse video. To select any other function, such as "Quit" here, type in the first letter of that word, which is the only thing shown in reverse video in that word.)

3. Create a Project (Figure 3.3)

Creating a new project requires entering a name for it, which must follow the rules of a DOS file name, but without an extension. In Figure 3.3 you see how we have entered the name STARTUP at the bottom of the screen. We'll use our STARTUP project to contain the first programs we work with, which come from the diskettes supplied with this manual. You can name a project anything you like, such as TEST for test programs, CHAPTER1 for programs from your textbook, and so forth. Each project can contain many programs. The project name must be on the default disk drive (usually drive C), so you can't enter this name with a disk letter.

4. Create a Project Description (Figure 3.4)

Every project may optionally carry a description of up to 40 characters to help you identify it. Figure 3.4 illustrates the screen display following entry of a new project name. RM/CO* will show you this description whenever you see the project name as you begin an RM/CO* session.

5. Go "Into" the Project (Figure 3.5)

After entering a project name and description, you will arrive at the screen shown in Figure 3.5. You can recognize that this is the same screen shown in Figure 3.2, except that now our STARTUP project is present. Go into the project (that is, "enter" the project) by pressing <*Enter*>.

6. Select "Add Member" (Figure 3.6)

When you go into a project, you'll see a list of all the programs contained in the project. In Figure 3.6, you see a blank screen for the STARTUP project, since we haven't yet added any programs to it. Each program is called a "member" of the project. Press the letter "A" to select the "Add Member" function. You'll notice that "A" is one of the only functions highlighted at this point. (Functions are highlighted when the first letter is presented in reverse video or in boldface.) Since you do not yet have any programs (members) in this project, your choice of action is presently limited.

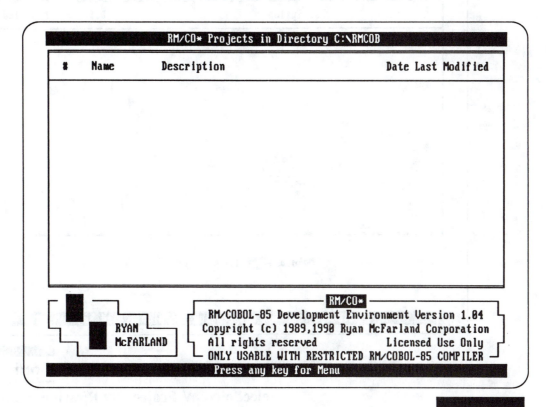

Figure 3.1

RM/CO* "Greeting" Screen

7. Add a Program to the Project (Figures 3.7 and 3.8)

At the "pathname" prompt at the bottom of Figure 3.7, enter the name FIRST1 without a file extension. You'll see the screen change to the appearance of Figure 3.8 as the FIRST1.CBL program is added to the project STARTUP.

8. Add More Programs to the Project (Figure 3.9)

Repeat steps 6 and 7 for the SAMPLE program and the ACCEPT1 program. When you finish adding the member, your "member list" screen should appear as in Figure 3.9.

End of Tutorial 1

You have now created a project and added three existing programs to it. You can press "Q" at the member list screen to quit RM/CO* or you can go on to Tutorial 2.

```
┌─────────────────────────────────────────────────────────────────┐
│  ████████████ RM/CO* Projects in Directory C:\RMCOB ████████████  │
│  ┌─────────────────────────────────────────────────────────────┐ │
│  │ #  Name      Description                 Date Last Modified  │ │
│  │ ─────────────────────────────────────────────────────────── │ │
│  │                                                             │ │
│  │                                                             │ │
│  │                                                             │ │
│  │                                                             │ │
│  │                                                             │ │
│  │                                                             │ │
│  │                                                             │ │
│  │                                                             │ │
│  └─────────────────────────────────────────────────────────────┘ │
│                                                                   │
│            Make a  New  Project, or  Q uit ?                      │
│                                                                   │
│  ████████ Select a function by pressing the highlighted key █████ │
└─────────────────────────────────────────────────────────────────┘
```

Figure 3.2

Select a NEW Project By Pressing *<Enter>*

```
┌─────────────────────────────────────────────────────────────────┐
│  ████████████ RM/CO* Projects in Directory C:\RMCOB ████████████  │
│  ┌─────────────────────────────────────────────────────────────┐ │
│  │ #  Name      Description                 Date Last Modified  │ │
│  │ ─────────────────────────────────────────────────────────── │ │
│  │                                                             │ │
│  │                                                             │ │
│  │                                                             │ │
│  │                                                             │ │
│  │                                                             │ │
│  │                                                             │ │
│  │                                                             │ │
│  │                                                             │ │
│  └─────────────────────────────────────────────────────────────┘ │
│                                                                   │
│     Type a name for the new Project (up to 8 letters/numbers)     │
│                                                                   │
│       (Press  Enter  when done,  Esc  to cancel)                  │
│                                                                   │
│  Project Name (1-8 Characters): STARTUP                          │
└─────────────────────────────────────────────────────────────────┘
```

Figure 3.3

Enter a Project Name Such as STARTUP

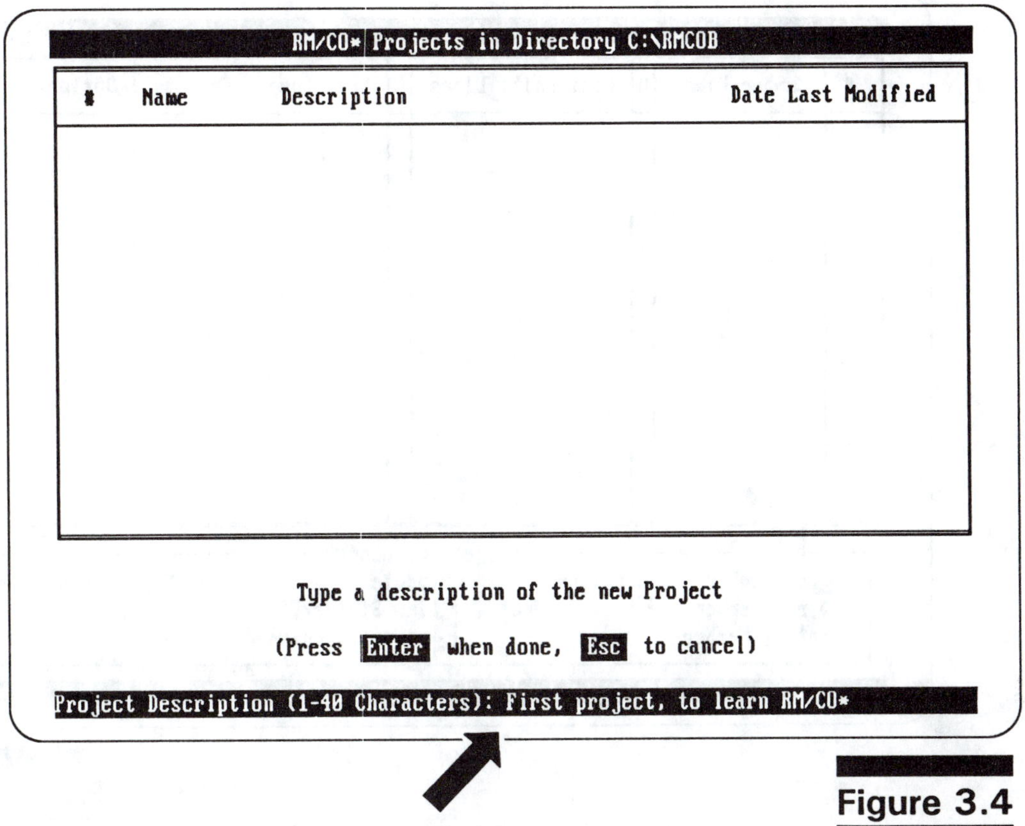

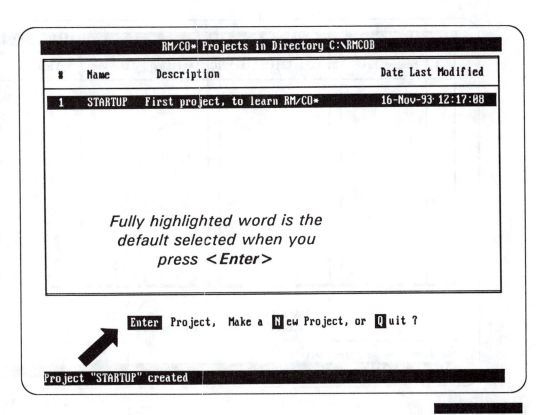

Figure 3.4

Enter a Project Description

Fully highlighted word is the default selected when you press <Enter>

Figure 3.5

Press <*Enter*> to Begin Working in the Project

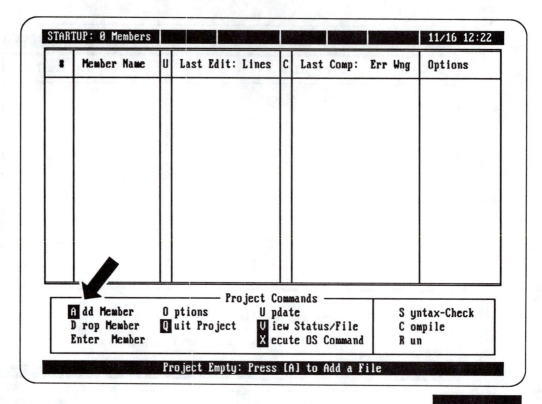

Figure 3.6

Enter "A" to Add a Program to the Project

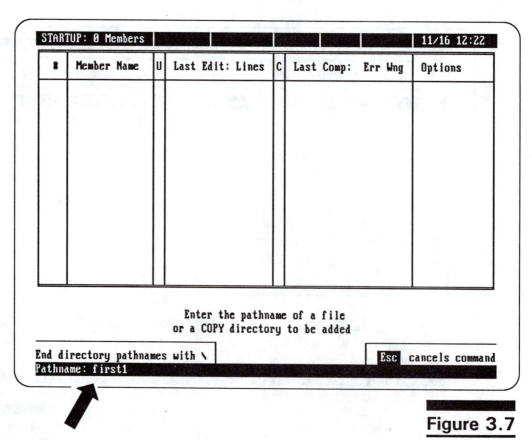

Figure 3.7

Add a Program By Entering its Name (No Extension)

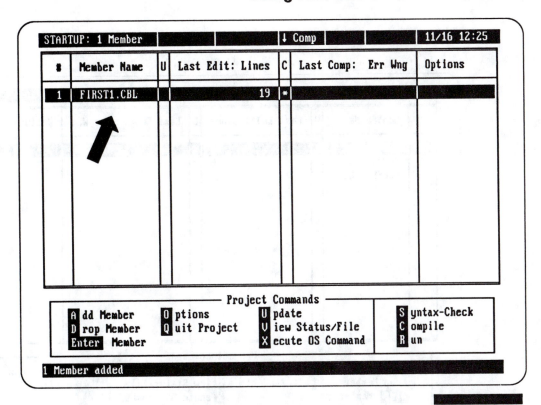

Figure 3.8

FIRST1.CBL Has Been Added to the Project

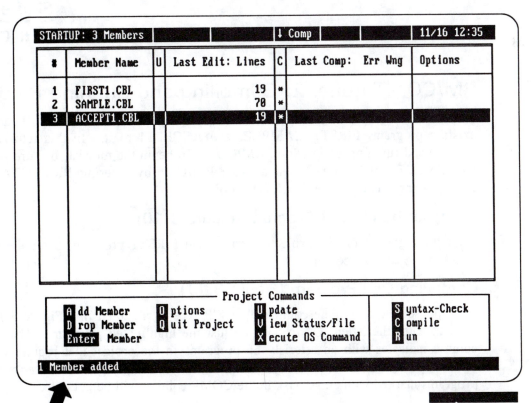

Figure 3.9

Member List Screen after Adding More Programs

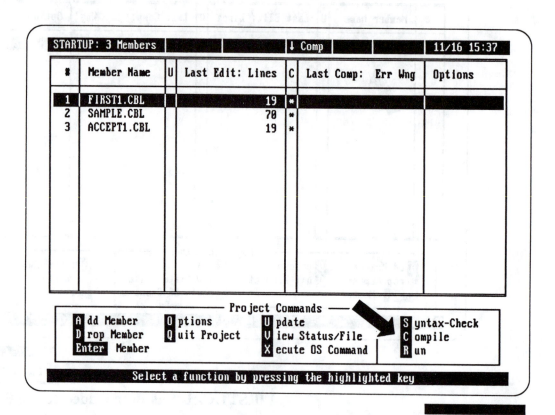

Figure 3.10

Put Highlight on a Program, Use "C" to Compile

3.6   RM/CO* Tutorial 2: Compiling and Running Programs

In tutorial 1, you used RM/CO* to create a project named STARTUP, and added existing programs FIRST1, SAMPLE, and ACCEPT1 to it. In this tutorial, you'll compile and run a program within RM/CO*. To begin the tutorial, be sure you are in the \RMCOB subdirectory, then activate RM/CO* by entering RMCOSTAR at the DOS prompt, and enter the STARTUP project.

1. Compile the FIRST1 Program (Figure 3.10)

With the highlight on the project menu on the FIRST1 program, enter the letter C, which is the compile command.

2. Compiling One Program (Figure 3.11)

In response to the compile command, you'll receive a screen like Figure 3.11. You need to enter the letter "O" to compile just the highlighted program. The "COMP" column indicates with an asterisk the programs in the project that require compiling since they are new to the project or modified. If you simply press <Enter> all of the programs marked with an asterisk in the COMP column will be compiled.

3. Result of a Compile (Figures 3.12)

When RM/COBOL-85 compiles a program it removes the asterisk in the COMP column, indicating that the program has been compiled. The highlighted line indicates how many program errors and warnings have been generated by the compilation. Messages at the bottom of the screen also indicate this. Press <Esc> to return to the project command menu or just the <Enter> key to view the electronic equivalent of the source code listing from the compiler.

4. Run the Program (Figure 3.13)

Using the arrow keys, position the highlight on the program you want to run. Then enter the command "R" to run the program.

5. Confirm the Program to Be Run (Figure 3.14)

It's possible to concatenate more than one program in a given set of source code. RM/CO* calls such a consolidated set of source code a "library." The screen you see in Figure 3.14 lets you indicate which program among programs in such a library you want to run. In most cases you'll just see one name on this screen, since we commonly store each program as a separate member. Just press <Enter> at this screen.

6. Debugging Mode Starts Running (Figures 3.15 and 3.16)

The educational version of RM/COBOL-85 starts program execution in debugging mode. This means one instruction at a time is executed, and the next instruction to be executed will be highlighted. This is at the bottom of Figure 3.15:

```
        ST   11   FIRST1   C? _
```

Debugger is in "step" mode at line 11 in program FIRST1   Your command? _

Enter "S" and press <Enter>, or simple press <Enter>, to step ahead to the next instruction. The "C?" is a prompt for you to enter a debugging command. You can enter here any of the debugging instructions discussed in Appendix D to display the contents of a data field, or type "e" to end the debugger and simply execute the program. *Enter "s" and press <Enter> four times now to make your screen look like Figure 3.16.*

7. Show Run Results (Figure 3.17)

If you press the <F10> key while stepping through a program, the screen will switch to show you the DISPLAYed output produced by the program. In Figure 3.17 you see the first few lines DISPLAYed by the FIRST1 program, which is currently waiting to execute line 15. Press <F9> to return to viewing the program source code listing with the next instruction highlighted. You can toggle back and forth from the run screen (Figure 3.16) to the program output screen (Figure 3.17) by using the <F9> and <F10> keys, as the message at the bottom of the screen reminds you.

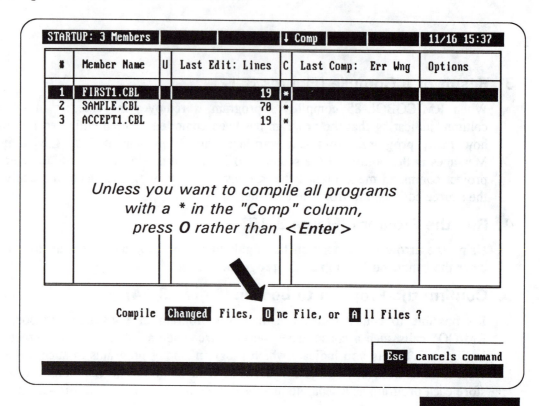

Figure 3.11

Enter "O" to Compile One Highlighted Program

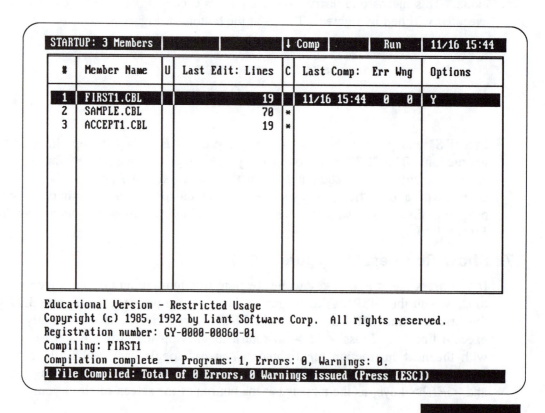

Figure 3.12

After Compiling, Press *<Esc>* to Return to Menu

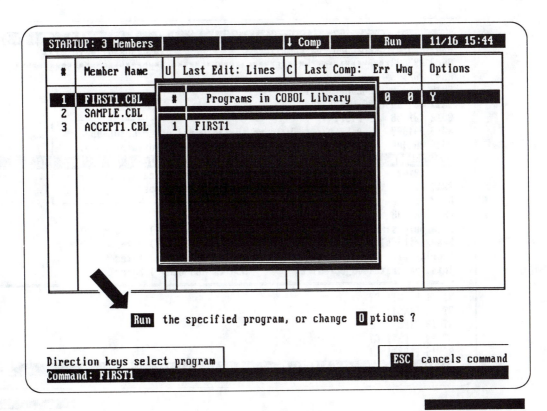

Figure 3.13

Run a Program with No * under "COMP" By Entering "R"

Figure 3.14

Press *<Enter>* to Run the Program

```
STARTUP: FIRST1.CBL    LISTING                              01,01
0007 000700* RM/COBOL-85 compiler            Jim Janossy, July 1993    *
0008 000800***********************************************************************
0009 000900
0010 001000 PROCEDURE DIVISION.
0011 001100 0000-MAINLINE.
0012 001200    DISPLAY '                                              '.
0013 001300    DISPLAY ' ┌────────────────────────────────────────┐ '.
0014 001400    DISPLAY ' │ Welcome to the world of RM/COBOL-85!    │ '.
0015 001500    DISPLAY ' │ Best wishes from Liant Software Corp.   │ '.
0016 001600    DISPLAY ' │          John Wiley & Sons, Inc.        │ '.
0017 001700    DISPLAY ' │          Nancy and Robert Stern         │ '.
0018 001800    DISPLAY ' │          Jim Janossy                    │ '.
0019 001900    STOP RUN.           └────────────────────────────────────────┘
Read only size:               638 (X"0000027E") bytes
Read/write size:               12 (X"0000000C") bytes
Overlayable segment size:       0 (X"00000000") bytes
Total generated object size:  650 (X"0000028A") bytes



ST 11 FIRST1 C?
At line 11 in Program FIRST1 Keys: [F9]=Edit [F10]=Show Run
```

Figure 3.15

Run Starts in Step Mode; Press <*Enter*> to Execute Next Instruction

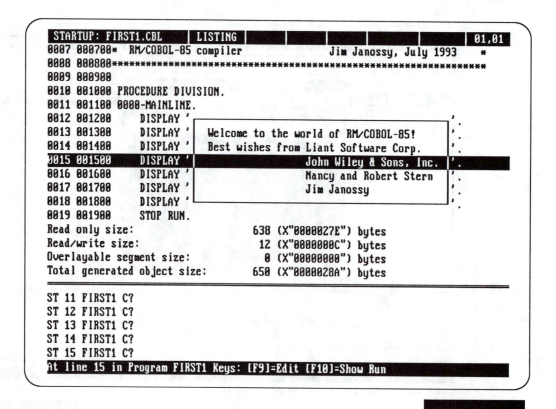

```
STARTUP: FIRST1.CBL    LISTING                              01,01
0007 000700* RM/COBOL-85 compiler            Jim Janossy, July 1993    *
0008 000800***********************************************************************
0009 000900
0010 001000 PROCEDURE DIVISION.
0011 001100 0000-MAINLINE.
0012 001200    DISPLAY '                                              '.
0013 001300    DISPLAY ' ┌────────────────────────────────────────┐ '.
0014 001400    DISPLAY ' │ Welcome to the world of RM/COBOL-85!    │ '.
0015 001500    DISPLAY ' │ Best wishes from Liant Software Corp.   │ '.
0016 001600    DISPLAY ' │          John Wiley & Sons, Inc.        │ '.
0017 001700    DISPLAY ' │          Nancy and Robert Stern         │ '.
0018 001800    DISPLAY ' │          Jim Janossy                    │ '.
0019 001900    STOP RUN.           └────────────────────────────────────────┘
Read only size:               638 (X"0000027E") bytes
Read/write size:               12 (X"0000000C") bytes
Overlayable segment size:       0 (X"00000000") bytes
Total generated object size:  650 (X"0000028A") bytes

ST 11 FIRST1 C?
ST 12 FIRST1 C?
ST 13 FIRST1 C?
ST 14 FIRST1 C?
ST 15 FIRST1 C?
At line 15 in Program FIRST1 Keys: [F9]=Edit [F10]=Show Run
```

Figure 3.16

Highlighted Line Shows Next Instruction to Be Executed

```
RM/COBOL-85 Runtime - Version 5.24.00 for DOS 2.00+.
Configured for 001 user.
Educational Version - Restricted Usage
Copyright (c) 1985, 1992 by Liant Software Corp.  All rights reserved.
Registration Number: GZ-0000-00860-01




                    This is the "Show Run" screen
                    you get by pressing <F10>
                    during debugging execution; press
                    <F9> to get back to debugging



  ┌─────────────────────────────────────────┐
  │ Welcome to the world of RM/COBOL-85!     │
  │ Best wishes from Liant Software Corp.    │
  └─────────────────────────────────────────┘
```

Figure 3.17

Press *<F10>* to See Program's DISPLAYed Output

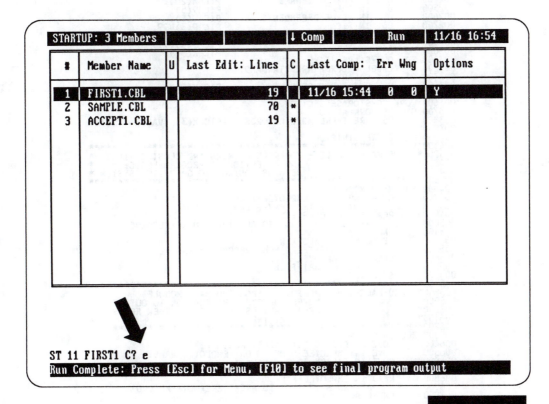

```
STARTUP: 3 Members                    ↓ Comp        Run     11/16 16:54

 #   Member Name   U  Last Edit: Lines  C  Last Comp:  Err Wng  Options

 1   FIRST1.CBL                    19      11/16 15:44   0   0   Y
 2   SAMPLE.CBL                    70   *
 3   ACCEPT1.CBL                   19   *












ST 11 FIRST1 C? e
Run Complete: Press [Esc] for Menu, [F10] to see final program output
```

Figure 3.18

Enter "e" to End Debugging, *<Esc>* to Return to Project Commands

8. End Debugging Mode, Execute Program to End (Figure 3.18)

To end debugging mode and simply run the program to its conclusion, enter the "e" debugging command, then press *<Esc>* to return to the project commands menu.

End of Tutorial 2

After running a program to its end, you can press *<F10>* to see its completed DISPLAY output, or press *<Esc>* to return to the project menu. As an exercise, compile and run the SAMPLE program that is already in your first project by repeating the actions at steps 1 through 8 above. SAMPLE1 source code looks like this:

```
000100 IDENTIFICATION DIVISION.
000200 PROGRAM-ID.  SAMPLE.
000300*************************************************
000400*  SAMPLE  -  UPDATES A FILE WITH EMPLOYEE    *
000500*                  NAMES AND SALARIES          *
000600*************************************************
000700
000800 ENVIRONMENT DIVISION.
000900 CONFIGURATION SECTION.
001000 SOURCE-COMPUTER. VAX-6410.
001100 OBJECT-COMPUTER. VAX-6410.
001200 INPUT-OUTPUT SECTION.
001300 FILE-CONTROL.
001400     SELECT IN-EMPLOYEE-FILE ASSIGN TO DISK 'DATA4E.DAT'
001500         ORGANIZATION IS LINE SEQUENTIAL.
001600     SELECT OUT-SALARY-FILE  ASSIGN TO DISK 'DATA4S.DAT'
001700         ORGANIZATION IS LINE SEQUENTIAL.
001800
001900 DATA DIVISION.
002000 FILE SECTION.
002100 FD  IN-EMPLOYEE-FILE
002200     LABEL RECORDS ARE STANDARD.
002300 01  IN-EMPLOYEE-REC.
002400     05   IN-EMPLOYEE-NAME        PIC X(20).
002500     05   IN-SALARY               PIC 9(5).
002600     05   IN-NO-OF-DEPENDENTS     PIC 9(1).
002700     05   IN-FICA                 PIC 9(3)V99.
002800     05   IN-STATE-TAX            PIC 9(4)V99.
002900     05   IN-FED-TAX              PIC 9(4)V99.
003000     05                           PIC X(37).
003100 FD  OUT-SALARY-FILE
003200     LABEL RECORDS ARE STANDARD.
003300 01  OUT-SALARY-REC.
003400     05   OUT-EMPLOYEE-NAME       PIC X(20).
003500     05   OUT-SALARY              PIC 9(5).
003600 WORKING-STORAGE SECTION.
003700 01  WS-WORK-AREAS.
003800     05   ARE-THERE-MORE-RECORDS  PIC X(3)  VALUE 'YES'.
003900*
004000 PROCEDURE DIVISION.
004100*************************************************************
004200*  100-MAIN-MODULE - CONTROLS OPENING AND CLOSING FILES   *
004300*                    AND DIRECTION OF PROGRAM LOGIC;       *
004400*                    RETURNS CONTROL TO OPERATING SYSTEM   *
004500*************************************************************
004600 100-MAIN-MODULE.
004700     OPEN INPUT  IN-EMPLOYEE-FILE
004800          OUTPUT OUT-SALARY-FILE.
004900     READ IN-EMPLOYEE-FILE
005000         AT END MOVE 'NO' TO ARE-THERE-MORE-RECORDS
005100     END-READ.
005200     PERFORM 200-CALC-RTN
005300         UNTIL ARE-THERE-MORE-RECORDS = 'NO '.
005400     CLOSE IN-EMPLOYEE-FILE
005500           OUT-SALARY-FILE.
005600     STOP RUN.
005700*************************************************************
005800*  200-CALC-RTN - PERFORMED FROM 100-MAIN-MODULE          *
005900*                 MOVES EMPLOYEE INFORMATION TO OUTPUT     *
006000*                 AREAS, WRITES THE RECORD, THEN READS     *
006100*                 THE NEXT INPUT RECORD                    *
006200*************************************************************
006300 200-CALC-RTN.
006400     MOVE SPACES TO OUT-SALARY-REC.
006500     MOVE IN-EMPLOYEE-NAME TO OUT-EMPLOYEE-NAME.
006600     MOVE IN-SALARY TO OUT-SALARY.
006700     WRITE OUT-SALARY-REC.
006800     READ IN-EMPLOYEE-FILE
006900         AT END MOVE 'NO' TO ARE-THERE-MORE-RECORDS
007000     END-READ.
```

3.7   RM/CO* Tutorial 3: Text Editing to Correct Errors

The RM/CO* text editor is easy to access and easy to use. In this tutorial you'll use it to introduce a simple mistake into a program, to see how the compiler reports syntax errors. Then you'll have a chance to apply your skill in removing the errors from a second program. To begin this tutorial, make sure you are in the \RMCOB subdirectory and activate RM/CO* by entering RMCOSTAR at the DOS prompt, then enter the STARTUP project.

1. Select the SAMPLE Program (Figure 3.19)

At the Project Commands menu, use the *<Arrow>* keys to move the highlight bar to the SAMPLE program, which you added to the STARTUP project in Tutorial 1. Then press the *<Enter>* key to "enter" into an edit of the SAMPLE program (member).

2. At the Edit Commands Menu (Figure 3.20)

When you start editing a program, you are at the "Edit Commands" menu shown in Figure 3.20. To begin modifying or manipulating the program lines, move the cursor down from the first line using the down, up, left and right arrow keys (the cursor is on the "F" in **** Top of File **** to start with). You will notice that the position of the cursor on the screen is indicated by the numbers at the upper-right corner of the screen once you move the cursor into the text area. The line number, shown first, is not too important, but the second number, which is the column in which the cursor is located, tells you if you are coding at the appropriate column (COBOL's "A" margin, where things such as FDs and paragraph names start, is at column 8, while the "B" margin, where ordinary statements start, is at column 12.)

3. At the Edit Operations Menu (Figure 3.21)

Once you have moved the cursor into the program lines, the position of the cursor is indicated at the upper right corner of the edit screen as "line, column." Now, the actions indicated at the bottom of Figure 3.21 become accessible. You access the functions listed in the first three columns by pressing the *<Alt>* key and the indicated key. Move the cursor down to line 7, which is initially entirely blank, and enter three **xxx**'s as shown in Figure 3.21. This makes line 7 invalid since these **xxx**'s have no legitimate place here. Press *<Esc>* once to get back to the Edit Commands menu, and press *<Esc>* a second time to get back to the Project Commands menu.

4. Compile the SAMPLE Program (Figure 3.22)

At the Project Commands menu, note that the column labeled "Update" now has an asterisk on the SAMPLE.CBL line. Your entry of "**xxx**" at line 7 of the program has changed the program, but RM/CO* has not actually changed the SAMPLE.CBL file. Instead, it records your changes in what it calls a "shadow" file. You can compile the program with the "C" command and the entries in the shadow file are automatically merged with the source code in the SAMPLE.CBL file. If you want to "update" the source code file with the changes, select the "U" Update command, which causes the changes to be merged with the program and the program saved in the altered form. When you update you'll see that the asterisk for the program in the Update column is removed. (Note that you don't have to do the update function in order to be able to

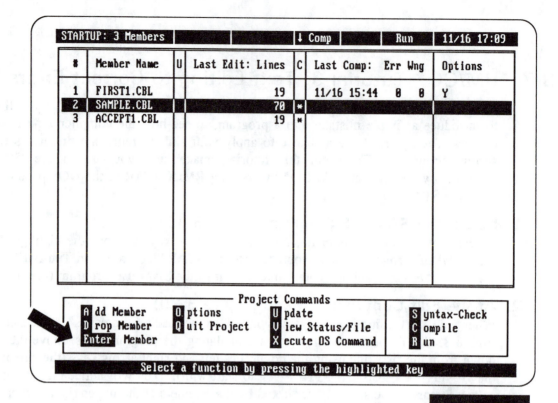

Figure 3.19

Press <*Enter*> to Begin Editing SAMPLE.CBL

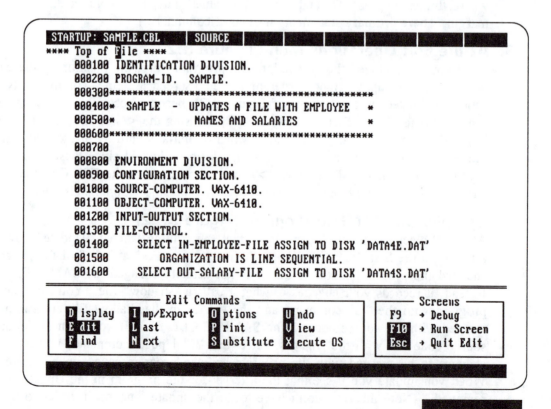

Figure 3.20

Cursor Starts at Top, Edit Commands at Bottom

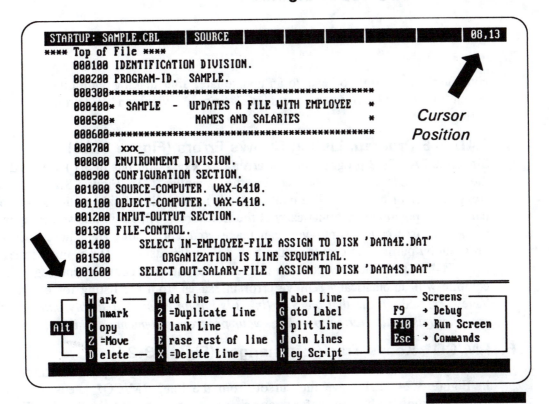

Figure 3.21

"Edit Operations" Menu Appears When You Move Cursor Down

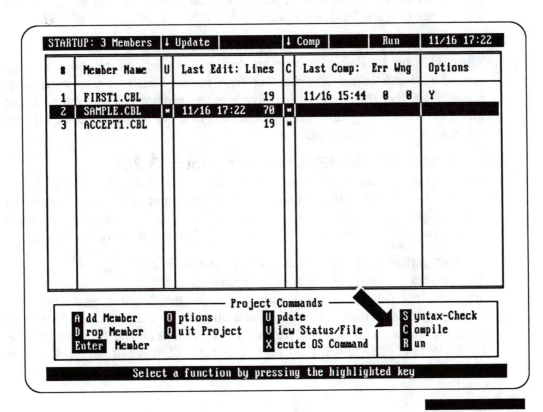

Figure 3.22

Compile the SAMPLE Program By Entering "C"

compile the program; you can do an update later after making additional changes to it.) When the compile finishes, press <*Enter*> to view an "electronic source code listing."

5. SAMPLE Program Listing Shows Errors (Figure 3.23)

Since the SAMPLE program has an error (the xxx's you put into it) we need to view the source code listing produced by the compiler. In Figure 3.23 you see the compiler's error message. The likely error is located directly above the $ symbol. The cursor will positioned automatically at the first error. Although this screen appears like a paper source code listing, you can make your corrections right here. Correct the program by putting the cursor on the first "x" and pressing <*Del*> three times. Then press "N" to automatically position the cursor to the next compiler message. The next compile will automatically remove error messages from the listing for errors that you have corrected. *(Note that the $ at line 8 is not an error, but simply indicates that the compiler has again started to analyze your program statements at this point.)*

6. RM/CO* Keeps Track of Changes (Figure 3.24)

When you make a change in a line of source code on the compiler's listing, as shown in Figure 3.24, and move the cursor from the line, RM/CO* keeps a copy of the original coding of the line, before your change. You can see such a line in Figure 3.24 at line 7. The "old" version of the line is shown in red on color monitor screens, and is filled with hyphens. The changed line appears like the unchanged source code lines. To find the next diagnostic message, press <*Esc*> to get to the Edit Commands menu (as shown in Figure 3.23), then press "N".

7. "Next Diagnostic" Entry (Figure 3.25)

When you are looking at a program listing that contains compiler messages about errors, it's handy to move to the next error message quickly, after correcting the first error. The "N" (Next) command produces the prompt at the bottom of this screen. Since the word "Diagnostic" is highlighted, press <*Enter*> to select "Diagnostic" as the type of item to go to next.

8. Recompile the SAMPLE Program (Figure 3.26)

After correcting source code errors in the listing (steps 6 and 7), press <*Esc*> twice to leave the Edit Operations Menu and the Edit Commands menu. You will be at the Project Commands menu again, as shown in Figure 3.26. Compile the program again by selecting the "C" function. Then use the "R" command to run the program.

9. Running the SAMPLE Program (Figure 3.27)

The corrected SAMPLE program compiles successfully, and running the program produces this debugging mode screen. Enter the "e" debugger command to end debugging execution of the program and allow it to execute to its logical end. The program reads a data file named DATA4E.DAT and creates a file named DATA4S.DAT. SAMPLE does not create any DISPLAYed output so you won't see much on the screen when it finishes.

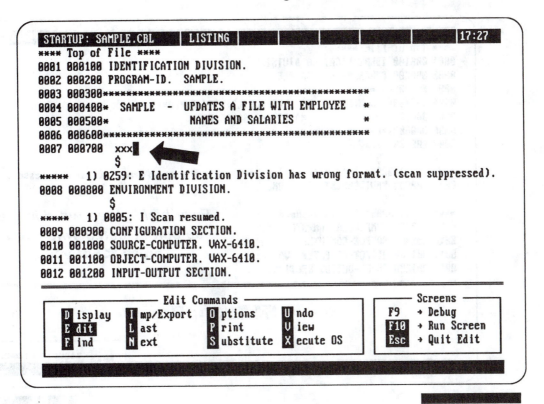

Figure 3.23

You Correct Errors Directly on the "Electronic Listing"

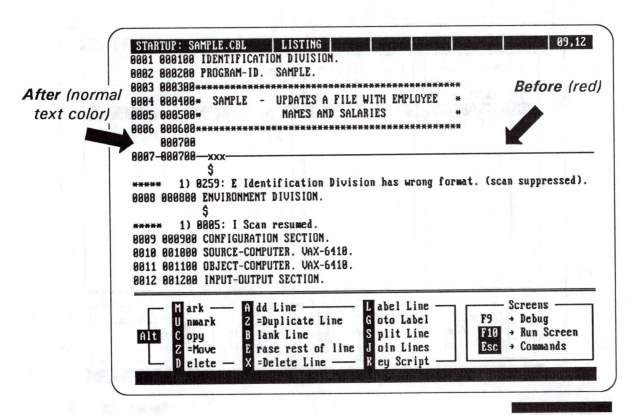

Figure 3.24

RM/CO* Shows "Before" and "After" Coding as You Edit

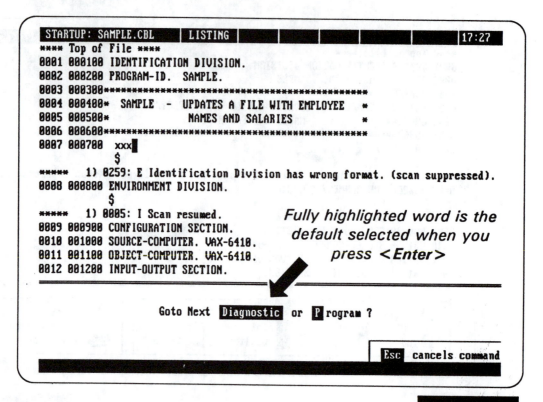

Figure 3.25

Press *<Enter>* **at the "Next" Edit Command to See the Next Error**

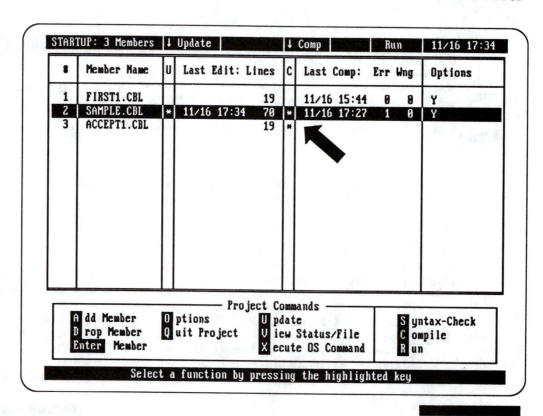

Figure 3.26

SAMPLE Program Has Changed (* In COMP Column); Recompile It

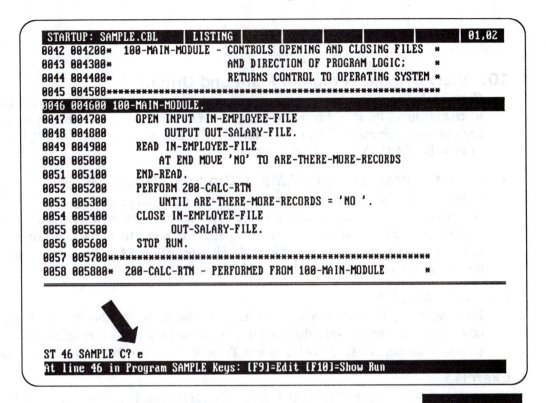

Figure 3.27

Running the SAMPLE Program: Enter "E" to Leave Debugger

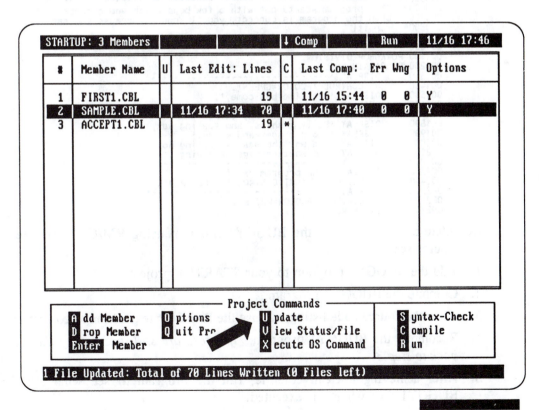

Figure 3.28

"U" (Update) Applies Changes to File and Removes * in "U" Column

10. View SAMPLE Program Input and Output

Entering "e" at the screen in Figure 3.27 will cause the SAMPLE program to execute to completion. Press <*Esc*> twice to return to the Project Commands menu. Then use the View command (V) to first view DATA4E.DAT (input to SAMPLE), and then to view DATA4S.DAT (output by SAMPLE).

11. Post Corrections to SAMPLE Program (Figure 3.28)

Figure 3.28 shows you the screen you receive after selecting the "U" (update) command and it completes successfully. The shadow file in which your source code corrections were stored has been used to apply changes to the actual program source code. Note that the asterisk in the "U" (Update) column has been removed, and that the word "Update" above the "U" column is gone also.

End of Tutorial 3

By completing Tutorial 3, you have learned how to access the RM/CO* text editor, how view messages produced by errors, and how to use the text editor to correct the errors. You can press "Q" twice to end Tutorial 3, or continue with an exercise.

Exercise

One program on your RM/COBOL-85 diskette (Diskette 1) is named BUGGY1.CBL:

```
000100 IDENTIFICATION DIVISION.
000200 PROGRAM-ID.  BUGGY1
000300 AUTHOR.  JIM JANOSSY, DEPAUL UNIVERSITY, CHICAGO.
000400
000500*******************************************************************
000600*   This program starts out with a few bugs which you correct.   *
000700*   When the program is correct, you'll know it because you can  *
000800*   run it!                                                      *
000900*******************************************************************
001000
001100 PORKCHOP DIVISION.
001200 0000!MAINLINE.
001300     DISPLAY '-----------------------------!
001400        CONTROL 'FCOLOR=GREEN'.
001500     DISPLAY 'The time has come,'.
001600     DUSPLAY 'the Walrus said,'.
001700     DISPLAY 'to talk of many things'.
001800     DISPLAY 'Sailing ships, and sealing wax,'.
001900     DISPLAY 'and cabbages and kings.'.
002000     DISPLAY 'And why the sea is boiling hot,'.
002100     DISPLAY 'and whether pigs have wings.'.
002200     DISPLEY '-----------------------------!.
002300     DISPLAY 'Your program ran fine!'
002400        BLINK LOWLIGHT CONTROL 'FCOLOR=RED'.
002500     DISPLAY '-----------------------------!
002600        CONTROL 'FCOLOR=WHITE'.
002700     STOOP RUN.
```

Complete these actions for the BUGGY1 program using RM/CO* (and be ready for some surprises):

1. Add the BUGGY1 program to your STARTUP project.

2. Compile the BUGGY1 program.

3. View the source code listing and use the RM/CO* text editor to correct errors.

4. Recompile the BUGGY1 program. *If errors are still detected by the compiler, go back to step 3.*

5. After achieving a clean compile, run the program to see what a fully correct BUGGY1 does when it is executed!

3.8 RM/CO* Tutorial 4: Creating a New Program

Your first three tutorials in using RM/CO* focused on adding existing programs to a project as members. This was a natural place to begin since we provide several programs for you to experiment with on the diskettes associated with this guide. We'll now shift attention to creating new programs with RM/CO*. We will focus on how you add a new member to a project, the automatic tab stops RM/CO* gives you, and the "editing operations" menu that reminds you of the keystrokes to use in working with items that you edit. To begin this tutorial, be sure you are in the \RMCOB subdirectory, activate RM/CO* by entering RMCOSTAR at the DOS prompt, then enter the STARTUP project.

1. Starting to Enter the NEW1 Program (Figure 3.29)

At the Project Commands menu, enter "A" to add a member. This will produce the screen you see in Figure 3.29. Enter the member name NEW1, which does not exist in your STARTUP project.

2. NEW1.CBL Does Not Exist (Figure 3.30)

Since you did not use a file extension RM/CO* assumes that NEW1 is to be a .CBL file, that is, a file that contains COBOL source code. Since NEW1.CBL does not exist, RM/CO* asks you to confirm that you really want to add it, as shown in Figure 3.30. Notice that the default for your response is "N", for "no, don't add it" (RM/CO* assumes that you have made a mistake in spelling the name of an existing member). If you simply press <*Enter*>, you will abort the "add member" action. You have to type "y" to confirm the creation of member NEW1, and press <*Enter*>.

3. Member NEW1.CBL Is Added and Is Empty (Figure 3.31)

As Figure 3.31 illustrates, when you add a new member it is established with 0 lines in it (the member is empty). Press <*Enter*> to begin inserting information into the member. As background, you should know that when you create a new member such as NEW1, a empty file is actually created in the subdirectory in which you are working, as well as a file named with the file extension .C00, such as NEW1.C00. Further work you do with the file will not immediately put data into the file. Instead, your actions are recorded in the .C00 file, which is the "shadow" or "history" file used by RM/CO* for the member. The update function at the Project Commands menu transfers information from the shadow file into the actual file.

4. Starting to Edit an Empty File (Figure 3.32)

When you go into ("enter") an empty member, the editing screen will appear as in Figure 3.32, with the cursor on the top line. To start putting in lines, press the edit command E, for "edit" or move the cursor downward. Either action will cause the bottom of the screen to change from the Edit Commands menu to the "editing operations" menu shown in Figure 3.33 (and which, unfortunately, is not labeled!).

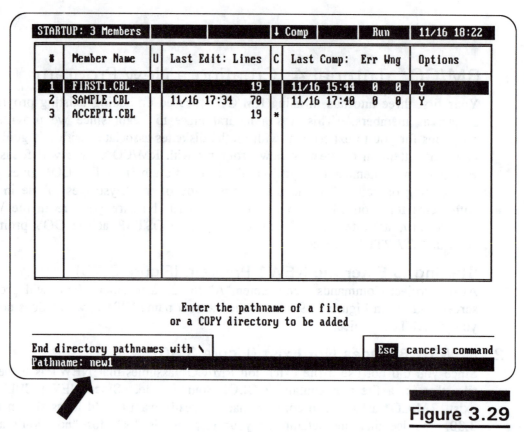

Figure 3.29

Starting to Enter the NEW1 Program

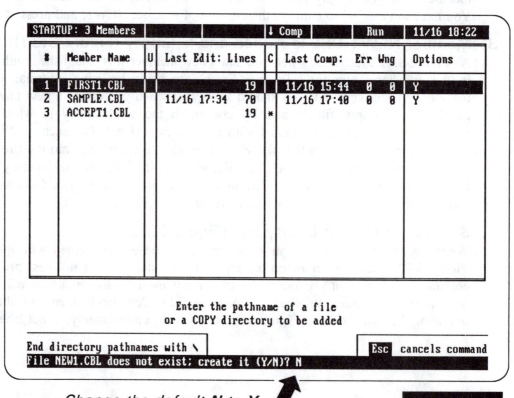

Change the default N to Y

Figure 3.30

NEW1 Program Does Not Exist; Confirm Intention to Create It

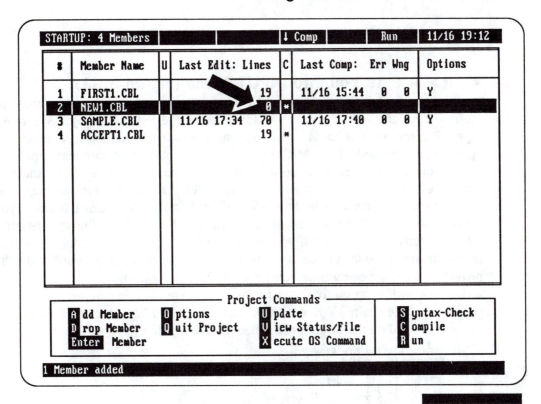

Figure 3.31

Member NEW1 Is Added and Is Empty

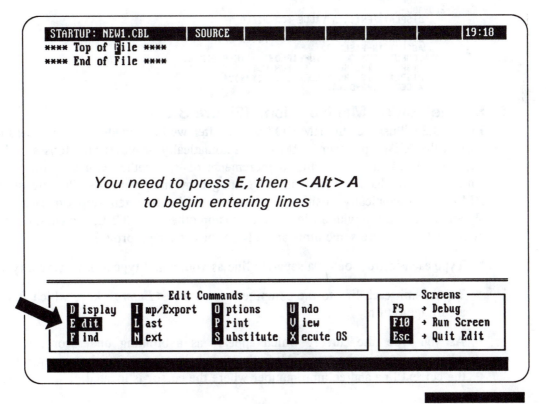

Figure 3.32

Starting to Edit an Empty Member (Program)

5. <Alt>/A Puts You into INPUT Mode (Figure 3.33)

In order to begin inserting lines into a new (or existing) member, you must press the *<Alt>* key, and, while holding it down, press the letter "a" key. We refer to this type of entry as *<Alt>/A*. Several such key combinations are used as editing operations commands by RM/CO*. Using the *<Alt>/A* command puts you into "input" mode at the first line, between the **** Top of File **** and **** End of File **** lines, as shown in Figure 3.33. *You can't put anything into a new member until you get into input mode with <Alt>/A.* You can tell when you are in input mode because the screen displays the word INPUT in the upper-right corner. Once you go into input mode, you will stay in it as long as you continue entering new lines. In input mode, the cursor will automatically move downward and leftward to provide a new line every time you press *<Enter>*. But once you move the cursor up a line, you will drop out of input mode. To move back into input mode you have to press *<Alt>/A* again. You can begin entering the NEW1 program now (this program is not contained on the diskettes supplied with this guide!):

```
IDENTIFICATION DIVISION.
PROGRAM-ID.  NEW1.
DATA DIVISION.
WORKING-STORAGE SECTION.
01  IN-FIELD-1       PIC 999.
01  IN-FIELD-2       PIC 999.
01  SUM-OUT          PIC 9999.
01  MORE-DATA        PIC X     VALUE 'Y'.
PROCEDURE DIVISION.
100-MAIN-MODULE.
    PERFORM 200-ADD-RTN
        UNTIL MORE-DATA = 'N'.
    STOP RUN.
200-ADD-RTN.
    DISPLAY 'ENTER A VALUE FOR FIELD 1'.
    ACCEPT IN-FIELD-1.
    DISPLAY 'ENTER A VALUE FOR FIELD 2'.
    ACCEPT IN-FIELD-2.
    COMPUTE SUM-OUT = IN-FIELD-1 + IN-FIELD-2.
    DISPLAY 'THE SUM IS ', SUM-OUT.
    DISPLAY 'IS THERE MORE DATA (Y/N)?'.
    ACCEPT MORE-DATA.
```

6. Simple Editing Manipulations (Figure 3.34)

Figure 3.34 illustrates the RM/CO* screen after we have made some progress entering part of the NEW1 program. RM/CO* automatically provides tab stops at columns 8, 12, 16, 20, 24, and so forth, in increments of 4, whether you are editing COBOL source code or data. When you are editing a member with the file extension .CBL, RM/CO* automatically positions the cursor at the first tab stop on each new line. When you edit a file with a file name extension other than .CBL, the cursor is placed at position 1. Here are some hints and advice for entering a program:

- Type each instruction on a separate line as you would type a line using a typewriter.

- To transmit each line to the computer, press the *<Enter>* key, which functions as a carriage return.

- As you type, the cursor, which appears as a blinking underscore, will indicate where you are in the text. Also, the upper-right corner of the screen will indicate the current line and column number where the cursor is located.

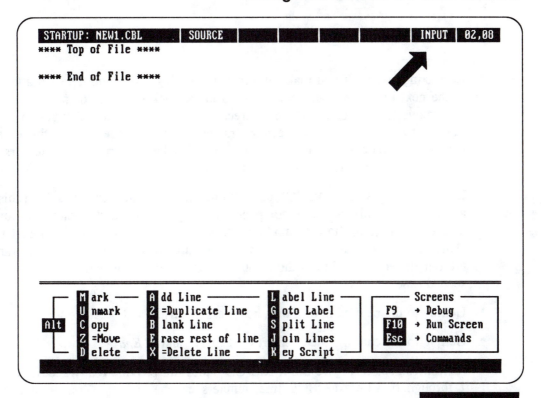

Figure 3.33

<*Alt*>/A Puts You into INPUT Mode ("Add Line")

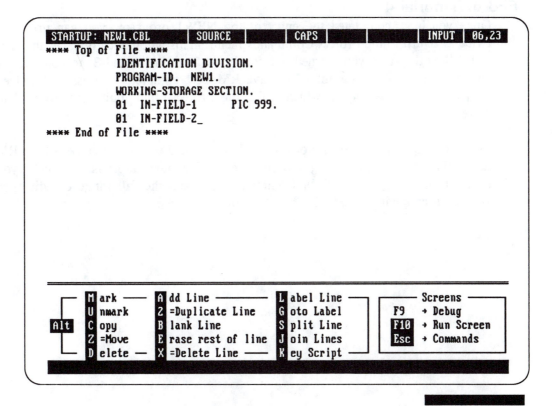

Figure 3.34

Making Progress in Entering a New Program

- Correcting errors: if you make an error in entering a line and detect it after moving to the next line, use *<Arrow>* keys to move back to the error point. *<Arrow>* keys move the cursor around the screen without making any changes to text. *The <Backspace>* key deletes each character directly to the left of the cursor and moves the cursor leftward. The *<Del>* key deletes characters at the cursor point and the cursor remains in the same position.

- Inserting a character: RM/CO* usually operates in "typeover" mode. In this mode, a character already at the cursor position is replaced by a character that you enter. You can change to "insert" mode by pressing the *<Ins>* key. In insert mode, a character keyed at an existing character position will insert the character and push the remainder of the line to the right. To return to typeover mode, press *<Ins>* a second time.

- Getting to the beginning of a member press *<Ctrl>* and *<Home>*.

- Getting to the end of a member press *<Ctrl>* and *<End>*.

- As you can see in Figure 3.34, RM/CO* does not provide ready access to positions 1 through 6, where COBOL line numbers can be coded. You do not need line numbers on COBOL source code, and we suggest that you simply do not use them. If you eventually wish to apply line numbers, see Chapter 4, where the "R" renumbering utility provided on diskette 1 is demonstrated.

End of Tutorial 4

Once you have completed the entry of the NEW1 program, you can press *<Esc>* twice to return to the Project Commands menu. This automatically saves the file. You can follow the steps you learned previously, in Tutorials 2 and 3, to compile, correct, and run the NEW1 program. To leave RM/CO* completely, press "Q" twice at the Project Commands menu, which quits the project, then quits the entire RM/CO* system.

In completing our first four tutorials you have learned the "big picture" of the RM/CO* text editor and programming environment. The next tutorials will help you gain detailed knowledge of the Edit Command menu and the full range of edit operations you can access with the RM/CO* text editor.

3.9 RM/CO* Tutorial 5: Using Advanced Editing Features and Help

We begin Tutorial 5 on RM/CO* with reference material about its two editing menus. We then illustrate how to use some of the advanced editing features provided by RM/CO*. After completing this tutorial you will be familiar with most of its editing facilities, and with its self-contained context-sensitive help system.

In this discussion, keep in mind that RM/CO* refers to the programs or files of test data that you put into a project as "members." We also call these items **members** here, although you might actually think of the programs and test data as DOS files, which is really what they are. A "project" is simply a records-keeping device that keeps track of the files (members) you have included in it.

Edit Commands Menu Reference

When you go into ("enter") an existing member, you see the Edit Commands menu at the bottom of your screen, as shown in Figure 3.35. This is the higher level of the two editing menus. "Edit Commands" appears when you have not yet moved the cursor within the member you are editing. Following is a description of what each edit command does.

D Display

Displays the member you have selected in either Source or Listing format. Source format shows you the contents of the member as you keyed it into the computer system, without the diagnostic messages produced by a compile. Listing format is the "electronic source code listing" with diagnostic messages from the compile.

E Edit

Edit put puts you into editing mode so that you can use the full screen text editor. Press this to begin editing when you go into an existing member, or simply move the cursor using the arrow keys. When you are adding a new member, you automatically begin in editing mode. To leave editing mode, press *<Esc>*.

F Find

You use Find to search for and jump to a character string or location in an existing member. This can be a string, line number, line label, top of file, end of file, or relative displacement. To select a compiler-applied line number the file must already have been compiled or sequence-checked.

I Import/Export

You use Imp/Export to copy in the contents of a file at the cursor location or copy marked lines out to a file. When you select Imp/Export, you are asked to choose whether you want to import or export. To import a file, you enter its file name when asked to do so. To export lines to a file, you first mark them using the *<Alt/M>* editing operations command, then enter the target file name when asked to do so. If you export to an existing file, the existing file is overwritten by the exported lines, so be careful that you do not destroy something you want when you export! If the file to be imported or exported is on a different disk drive or in a different subdirectory, enter this when the prompt for path name appears; if the file is in the same subdirectory as RM/CO*, just type the file name.

L Last

The most common use of the Last command is to go to the last diagnostic message in the program. You can use this command only after you have compiled or syntax checked a program.

N Next

Next locates the next diagnostic message in the listing of a compiled program. You can use this command only after you have compiled or syntax checked a program.

O Options

Options changes compile, runtime, and RM/CO* options. We show you how to these options in Tutorial 6, and we explain what many of the options do in Appendix C.

P Print

This prints all or part of a member or file. You will be prompted for All or Part, and if you select Part, you will be given instruction on how to specify the part.

S Substitute

Substitute replaces one or more occurrences of a character string with another character string. We show you how to use this command later in this tutorial.

U Undo

Undo "undoes" your most recent editing change, or all changes since you began the current editing session. Undo works only in the current editing session. Once you leave a member by pressing <Esc>, changes are saved and you cannot undo them.

V View

The most common use of View is to see the contents of a member, which you do by using this command and entering the name of the file you wish to view. You can also use this command to view the "status" of the member you are editing. Status information is somewhat redundant to the housekeeping information you see on the Project Commands menu about each member.

X eXecute

"Xecute OS" means "execute DOS command." If you select this function RM/CO* will allow you to enter an ordinary DOS command such a "copy." After executing a DOS command, you press the <Enter> key to return to RM/CO*.

<F9> Toggle Edit and Debugging Screens

The <F9> key gets you back to the program execution debugging screen when you have entered edit from the debugging screen.

<F10> See Run Screen

<F10> shows you the most recent run screen, just as it does when you are running a program with the debugger. Pressing <F10> a second time brings you back to the edit.

<Esc> Leave Edit

Pressing *<Esc>* from the Edit Commands screen takes you back to the Project Commands screen. Note that this automatically saves any changes you have made to the member, but puts those changes only into the "shadow" file name with the suffix .C00. To actually apply these changes to the real file you have been editing, you must run the "U" Update command at the Project Commands screen.

Tutorial 5, Part A: Using Edit Commands

We now use some of the Edit Commands to give you hands-on experience with them, and also to see how RM/CO* provides built-in help screens.

1. Activate RM/CO*

Activate RM/CO* by entering the RMCOSTAR at the DOS prompt and press any key to arrive at the Project Commands menu.

2. Choose the NEW1 Program

Use the *<Arrow>* keys to move the highlight to the NEW1.CBL program you entered in Tutorial 4.

3. Begin Editing the NEW1 Program

After positioning the highlighted line as described in step 2, press *<Enter>* to go into (to "enter") the NEW1.CBL program for editing. Your screen should look like Figure 3.35 after you have begun the edit of NEW1.CBL, with the Edit Commands menu at the bottom.

4. Select the "S" Command for Substitution (Figure 3.35)

Enter "S" to select the substitute command from Edit Commands shown in Figure 3.35. We will use this to change all occurrences of the data name IN-FIELD-1 to IN-FIELD-ONE throughout the program.

5. Enter the Current and New Substitute Values (Figure 3.36)

The substitute command is entered as you see at the bottom of Figure 3.36. The first value is the way the character string currently appears and the second value is the way we want to make it appear. The slashes / are delimiters. The final * * indicate that we want all occurrences of the current value in each line, from the cursor position onward in the member, to be changed.

6. Confirm the Substituted Values (Figure 3.37)

After execution of the substitute command, you will see the old version of each affected line in red, filled with a horizontal line. Your screen should appear as in Figure 3.37. A message at the bottom of the screen indicates how many occurrences of the original

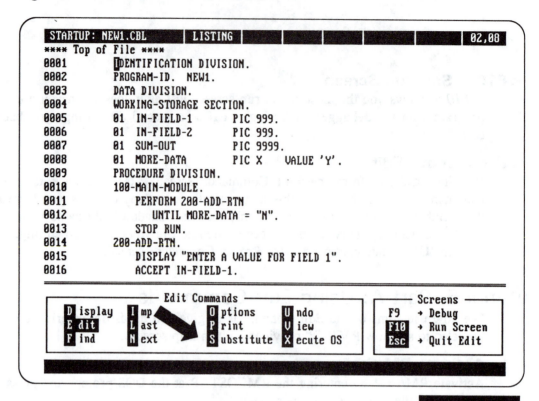

Figure 3.35

Select the "Substitute" Command By Entering "S"

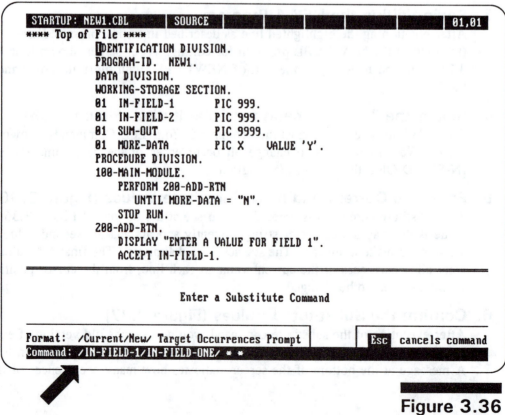

Figure 3.36

Type in the Substitute Command: Old and New Strings

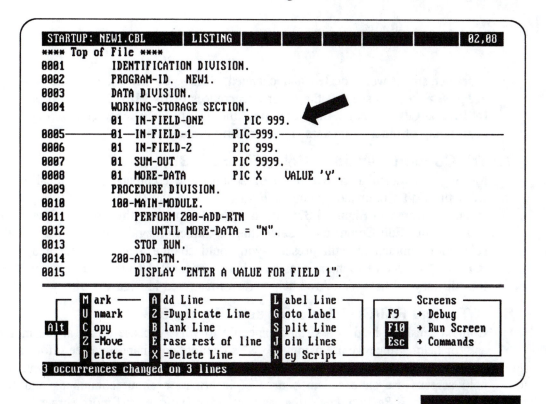

Figure 3.37

Substitute Command Has Executed; Lines Changed

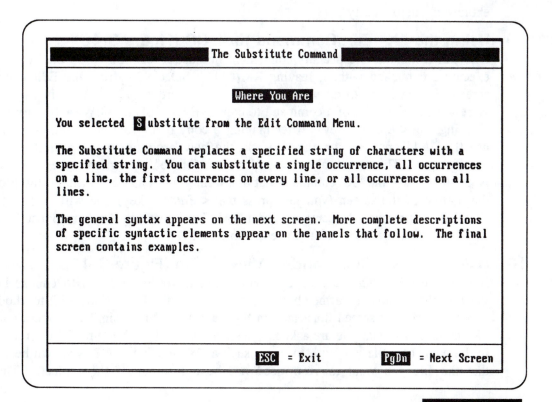

Figure 3.38

Initial Context-Sensitive Help Screen for "Substitute" Command

character string were located and changed. Move downward with the *<Arrow>* or *<PgDn>* keys to see that the other occurrences of IN-FIELD-1 have been changed to IN-FIELD-ONE. Note that changing the length of a character string affects the positioning of other characters rightward on the same line.

7. Try Context-Sensitive Help (Figure 3.38)

Moving downward after execution of a substitute command automatically takes you from the Edit Commands menu in Figure 3.35 to the (unlabeled) Editing Operations menu illustrated in Figure 3.37. Press *<Esc>* to leave the Editing Operations menu and return to Edit Commands. Select the "S" function again and you will see that your substitute command is still present; you could change it and execute it again. Press *<F1>* to receive context-sensitive help from RM/CO* and you will see the introductory "Where You Are" help screen illustrated in Figure 3.38.

8. A Typical RM/CO* Help Screen (Figure 3.39)

Context-sensitive help is assistance specific to what you are doing at the moment you ask for help. Since we are using the "S" substitute command, we see information about the substitute command as shown in Figure 3.39 by pushing the *<F1>* key. RM/CO* help screens are an excellent source of information about commands and functions. Pressing the *<PgDn>* key often, as here, gives you several more screens with advice and examples. Press *<Esc>* to leave help screens and return to the Edit Commands menu. Since helpful information is built right into RM/CO*, we suggest you select a few more edit commands, one at a time, and press *<F1>* after each selection to explore the help facility.

9. Using the "X" Edit Command for DOS (Figure 3.40)

One edit command is especially convenient because it lets you "drop out" to DOS and execute a command without leaving RM/CO*. Select "X" from the Edit Commands screen (Figure 3.35) to do this. You will see a screen as illustrated in Figure 3.40. Here you see the entry of a command to copy NEW1.CBL to NEW2.CBL, followed by pressing the *<Enter>* key. After making a copy of a program in this way, you can use the "Add" project command to add the new program to the project, and begin modifying it. This is a straightforward way to "clone" a program to begin a new one. Note: If you use the "X" command but don't enter any DOS command at the prompt at the bottom of the screen (you just press the *<Enter>* key) you will drop out to the actual DOS prompt. No entry is what RM/CO* means by "null response." In that case, you enter the word "exit" to return to RM/CO*.

10. Using the "V" Command to View a File (Figure 3.41)

If you select V from the Edit Commands menu, you'll be asked to choose between viewing the "status" of a member or the contents of a file. Enter "F" to choose file viewing to see the screen illustrated in Figure 3.41. This is similar in operation to the "X" command in that you are asked to make an entry at the bottom of the screen. Type in the name of a file you wish to view, such as WORKERS.DAT as shown here. Note that the file you want to view need not be a member of the project. The view

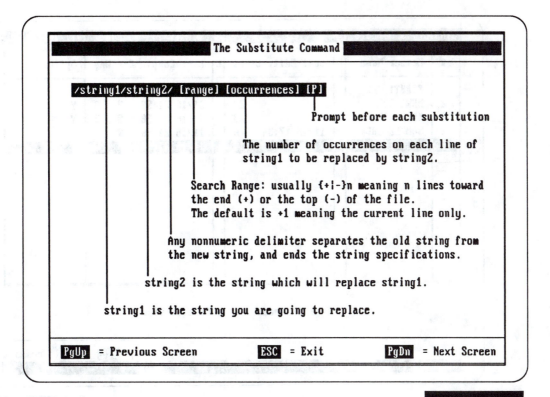

Figure 3.39

Internal Help Screens Like This Document Most of RM/CO*

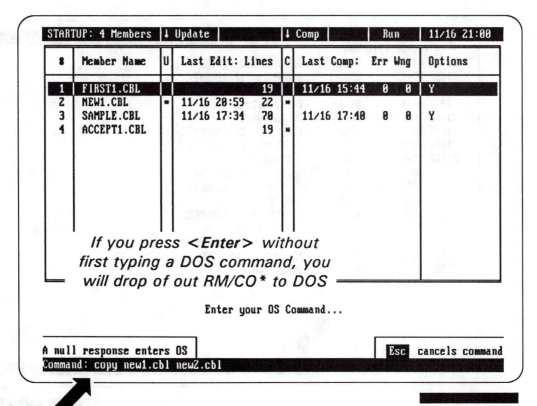

Figure 3.40

Using the "X" Edit Command to Enter a DOS Command

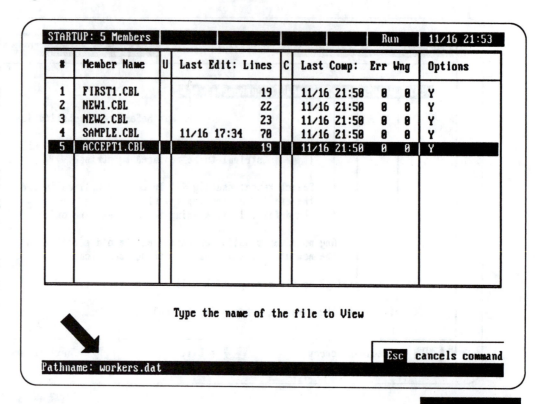

```
STARTUP: 5 Members                              Run    11/16 21:53

 #  Member Name  U Last Edit: Lines C Last Comp:  Err Wng  Options

 1  FIRST1.CBL                19      11/16 21:50   8   8   Y
 2  NEW1.CBL                  22      11/16 21:50   8   8   Y
 3  NEW2.CBL                  23      11/16 21:50   8   8   Y
 4  SAMPLE.CBL   11/16 17:34  78      11/16 21:50   8   8   Y
 5  ACCEPT1.CBL               19      11/16 21:50   0   0   Y




            Type the name of the file to View



                                             Esc cancels command
Pathname: workers.dat
```

Figure 3.41

A File Does Not Have to Be "in" a Project to Be Viewed

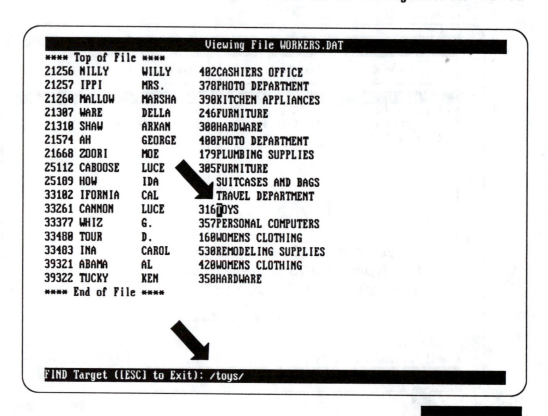

```
                  Viewing File WORKERS.DAT
**** Top of File ****
21256 NILLY     WILLY    402CASHIERS OFFICE
21257 IPPI      MRS.     378PHOTO DEPARTMENT
21260 MALLOW    MARSHA   390KITCHEN APPLIANCES
21307 WARE      DELLA    246FURNITURE
21310 SHAW      ARKAN    300HARDWARE
21574 AH        GEORGE   400PHOTO DEPARTMENT
21668 ZOORI     MOE      179PLUMBING SUPPLIES
25112 CABOOSE   LUCE     305FURNITURE
25109 HOW       IDA         SUITCASES AND BAGS
33102 IFORNIA   CAL         TRAVEL DEPARTMENT
33261 CANNON    LUCE     316TOYS
33377 WHIZ      G.       357PERSONAL COMPUTERS
33480 TOUR      D.       160WOMENS CLOTHING
33483 INA       CAROL    530REMODELING SUPPLIES
39321 ABAMA     AL       420WOMENS CLOTHING
39322 TUCKY     KEN      350HARDWARE
**** End of File ****




FIND Target ([ESC] to Exit): /toys/
```

Figure 3.42

The "View" Edit Command Has a Built-in "Find" Feature

command makes it unnecessary for you to add each data file your programs will read or create to the project in order to examine their contents.

11. Using the Find Feature of View (Figure 3.42)

The file viewing feature of RM/CO* includes a "find" feature to locate the occurrences of any character string you specify. In Figure 3.42, we use the "find" feature to locate the word "toys" in the file being viewed. Note that you must frame the character string with slashes or another nonnumeric literals such as apostrophes. After locating one occurrence of a character string you can press <Enter> to repeat the search to find the next occurrence of the character string.

End of Tutorial 5, Part A

This concludes Tutorial 5, Part A. You can press <Esc> to end viewing and reach the Project Commands menu, and "Q" twice to leave RM/CO*, or you can continue on with the Part B of this tutorial.

Edit Operations Menu Reference

The "Edit Commands" menu appears first when you begin editing a member. When you select the "E" function for editing, or simply move the cursor with the <Arrow> keys, you change into the "edit operations" menu shown in Figure 3.43. Following is a description of what each edit operation does. Remember that edit commands use combination keys as commands. For example, in order to begin inserting lines into a new (or existing) member, you must press the <Alt> key, and, while holding it down, press the letter "a" key. We refer here to this type of entry as <Alt>/A, which you might want to pronounce as "<Alt> plus A".

<Alt>/M Mark

You mark one or more lines of text (a "block" of line) by moving the cursor to the first line to be marked pressing <Alt>/M. Then move the cursor to the intended end of the block and press <Alt>/M again. The block will appear highlighted and you can now copy, move, or delete it.

<Alt>/U Unmark

Unmarks a block of text, removing the highlighting from it.

<Alt>/C Copy

Copies a marked line or block of lines to the line after the cursor position. To copy one or more lines you mark them first using the <Alt>/M command, then move the cursor to the intended location for the copied lines, and press <Alt>/C. You then unmark the lines by pressing <Alt>/U.

<Alt>/Z Move

Moves a marked line or block of lines to the line after the cursor position. To move one or more lines you mark them first using the <Alt>/M command, then move the cursor to the intended location for the moved lines, and press <Alt>/Z. You then unmark the lines by pressing <Alt>/U.

\<Alt\>/A   Add Line (Start INPUT Mode)

Creates a blank line and puts you into "input" mode. As long as you continue to enter characters and press the \<Enter\> key at the end of new lines, input mode continues to give you new lines. You leave input mode when you move the cursor upward using the \<Arrow\> keys.

\<Alt\>/2   Duplicate a Line

Duplicates the line on which the cursor is positioned. You simply hold down this key combination to quickly generate multiple copies of the same line.

\<Alt\>/B   Erase a Line

Erases the line on which the cursor is located, from the beginning of the line to the end.

\<Alt\>/E   Erase to End of Line

Erases the contents of the line from the cursor position rightward.

\<Alt\>/X   Delete

Deletes the entire line, and moves the text below it up one line. If you hold this key combination down, lines below the cursor are quickly deleted. (If you delete too many lines, press \<Esc\> to go to the Edit Commands menu, and restore the lines with the "U" Undo command.) If you have marked a block of lines, pressing \<Alt\>/X will delete the entire block at once. (Remember that blank lines are acceptable in COBOL programs and you can use them to provide "white space" to aid program readability.)

\<Alt\>/L   Label a Line

Labels a line for an easy return to it later on. You are prompted to press a Label key (any letter A through Z, upper- or lowercase. You can later select Goto Label by pressing \<Alt\>/G, type in the label key, and jump immediately to the labeled line.

\<Alt\>/G   Goto Label

"Goes" to a line you have labeled previously, using the \<Alt\>L command. When you press \<Alt/G\> you are prompted to enter the label letter for the line you wish to go (jump) to.

\<Alt\>/S   Split Line

Splits a line; the characters rightward of the cursor are placed on the next line. The cursor remains in the same position. This allows you to add more characters in the middle of the line. You can then press \<Alt\>/J to rejoin the present line with the characters that had been shifted downward.

\<Alt\>/J   Join Lines

Rejoins lines previously split with the \<Alt\>/S command. The cursor remains at the same point.

\<Alt\>/K   Key Script (Macro)

Allows you to establish the 10 function keys as "macro instruction" keys, or "macros." A macro enables you to set up a series of keystrokes and have them entered automatically every time you press the function key. To establish a macro for a function key, enter < *Alt* > */K* and press the function key you want to assign the keystrokes to. Then press the keys to be assigned to it. When you want to stop recording keys to be stored as the macro, again press the function key receiving the assignment. Several function keys are already predefined with these macro instructions:

< *F1* > is preassigned < *Alt* > */H,* which accesses the RM/CO* help facility

< *F2* > is preassigned < *Alt* > */A* to add a line and begin input mode

< *F3* > is preassigned < *Esc* > < *Esc* > to quickly end an edit, save changes, and move from the edit operations screen to the Project Commands menu

< *F4* > is not preassigned; experiment with it if you like!

< *F5* > is preassigned < *Alt* > */B* to erase the line on which the cursor is located

< *F6* > is preassigned < Alt > /E to erase to the end of the line on which the cursor is located

< *F7* > is preassigned < *Esc* > */D/T* to move from edit operations to Edit Commands, select Display, and select Toggle between the source code edit screen and the listing screen

< *F8* > is preassigned < *Esc* > */U/L* to undo your last command. Press this while you are in the edit operations screen and you will see that it is much handier than manually entering < *Esc* >, then "U", then "L".

< *F9* > is preassigned < *Alt* > */W* to toggle between the editing screen and the debugging screen

< *F10* > is preassigned < *Alt* > */R* to toggle between the debugging screen and the "run" screen, which shows the DISPLAYed output of the program and runtime system messages.

Tutorial 5, Part B: Using Edit Operations Commands

This is a continuation of Tutorial 5, and step 12 below follows step 11 of Part A. If you ended your work with RM/CO* after Part A of the tutorial, activate RM/CO* again by entering RMCOSTAR at the DOS prompt and press any key to arrive at the Project Commands menu.

12. Choose the NEW1 Program
Use the < *Arrow* > keys to move the highlight to the NEW1.CBL program.

13. Begin Editing the NEW1 Program (Figure 3.43)

Go into ("enter") the NEW1.CBL program for editing. Your screen should look like Figure 3.43 after you have begun the edit of NEW1.CBL, with the Edit Commands menu at the bottom, except that no lines will yet be highlighted.

14. Marking Two Lines for Moving (Figure 3.43)

Using the *<Arrow>* keys move the cursor to the line where IN-FIELD-1 is coded. Press *<Alt>/M,* which will cause the line to become highlighted. Then move the cursor down one line and press *<Alt>/M* a second time. This completes a marking action, and the lines will remain highlighted as shown in Figure 3.43 as you move the cursor again.

15. Moving Marked Lines (Figures 3.44 and 3.45)

Using the *<Arrow>* keys, move the cursor so that it rests on the line where MORE-DATA is coded. Then press *<Alt>/Z* to move the marked block of lines to the point following the line on which the cursor is located, followed by *<Alt>/U* to remove the marking. Figure 3.44 shows you how the listing screen appears after the marked lines have been moved and unmarked. If you do not see the "struck out" lines in their previous location (lines 5 and 6 in Figure 3.44) press the *<F7>* key to toggle to this listing screen. Press *<F7>* again to switch to the source screen shown in Figure 3.45.

16. Marking a Block of Lines for Export (Figure 3.46)

Using the *<Arrow>* keys, move the cursor to the first line of WORKING-STORAGE and press *<Alt>/M* to begin marking a group of lines. Then move the cursor to the last line of WORKING-STORAGE and press *<Alt>/M* again. The four lines in WORKING-STORAGE are now marked and should be highlighted as shown in Figure 3.46.

17. Exporting a Block of Lines (Figure 3.47)

Press *<Esc>* to leave the editing operations menu and go to the Edit Commands menu. Select "I" for "Imp/Export." You will be prompted to enter "I" for import or "E" for export. Enter "E" and you will see a screen similar to Figure 3.47. At the bottom of the screen, enter STUFF.CBL as the name of a file to which the marked lines will be written. The press *<Alt>/D* to delete the marked lines.

18. Installing COPY to Acquire the Exported Lines (Figure 3.48)

One reason you export lines of code from a program to a file is to make those lines of coding accessible to any program. COPY is a directive that tells the compiler to copy in lines at compile time. This is handy for record descriptions shared by many programs, as well as for any standard coding. In Figure 3.48 we have used *<Alt>/A* to insert line 6 and coded the appropriate COPY command on it to copy in STUFF.CBL, the file containing the lines of code we exported in step 17. Insert this copy command in your NEW1.CBL program as shown. Then press *<F3>* to get to the Project Commands menu and compile the NEW1 program. *<F3>* is a

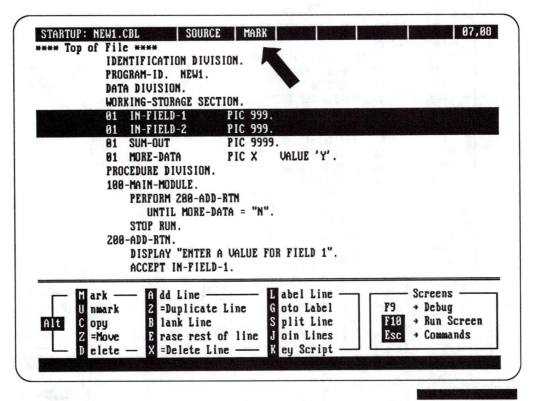

Figure 3.43

Using the _<Alt>_/M Edit Operation to Mark a Block for Moving

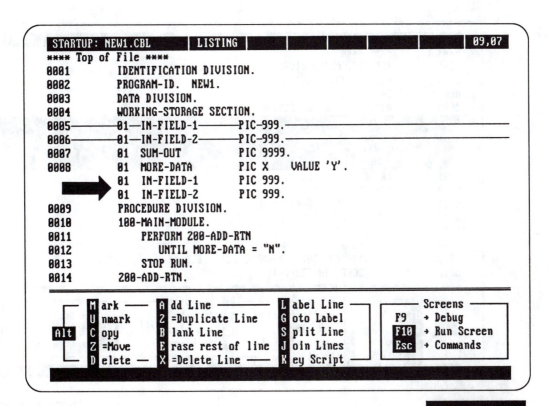

Figure 3.44

Marked Block Has Been Moved Using the _<Alt>_/Z Edit Operation

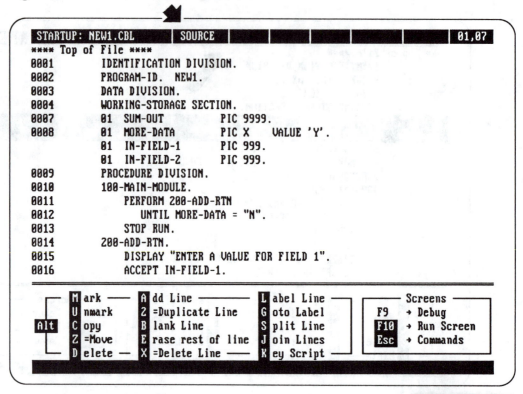

Figure 3.45

Press <*F7*> to Toggle (Switch) to the SOURCE Screen

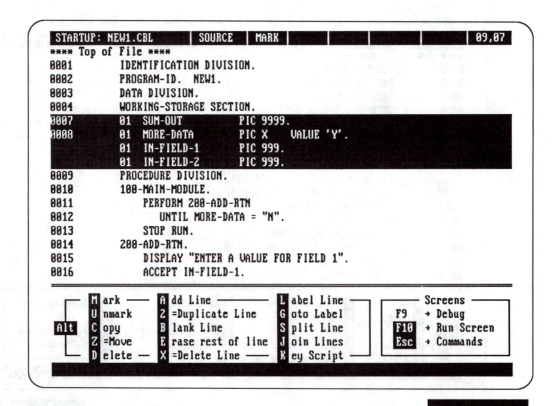

Figure 3.46

Using <*Alt*>/*M* to Mark a Block of Lines for Export

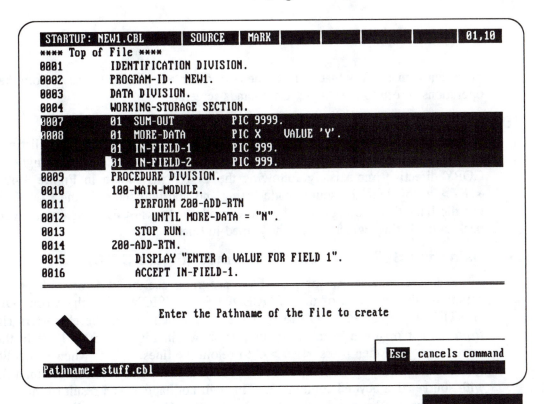

Figure 3.47

Using the Export Edit Command to Create a COPY Item

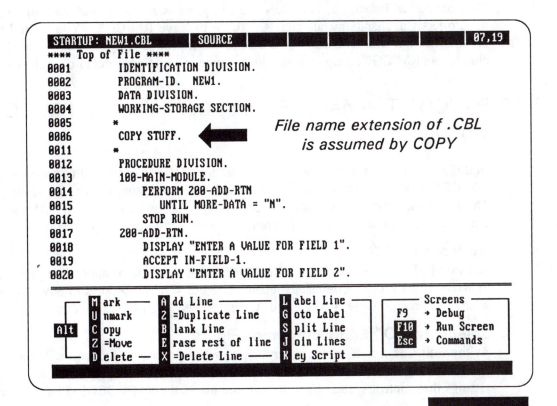

Figure 3.48

Program after Deleting Exported Lines and Installing COPY

preassigned macro key that "emits" the two $<Esc>$'s needed to move from the editing operations screen to the Project Commands screen.

19. Seeing Copied-In Lines (Figure 3.49)

At the Project Commands screen, press $<Enter>$ to go into the listing of the freshly-compiled NEW1 program. You will see the lines of coding brought in by the COPY directive immediately following the COPY, as shown in Figure 3.49. Press $<F7>$ to toggle to the source code listing and you will see only the COPY directive, not the lines that are copied in by the compiler. Press $<F7>$ again and you toggle back to the listing, which shows the copied-in lines.

20. Using the Split and Join Commands (Figure 3.50)

In the source code screen for the NEW1 program, use the $<Arrow>$ keys to put the cursor on the first line of the PROCEDURE DIVISION, after the words DISPLAY "ENTER A. Press $<Alt>$/S to split the line, which moves the characters rightward from the cursor down to the next line, as shown in Figure 3.50. Type in the added word "new" and then press $<Alt>$/J to rejoin the lines. Note: when you split a line, type more words into the line, and rejoin it, you can create lines longer than 80 bytes, with source code beyond column 72. This will not happen as a result of this step in the tutorial, but can happen in actual work you do. You can view lines longer than 80 bytes by moving the cursor rightward on such a line, using the $<Right\ Arrow>$ key.

End of Tutorial 5, Part B

This concludes Tutorial 5, Part B. You can press $<Esc>$ to end viewing and reach the Project Commands menu, and "Q" twice to leave RM/CO*. You should now be familiar enough with RM/CO* to be able to use it productively, and you should now be able to use RM/CO*'s help facilities to continue to build your depth of understanding.

3.10 RM/CO* Tutorial 6: Setting Compiler and RM/CO* Options

In this final tutorial we show you how to use the "O" edit command to set compiler and RM/CO* options for either the file (member) you are editing or for the whole project. The skills you learn in this tutorial round out your knowledge of RM/CO* and let you tailor its operation to suit your preference in compiler output and operation.

1. Activate RM/CO*

Activate RM/CO* by entering the RMCOSTAR at the DOS prompt, then press any key to arrive at the Project Commands menu. Use the $<Arrow>$ keys to any program you wish, and press $<Enter>$ to go into (to "enter") editing of the program.

2. Select the "O" Edit Command (Figure 3.51)

At the Edit Commands menu, enter "O" to select "options" and you will see a screen similar to Figure 3.51. The window displays a list of compiler options, which are settings that control special features and outputs of the RM/COBOL-85 compiler. The

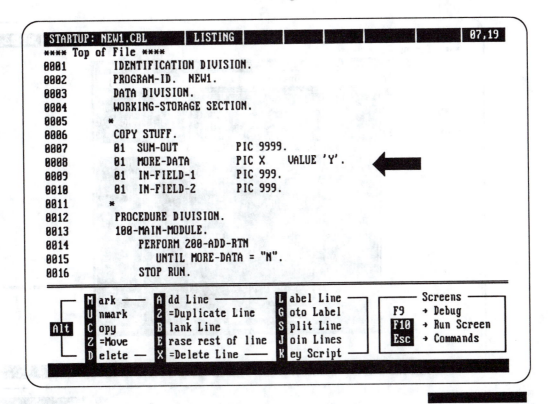

Figure 3.49

Copied-in Lines Appear in Red on the Compiled Listing

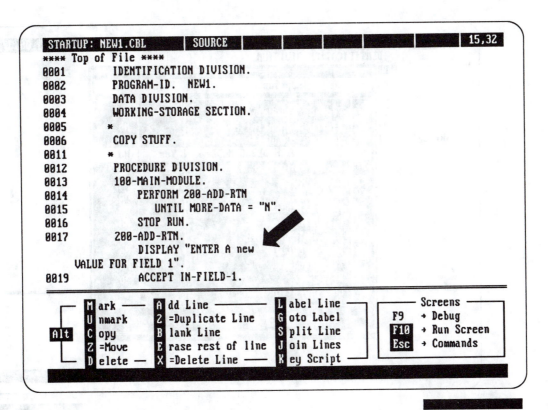

Figure 3.50

Using the <Alt>/S "Split" Command at Line 0018

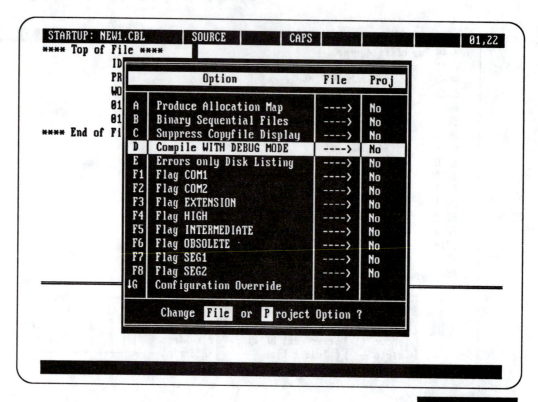

Figure 3.51

Select "O" Options from Edit Commands to Get This Window

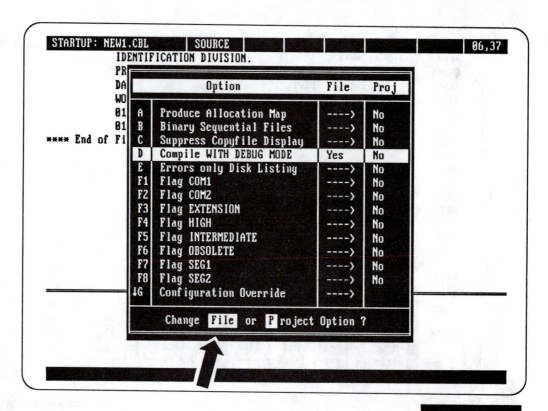

Figure 3.52

Press "F" to Change the Option Setting for the File (Member)

nature of these options is documented for you in Appendix C. Move the highlighted bar down using the *<Down Arrow>* key so that the "Compile WITH DEBUG MODE" option is highlighted. This option, when activated, makes lines coded with "D" in column 7 (usually treated as comments) act as normal executable lines.

3. Press "F" to Change Option for the File (Figure 3.52)

You can activate or deactivate the highlighted option for either the single file (member) you are editing or for the entire project. To change the option for the file, you can press the letter "F". To change the option for the entire project, you can press the letter "P". Press "F" several times now. You will see in Figure 3.52 that the ----> changes to "Yes" the first time you press "F". Press "F" again and the setting changes to "No", then back to ----> each time you press "F." "Yes" means the option is activated, "No" means the option is turned off, and ----> means that the option setting for the file is taken from that for the project. (It's unfortunate that RM/CO* is inconsistent in its terminology. "File" means the same thing here as "member.")

4. Press "P" to Change Option for the Whole Project (Figure 3.53)

In Figure 3.53 we have moved the highlight bar up to the "Produce Allocation Map" option. Pressing "P" changes this option for the whole project. Setting the option to "Yes" for the project means that every program in the project, when compiled, will have an allocation map at the end of its compile listing.

5. Second Compiler and RM/CO* Options Screen (Figure 3.54)

Press the *<Page Down>* key while the option window is visible to scroll the contents of the window downward and see additional compiler and RM/CO* options, as shown in Figure 3.54. Use this window now to set the "X" option on for the whole project. This option generates a useful data name cross-reference that lists data names in alphabetical sequence and shows what line each data name is defined on. If you set the "V" option you can dispense with coding ORGANIZATION IS LINE SEQUENTIAL as discussed in Appendix C. Note that the five items at the bottom of this last option screen are not compiler options, but options to control the way RM/CO* works. If you set the Automatic Update option on for the file (member) you will not have to manually perform the "U" Update function to apply changes to the actual file in which the member is stored.

6. Compile the Program with Options Now Set

Press *<Esc>* to leave the options window, then press *<Esc>* again to arrive at the Project Commands menu. Compile the program you selected in step 1, and view the compiler listing. You will see that an allocation map and cross-reference are now provided at the bottom of the listing as a result of the option settings. Appendix C illustrates how to interpret each of these.

End of Tutorial 6

This concludes Tutorial 6, our final tutorial on the use of RM/CO*. By completing these six tutorials you have gained the skill needed to use RM/CO* for your programming work in introductory and advanced COBOL courses. Best wishes in using RM/CO* for your programming assignments!

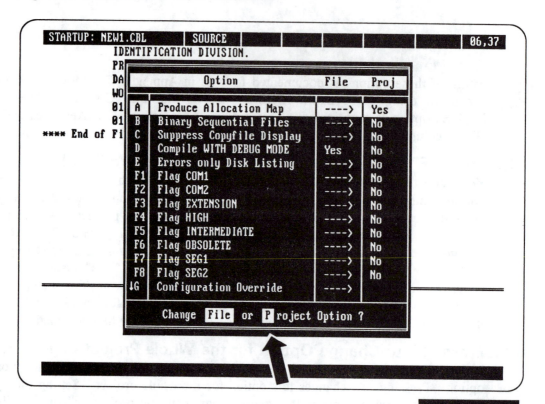

Figure 3.53

Press "P" to Change the Option Setting for the Whole Project

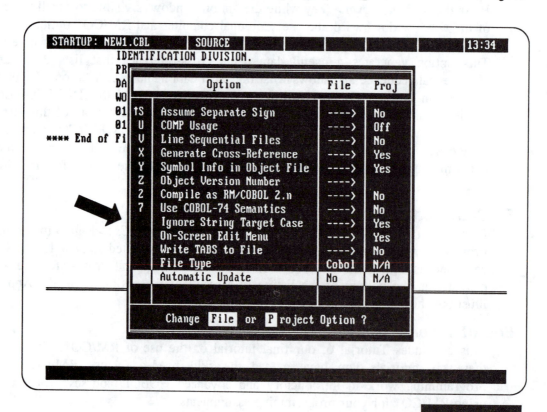

Figure 3.54

Options to Control RM/CO* Are at the Bottom of the Options List

Chapter 4

Using RM/COBOL-85 from the DOS Prompt

4.1 Creating Programs and Data as ASCII Files

T he RM/CO* package provides a convenient text editor integrated with access to the RM/COBOL-85 compiler. You may already use a word processor, however, and find yourself comfortable and productive with its particular keystrokes for manipulating text. Instead of using the RM/CO* text editor, you can use your own word processor to prepare COBOL source code and data for your RM/COBOL-85 programs. We explain how to do this in Chapter 4, and show you how to use the RM/COBOL-85 compiler and runtime system directly from the DOS prompt.

4.2 Differences between ASCII and Word Processed Files

An ASCII file, also sometimes called a "DOS" file, is simply a file of characters as entered from the keyboard, including the characters generated by the < Return > or < Enter > key at the end of each line. The file contains the bit patterns generated by your keystrokes, and each line is only as long as the number of characters you entered into it. Each line contains only your keystrokes, and no other formatting or printing control symbols, except the end of line symbols.

An ASCII file is the common denominator of electronic information interchange. Since the ASCII character set is standard, anyone can accept and view an ASCII file, so long as they can physically read the disk or tape on which the file is conveyed. When you use a simple text editor or word processor such as the editor supplied with DOS, you create an ASCII file. Shareware word processors such as PC-WRITE, available at negligible cost via public software bulletin boards and shareware distributors (check PC magazine ads), also produce files of this type. More sophisticated word processors such as WordPerfect, Microsoft Word, and Ami Pro can also produce ASCII files, but do not do so by default.

You can use any text editor or word processor to capture your keystrokes on a PC, and the words you place on the screen will look readable. But most word processors actually store information in a non-ASCII format. This happens because word processors often use the eighth bit of a byte, which is not necessary for the storage of the 128 ASCII characters, to indicate line or paragraph endings. Many word processors also include extra nonprinting control characters within your stored text to retain information about line width, page size, indentation, and your use of different fonts and typefaces. These extra characters are interpreted by the word processing software as you display or print your text, and they are not made visible (unless you use a "see codes" feature of a word processor to give them a visual presence).

Extra word processor-generated text-formatting symbols do not belong in either your program source code or data you prepare for input to a program. If you use a word processor to create programs or data, you must be careful to output what you are creating using the word processor's option to save the file in ASCII format. Different word processing software uses different terminology for ASCII files. WordPerfect and others, for example, refer to these as "DOS" or text files.

Every line of an ASCII file actually ends with two characters: line feed, and carriage return. Some word processors call these "hard returns." These characters are both generated automatically when you press the <*Enter*> or <*Return*> key on a PC keyboard. These special characters don't cause printed symbols to appear on a screen or printer. Rather, they cause the cursor on the screen or the print head to do just what their names say. The line feed character causes the cursor to drop down a line or the paper in a printer to advance one line. The carriage return causes the cursor to move to the left edge of the screen, or the print head of a printer to move to the left side.

Line feed and carriage return are machine control signals. When you direct an ASCII file to the screen by copying it from a file to the screen using the DOS TYPE command, it is the line feed and carriage return characters at the end of each line that cause the cursor to move down and to the left at the appropriate times.

4.3   Demonstrating What an ASCII File Is

If you enter the following command while in your \RMCOB subdirectory, you should see the source code for the FIRST1.CBL program as you would expect it to look:

```
c:> type first1.cbl  <Enter>
```

Trying to type out a file like this is a good way to check and see if it really is an ASCII file. If the file is not in ASCII format, the material will not look normal when typed out. If you use the DOS TYPE command on a file in this way and the text jumps around the screen, some characters appear as unusual symbols, and random beeps are generated, it's a clear indication that it is not an ASCII file.

4.4   Converting a Non-ASCII File to an ASCII File

Non-ASCII files can't be processed by RM/COBOL-85 as source code, and can't readily be input as raw keyed data by COBOL programs you create. If you have created a program or data file in a non-ASCII format by accident, you may be able to salvage all or most of it. Activate the word processor you used to create the file, and read in the file. Then select the appropriate word processor command to output (save) the file as an ASCII file. This should cause your word processor to convert the file to ASCII format, removing the unique nonprinting symbols the word processor ordinarily uses to control print formatting.

4.5   RM/COBOL-85 File Naming Conventions

RM/COBOL-85 expects to read COBOL source code from files named with the extension .CBL. You should, therefore, create any program source code as an ASCII file named similar to FIRST1.CBL. The first eight characters (the DOS "filename") can be any name you desire, in keeping with DOS file naming requirements. You can use letters or numbers, many symbols such as !, @, #, $, %, _, ^, &, -, and the twiddle ~ within file names. You should use the file extension .DAT to name data files being read or written by your programs.

4.6   Column Usage in RM/COBOL-85

RM/COBOL-85 follows COBOL standards for the placement of COBOL statements in columns on each line of source code. If you use your own text editor or word processor to create programs, you will have to either place line numbers in columns 1 through 6, or simply skip over these columns and put spaces there. RM/COBOL-85 will not examine what you put into columns 1 through 6, and we suggest that you leave them blank, then renumber them after entry using the "R" utility (see section 4.16). You might find it handy to set a tab stop in your word processor at column 7, to make it especially easy to skip over these positions in the line.

According to COBOL standards, you can code only these characters in column 7 of each line of source code:

- A space (for ordinary active lines of source code)

- An asterisk to make a line a comment

- A slash to cause a source code listing produced by a compiler to start on a new page at this point

- A "D" to make the line a conditionally compiled "debugging" line. A conditionally compiled line will be treated either as a comment or as an active line depending on an option you can specify at the time you compile the program (Appendix C describes and discusses compiler options). You can also control this with a phrase coded on the SOURCE-COMPUTER line, but that coding is much less convenient than using a compiler option.

Column 8 of each line of active source code is called the "A" margin and column 12 is called the "B" margin. As your COBOL textbook shows you, certain elements of COBOL must begin at either the A or B margin. RM/COBOL-85 follows the COBOL standards and you will also find it convenient to set tab stops in your word processor at columns 8 and 12. COBOL standards do not prescribe any additional column placement requirements for source code after column 12.

The last column in which you can code anything on a line of source code is column 72. Anything you enter on a line after column 72 will be invisible to the RM/COBOL-85 compiler. Since your screen is 80 characters wide, however, it is easy to go a bit too far and extend your coding beyond where it should be on a line. This can produce frustrating problems because the compiler does not "see" what you see on the screen, and you may not readily grasp what it is complaining about. We suggest that you set your word processor right margin to column 72, so that normal word wrap will occur if you try to code beyond column 72 on a line. The word wrap will not produce useful coding; you can't just hop to the start of the next line to continue coding in columns 1

```
C:\RMCOB> rmcobol copyit l

RM/COBOL-85 Compiler - Version 5.24.00 for DOS 2.00+.
Configured for 001 user.
Educational Version - Restricted Usage
Copyright (c) 1985, 1992 by Liant Software Corp.  All rights reserved.
Registration number: GY-0000-00860-01

Total generated object size:      1078 (X"00000436") bytes

Errors: 0, Warnings: 0, Lines: 67 for program COPYIT.

Compilation complete -- Programs: 1, Errors: 0, Warnings: 0.

C:\RMCOB>
```

Figure 4.1

Compiling the COPYIT Program

Compiling a program with the RMCOBOL command produces an object file named with the file extension .COB. The "L" compile option produces a source code listing file named with the file extension .LST. This produces a source code file named COPYIT.LST in this case.

through 6. But the word wrap will warn you that you were trying to form too long a line of source code.

4.7   Compiling RM/COBOL-85 Programs from DOS

Compiling a program from the DOS prompt using RM/COBOL-85 is simple. Assuming your source code file is in the same subdirectory as the compiler and the name of the program is COPYIT.CBL, enter the RMCOBOL command:

```
c:> rmcobol copyit <Enter>
```

The compiler assumes a file extension of .CBL, that is, it will process the source code it finds in a file named COPYIT.CBL. Of course, COPYIT.CBL is just an example here, the name of one of the sample programs included on your RM/COBOL-85 diskette (Diskette 1). In response to a command to compile a program, RM/COBOL-85 reads and analyzes the source code in the file you have named at the compile command, as shown in Figure 4.1. If it finds no syntax errors in your program source code, it produces an object file on the same disk and in the subdirectory as the source code. The object file has the same name as the source code file, and the extension .COB. In this case you can execute the object file as described in section 4.12. (VAX minicomputers use the file extension .COB for source code, and

.OBJ for object files. If you are coming from the VAX environment the use of file extensions made by RM/COBOL-85 may seem a bit strange!)

If the compiler finds one or more errors in your source code, it produces on the screen one or more descriptive error messages. You must then use your text editor to edit your source code to correct the errors, and recompile the program. You may need to repeat the process of editing and recompiling several times before all syntax errors are eliminated.

After trying out the RM/COBOL-85 compiler, and reading the sections 4.9, 4.10, and browsing Appendix C, you will understand why the basic command to compile a program is enhanced by entering it as:

```
c:> rmcobol copyit l,a,x,y  <Enter>
```

The characters "l,a,x,y" invoke useful compiler options. The "l" option generates a source code listing file, "a" adds extra information called an "allocation map" into the listing, "x" puts a cross-reference of data names into the listing, and "y" includes things in the object file that make interactive debugging easier.

4.8   Producing a Source Code Listing

If you receive syntax error messages from the compiler, you almost always have to examine a source code listing, which you can have the compiler produce. Unless your program is very tiny, some error messages will have scrolled off the top of the screen by the time the compiler completes its work. The source code listing will contain each error message immediately following the line that contains the error.

To tell the compiler to produce a source code listing, compile a program with the compiler option L:

```
c:> rmcobol copyit L  <Enter>
```

While the L is shown as a capital letter in this example, a lowercase l would work just as well. In response to this specification, RM/COBOL-85 creates a file named COPYIT.LST, in other words, a file with the same file name and the file extension .LST. You can examine this file using your text editor. Figure 4.2 illustrates how such a listing appears on the screen.

The source code listing produced by the RM/COBOL-85 compiler is 132 print positions wide, as you can see in Figure 4.3. When viewing this listing on the screen, you'll have to scroll the screen to the right to see the full text of the message or the location of the $ symbol that the compiler prints under each apparent error.

4.9   Printing a Source Code Listing

You can copy a source code listing file to the printer using a COPY command like this:

```
c:> copy copyit.lst lpt1  <Enter>
```

```
RM/COBOL-85 (Version 5.24.00) for DOS 2.00+    10-05-93  14:14:29    Page 1
Source file: COPYIT                        Options: L

  LINE    DEBUG      PG/LN -A 1 B..+....2....+....3....+....4....+....5....+....6..

     1               000100 ID DIVISION.
     2               000200 PROGRAM-ID.  COPYIT.
     3               000300 AUTHOR.  JIM JANOSSY, DEPAUL UNIVERSITY, CHICAGO.
     4               000400
     5               000500********************************************************
     6               000600*  This program is originally appeared in Practical MVS
     7               000700*  Examples by Jim Janossy (John Wiley & Sons, Inc. 1993
     8               000800*  is reprinted here by permission of the publisher.
     9               000900*  This program reads a file of records named WORKERS.DA
    10               001000*  and prints a simple report to demonstrate file handli
    11               001100*  using RM/COBOL-85 Version 5.24.        J. Janossy, Jul
    12               001200********************************************************
    13               001300
    14               001400 ENVIRONMENT DIVISION.
    15               001500 INPUT-OUTPUT SECTION.
    16               001600 FILE-CONTROL.
    17               001700     SELECT INPUT-FILE          ASSIGN TO DISK 'WORKERS.
    18               001800         ORGANIZATION IS LINE SEQUENTIAL.
    19               001900     SELECT OUTPUT-FILE         ASSIGN TO DISK 'WORKERS.
```

Figure 4.2

Viewing a .LST Source Code File

You can view the .LST "listing" file from a compile on your screen using your text editor, but it is actually designed to be printed. The listing contains line numbers at the left side, applied by the RM/COBOL-85 compiler, and imbedded error messages if source code syntax errors are present. Scroll your view to the right to see more of the source code lines and error message text if you view .LST files this way.

You may have to copy the file EJECT.DAT to the printer immediately after this copy action to force your printer to eject the final page of the printed listing, or press its "form feed" button. You can also get a printed copy of the source code listing by compiling with the P option, which automatically creates the listing and copies it to the printer (LPT1):

```
c:> rmcobol copyit P <Enter>
```

Once again, you may have to copy the file EJECT.DAT to the printer immediately after this copy action to force your printer to eject the final page of the printed listing, or press its "form feed" button. You can also ask for both a disk-stored source code listing file and a printed copy in one action:

```
c:> rmcobol copyit L,P <Enter>
```

4.10 Compiler Options

The L and P compiler options described in section 4.8 and 4.9 are only two of many optional services that you can request from the RM/COBOL-85 compiler. Other options can produce a sorted cross-reference of data names, create an "allocation map" describing all the data fields in the program, identify your usage of obsolete syntax elements, and alter the way files are processed, among other things. All told, over 20 RM/COBOL-85 compiler options exist.

You can find documentation about RM/COBOL-85 compiler options in Appendix C. The same options available by letter code when you compile a program from the DOS prompt are available within RM/CO* if you use it to compile your programs. In RM/CO*, you set your option choices interactively using the menu that appears when you select the "options" function from the Project Commands menu.

4.11 Source Code (Compile) Errors

RM/COBOL-85 categorizes its compiler messages as I (information), W (warning), E or (execution). A program that has one or more E errors will not run until the errors are corrected. A program that has only warning messages may or may not run properly. "I" messages are informational only and do not indicate a serious problem.

In the source code listing, $ is printed under any coding flagged as an error. A message indicating SCAN RESUME is displayed on the listing at the point where syntax checking continues after the error. Sometimes errors are difficult for the compiler to identify, with the effect that several entries may be designated as errors until the compiler can recognize an appropriate item. SCAN RESUME states that the compilation process is starting again at this point.

All types of compiler messages are identified with a specific message number, and the compiler-produced message text is self-explanatory. Some error messages are more difficult to decipher than others. Some types of errors cause multiple error messages. For example, if you misspell a data name in your WORKING-STORAGE section, and use its correct spelling in seven places in the program, you will receive seven error messages. Why? Because none of the seven uses of the data name refers to a defined data name. Rather than having seven corrections to make, however, you can correct the single data name declaration error, which may not even be flagged by the compiler!

Do not be surprised and certainly do not despair if you receive error messages that you have difficulty deciphering. Do your best to find the source of error in a few minutes and if you cannot, then ask for help from someone with more knowledge. We think it is best for you to try to isolate errors yourself first, in a reasonable period of time, and then consult an expert. To agonize over an error for hours when the problem may be minor will only lead to frustration.

```
RM/COBOL-85 (Version 5.24.00) for DOS 2.00+   10-05-93   14:14:29   Page 1
Source file: COPYIT                            Options: L

LINE  DEBUG   PG/LN -A 1 B..+....2....+....3....+....4....+....5....+....6....+....7..IDENTFCN

1     000100 ID DIVISION.
2     000200 PROGRAM-ID.  COPYIT.
3     000300 AUTHOR.  JIM JANOSSY, DEPAUL UNIVERSITY, CHICAGO.
4     000400 ***************************************************************
5     000500*                                                             *
6     000600* This program is originally appeared in Practical MVS JCL    *
7     000700* Examples by Jim Janossy (John Wiley & Sons, Inc. 1993) and  *
8     000800* is reprinted here by permission of the publisher.           *
9     000900* This program reads a file of records named WORKERS.DAT      *
10    001000* and prints a simple report to demonstrate file handling     *
11    001100* using RM/COBOL-85 Version 5.24.      J. Janossy July 1993    *
12    001200 ***************************************************************
13    001300
14    001400 ENVIRONMENT DIVISION.
15    001500 INPUT-OUTPUT SECTION.
16    001600 FILE-CONTROL.
17    001700     SELECT INPUT-FILE       ASSIGN TO DISK 'WORKERS.DAT'
18    001800         ORGANIZATION IS LINE SEQUENTIAL.
19    001900     SELECT OUTPUT-FILE      ASSIGN TO DISK 'WORKERS.REP'
20    002000         ORGANIZATION IS LINE SEQUENTIAL.
21    002100
22    002200 DATA DIVISION.
23    002300 FILE SECTION.
24    002400 FD INPUT-FILE
25    002500    RECORD CONTAINS 60 CHARACTERS.
26    002600 01 INPUT-RECORD                  PIC X(60).
27    002700 FD OUTPUT-FILE
28    002800    RECORD CONTAINS 60 CHARACTERS.
29    002900 01 OUTPUT-RECORD                 PIC X(60).
30    003000
```

```
RM/COBOL-85 (Version 5.24.00) for DOS 2.00+   10-05-93   14:14:29   Page 2
Source file: COPYIT                            Options: L

LINE  DEBUG   PG/LN -A 1 B..+....2....+....3....+....4....+....5....+....6....+....7..IDENTFCN  COPYIT

31    003100/
32    003200 WORKING-STORAGE SECTION.
33    003300 01 WS-FLAG           PIC X(1)   VALUE 'M'.
34    003400 01 WS-COUNT          PIC 9(5)   VALUE 0.
35    003500 01 WS-COUNT-Z        PIC ZZ,ZZ9.
```

Figure 4.3 Source Code Listing COPYIT.LST

Compiling a program with the "L" option produces a .LST file that you can send to the printer. Compiling with the "P" option sends this listing to the printer automatically.

4.12 Running RM/COBOL-85 Programs from DOS

Once you have compiled a program without any major errors, you can run it. For example, to run a successfully compiled program named COPYIT, you enter:

```
c:> runcobol copyit <Enter>
```

The educational version of RM/COBOL-85 automatically invokes an interactive debugger. You will receive a line such as the following on your screen when you use the RUNCOBOL command (here, I am running the program named COPYIT):

```
ST 38 COPYIT C? _
```

ST stands for "step" and the number "38" is the line number of the next instruction to be executed. COPYIT in this line is the name of the program being run, and is taken from the program's PROGRAM-ID sentence, *not* the DOS file name. The cursor rests after the C? prompt, which asks you to enter a debugging command.

If you press the *<Enter>* key or type the letter "s" and press *<Enter>*) at the C? prompt, the runtime system will execute just the next instruction in your program, and will produce another prompt similar to this one. (Just pressing *<Enter>* is fine to begin step-by-step program operation, but entering "s" and then *<Enter>* is necessary after entry of a debugging instruction, as described in Appendix D covering the interactive debugger.) Pressing *<Enter>* again will cause execution of the next step, and so forth.

Step-by-step execution is part of RM/COBOL-85's interactive debugger, and execution of all programs compiled and run with the educational version of RM/COBOL-85 begin in debugging mode. The interactive debugger permits you to view the actual sequence of steps as they are executed, since the line number changes to show the passage of control through the program. Figure 4.4 illustrates this method of execution for the COPYIT program.

If this program used the DISPLAY verb, you would see the DISPLAYed lines produced by the program on the screen interpersed between the ST prompt lines. Try step-by-step debugging with the FIRST1 program, for example, and you will see output as shown in Figure 4.5.

Step-by-step execution can be a very useful debugging aid with DISPLAY or with the use of interactive debugging commands. Appendix D shows you debugging commands you can enter at the C? prompt to set breakpoints (places where program execution will stop), traps (conditions that when met cause the program to stop), and commands to view the contents of data fields in the program. One of the debugging commands will execute the program completely, without the need to press the *<Enter>* key to proceed with execution step by step. To execute the program, enter the command E at the C? prompt:

```
ST 38 COPYIT C? e
```

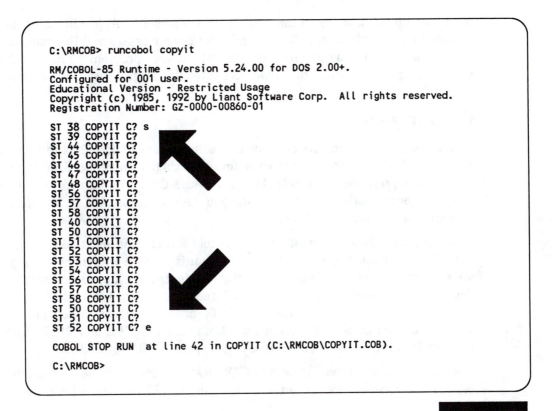

```
C:\RMCOB> runcobol copyit

RM/COBOL-85 Runtime - Version 5.24.00 for DOS 2.00+.
Configured for 001 user.
Educational Version - Restricted Usage
Copyright (c) 1985, 1992 by Liant Software Corp.  All rights reserved.
Registration Number: GZ-0000-00860-01

ST 38 COPYIT C? s
ST 39 COPYIT C?
ST 44 COPYIT C?
ST 45 COPYIT C?
ST 46 COPYIT C?
ST 47 COPYIT C?
ST 48 COPYIT C?
ST 56 COPYIT C?
ST 57 COPYIT C?
ST 58 COPYIT C?
ST 40 COPYIT C?
ST 50 COPYIT C?
ST 51 COPYIT C?
ST 52 COPYIT C?
ST 53 COPYIT C?
ST 54 COPYIT C?
ST 56 COPYIT C?
ST 57 COPYIT C?
ST 58 COPYIT C?
ST 50 COPYIT C?
ST 51 COPYIT C?
ST 52 COPYIT C? e

COBOL STOP RUN  at line 42 in COPYIT (C:\RMCOB\COPYIT.COB).

C:\RMCOB>
```

Figure 4.4

Step-by-Step Execution of the COPYIT Program

The interactive debugger is always invoked when you execute (run) a program compiled with the educational version of RM/COBOL-85. If you enter "s" and press <*Enter*> you will step through the program one instruction at a time, and the prompt tells you the compiler-assigned line number of the next instruction to be executed. If you enter the "e" ("end debugging") command, the program executes to completion.

E means "end" and ends involvement with the debugger, letting the program simply execute to completion. You actually don't need to begin stepping through a program one instruction at a time in order to use the E command. Just enter E as soon as you receive the first ST command and the entire program will execute to completion.

4.13 Runtime Errors

It is quite possible for a program to compile successfully but fail when you run it. When this happens, you will receive a runtime error number on the screen. Such an error message and number are shown in Figure 4.6. To resolve this type of error, you must look up the meaning of the runtime error number in Appendix E. Runtime errors include file, procedure, and data errors. The error message and line number shown on the screen will help you diagnose the problem in your program. You will then have to edit the program to correct the error, recompile the program, and run it again.

4.14 Creating Data Files

You can use your word processor or text editor to create data files to be read by your RM/COBOL-85 programs. On each line you simply enter the data in the positions desired and press the *<Enter>* key to indicate the end of a record. As with your program source code files, make sure you save these as ASCII files rather than as formatted word processing files.

Since data records will be read in a fixed-field format, you must take particular care to align fields consistently within your data records. Use a column ruler as provided by your word processor to make sure that fields are positioned to match the record descriptions you will be using to read records. Figure 4.7 shows you how the WORKERS.DAT file read by the COPYIT program appears when presented on the screen using the DOS TYPE command. Both COPYIT.CBL and WORKERS.DAT are on your Diskette 1, and should already be in your \RMCOB subdirectory.

With the commercial version of RM/COBOL-85, records can be any length. With the educational version, records can be a maximum of 132 characters long.

4.15 Viewing Output Disk Files

Once your program runs to completion, you need to carefully check the contents of output disk files to ensure that they contain the correct information. There are three ways to view the contents of a disk file:

- Before coding a WRITE to a file in a program, include a DISPLAY statement. Have this DISPLAY statement make the record to be written to a file appear on the screen.

- Use the DOS TYPE command or your text editor or word processor to view any data files produced by the program. The name of the file you TYPE or view must be the DOS file name and extension of the output file.

- Use the DOS DEBUG utility to see file contents in hexadecimal and characters formats.

Neither of the first two approaches is suitable if the file you must examine contains packed decimal numbers or signed numbers. The third method to view the contents of a file overcomes the limitations of the first two file viewing methods. The following example shows you how to view the contents of the WORKERS.DAT file supplied on Diskette 1, using DEBUG. Enter the following command:

```
c:> debug workers.dat  <Enter>
```

```
C:\RMCOB> runcobol first1

RM/COBOL-85 Runtime - Version 5.24.00 for DOS 2.00+.
Configured for 001 user.
Educational Version - Restricted Usage
Copyright (c) 1985, 1992 by Liant Software Corp.  All rights reserved.
Registration Number: GZ-0000-00860-01


ST 11 FIRST1 C? s
ST 12 FIRST1 C?

ST 13 FIRST1 C?
   Welcome to the world of RM/COBOL-85!
ST 14 FIRST1 C?
   Best wishes from Liant Software Corp.
ST 15 FIRST1 C?
                   John Wiley & Sons, Inc.
ST 16 FIRST1 C?
                   Nancy and Robert Stern
ST 17 FIRST1 C?
                   Jim Janossy
ST 18 FIRST1 C?

ST 19 FIRST1 C?
COBOL STOP RUN  at line 19 in FIRST1 (C:\RMCOB\FIRST1.COB).
SR 19 FIRST1 C?

C:\RMCOB>
```

Figure 4.5

Step-by-Step Execution of the FIRST1 Program

```
C:\RMCOB> runcobol copyit

RM/COBOL-85 Runtime - Version 5.24.00 for DOS 2.00+.
Configured for 001 user.
Educational Version - Restricted Usage
Copyright (c) 1985, 1992 by Liant Software Corp.  All rights reserved.
Registration Number: GZ-0000-00860-01




ST 38 COPYIT C? e
COBOL I/O error 35 on INPUT-FILE file C:\RMCOB\WORKERS.DAT.
COBOL I/O error  at line 45 in COPYIT (C:\RMCOB\COPYIT.COB) compiled 93/10/05
14:14:29.

C:\RMCOB>
```

Figure 4.6

A Runtime Error Reported by RM/COBOL-85

```
21256 NILLY      WILLY     402CASHIERS OFFICE
21257 IPPI       MRS.      378PHOTO DEPARTMENT
21260 MALLOW     MARSHA    390KITCHEN APPLIANCES
21307 WARE       DELLA     246FURNITURE
21310 SHAW       ARKAN     300HARDWARE
21574 AH         GEORGE    400PHOTO DEPARTMENT
21668 ZOORI      MOE       179PLUMBING SUPPLIES
25112 CABOOSE    LUCE      305FURNITURE
25189 HOW        IDA       005SUITCASES AND BAGS
33102 IFORNIA    CAL       200TRAVEL DEPARTMENT
33261 CANNON     LUCE      316TOYS
33377 WHIZ       G.        357PERSONAL COMPUTERS
33480 TOUR       D.        160WOMENS CLOTHING
33483 INA        CAROL     530REMODELING SUPPLIES
39321 ABAMA      AL        420WOMENS CLOTHING
39322 TUCKY      KEN       350HARDWARE
```

Figure 4.7

Data Read by the COPYIT Program

This data is housed in a file named WORKERS.DAT. It is read by the COPYIT program and used to produce a simple report. The fields of information in each record are employee id number, last name, first name, number of hours worked during the week (as a PIC 99V9 number), and the department of a department store in which the employee works.

This will change the prompt character to the hyphen. Then enter:

    - d 100 <Enter>

This DEBUG command says "display the data in memory at displacement 100 (hex)." The data you are attempting to view has been copied into memory at this point. This command produces a hexadecimal and character dump as shown in Figure 4.8. With the DEBUG hexadecimal format of data display, data is shown with 16 bytes on each line. The left side of a line shows the contents of the 16 bytes in hexadecimal, with each byte described with two characters. The two characters, such as 4E in the seventh position of the first data line in Figure 4.8, are an abbreviation for the bit pattern housed at that location. The character form of output produced by this particular bit pattern is located at the seventh position, at the right side of the screen, which shows whatever prints when the bit pattern is sent to the printer.

DEBUG shows you eight lines of a file dump at a time, which is 8 x 16 = 128 bytes at a time. After starting the dump with the command "d 100" you can continue to see subsequent 128-byte chunks of the file by simply entering the command "d" at the hyphen prompt without any number:

    - d <Enter>

To exit DEBUG, enter the "q" (quit) command at DEBUG's hyphen prompt:

    - q <Enter>

```
C:\RMCOB>debug workers.dat                    Same byte of data

-d 100

20A0:0100  32 31 32 35 36 20 4E 49-4C 4C 59 20 20 20 20 20   21256 NILLY
20A0:0110  20 57 49 4C 4C 59 20 20-20 20 20 34 30 32 43 41    WILLY     402CA
20A0:0120  53 48 49 45 52 53 20 4F-46 46 49 43 45 0D 0A 32   SHIERS OFFICE..2
20A0:0130  31 32 35 37 20 49 50 50-49 20 20 20 20 20 20 20   1257 IPPI
20A0:0140  4D 52 53 2E 20 20 20 20-20 20 33 37 38 50 48 4F   MRS.      378PHO
20A0:0150  54 4F 20 44 45 50 41 52-54 4D 45 4E 54 0D 0A 32   TO DEPARTMENT..2
20A0:0160  31 32 36 30 20 4D 41 4C-4C 4F 57 20 20 20 20 20   1260 MALLOW
20A0:0170  4D 41 52 53 48 41 20 20-20 20 33 39 30 4B 49 54   MARSHA    390KIT

-d

20A0:0180  43 48 45 4E 20 41 50 50-4C 49 41 4E 43 45 53 0D   CHEN APPLIANCES.
20A0:0190  0A 32 31 33 30 37 20 57-41 52 45 20 20 20 20 20   .21307 WARE
20A0:01A0  20 20 44 45 4C 4C 41 20-20 20 20 20 32 34 36 46     DELLA     246F
20A0:01B0  55 52 4E 49 54 55 52 45-0D 0A 32 31 33 31 30 20   URNITURE..21310
20A0:01C0  53 48 41 57 20 20 20 20-20 20 20 41 52 4B 41 4E   SHAW       ARKAN
20A0:01D0  20 20 20 20 20 33 30 30-48 41 52 44 57 41 52 45        300HARDWARE
20A0:01E0  0D 0A 32 31 35 37 34 20-41 48 20 20 20 20 20 20   ..21574 AH
20A0:01F0  20 20 20 47 45 4F 52 47-45 20 20 20 20 34 30 30      GEORGE    400

-q

C:\RMCOB>
```

Figure 4.8

DEBUG Utility Display of WORKERS.DAT

You can view data in both hexadecimal and character formats using the DEBUG utility provided by DOS. Data you load to memory with debug begins at memory displacement 100 (hex). The command "d 100" indicates that you want to display this data in the "dump" format you see here, hex at left, character format at right. Hexadecimal format lets you see the contents of any byte even if the bit pattern present is not associated with a printable symbol. The "q" command quits DEBUG; see DOS documentation for more DEBUG information.

For debugging purposes it's useful to get printouts or displays of both the input and the output disk files so that you can manually check that the program is running properly. You can print the hexadecimal dump produced by the DEBUG utility by pressing <Shift> and <PrtSc>. DEBUG is a powerful DOS utility that allows you to change file contents as well as view them. You can find more information about DEBUG in the DOS documentation supplied with your PC.

4.16 Hints and Suggestions for Coding Productivity

If you use a word processor to create your program source code you will find it handy to have a few small files and executable utility programs in your \RMCOB subdirectory. These will speed your development of source code as well as help you convert any VAX COBOL programs to standard ANSI format for use with RM/COBOL-85. We have included these as tools on the RM/COBOL-85 diskette with the file names shown in the following descriptions.

Comment/Ruler Line

Figure 4.9 shows you a special comment line that marks the several important column positions in a line of COBOL source code. This comment line shows the comment column 7, the A and B margins, and a column ruler useful to align various source code elements. The ruler ends at column 72, where your source code must end. This comment/ruler is contained in file RULER.CBL. Copy it into a program at any point where you need to confirm the positioning of source code elements.

Comment Box

Figure 4.10 illustrates a template for a box made up of comment lines. You can copy this box into a program at any point where you intend to place descriptive comments, and simply put comments into the box. You can repeat the middle lines to make the comment box longer. Using this template will help you maintain a standard appearance in your documentation without having to spend time manually outlining comments with rows of asterisks.

Line Numbering/Renumbering Utility

RM/COBOL-85 does not require that source code have line numbers, and it does not pay attention to anything coded in the line number area, columns 1 through 6. But you may find it convenient to apply lines numbers as an aid to resolving runtime errors in which the line number is reported. You should not waste your time keying in line numbers!

Figure 4.11 shows you how to invoke and use a program named R, a COBOL source code renumbering utility that originally appeared in *VS COBOL II Highlights and Techniques* by James Janossy, published by John Wiley & Sons., Inc, in 1992. You can use R to create a backup copy of a program and apply consistent COBOL line numbers.

Converting Programs from VAX COBOL Terminal Format

If you have already developed COBOL programs using a Digital Equipment Corporation VAX computer, you may be interested in converting them to work with RM/COBOL-85. VAX COBOL terminal format begins each line of source code in column 1 instead of column 7 or 8, and uses some screen handling words different from RM/COBOL-85.

Figure 4.12 demonstrates how you can use a program named TERMTORM ("TERMinal TO RM") to quickly convert programs written in VAX COBOL terminal format into a format that you can compile using RM/COBOL-85. TERMTORM is a

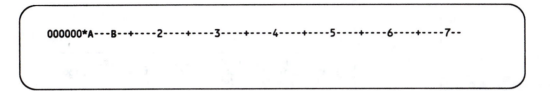

Figure 4.9

Ruler Line to Guide COBOL Program Entry

If you use an ordinary text editor or word processor to enter your COBOL source code into an ASCII file, it will help to have ruler lines like this in your programs. You can copy this from the RM/COBOL-85 diskette that accompanies this guide. It is stored as RULER.CBL.

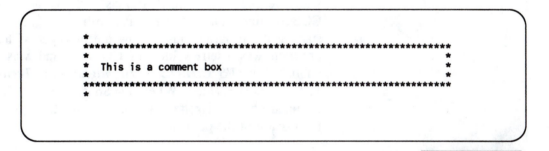

Figure 4.10

Comment Box for COBOL Program Entry

You can copy this pattern for a comment box from BOX.CBL on the RM/COBOL-85 diskette that accompanies this guide. Insert it into your programs ay whatever points you want to include explanatory comments. You can lengthen the box by repeating the third line as many times as needed.

part of materials associated with another Wiley book, *VAX COBOL On-Line,* by James Janossy (John Wiley & Sons, Inc., 1992) and is provided on the RM/COBOL-85 diskette as a convenience to you by permission of the publisher. While the TERMTORM program does much of the work of conversion, you may still have to make minor changes and cleanups yourself to achieve a completely converted program. This is especially true if the VAX COBOL program has used lines longer than 66 characters (VAX COBOL allows source code lines to be up to 255 characters long).

```
C:\RMCOB> r

                        R    The COBOL Renumbering Utility
             Featured in VS COBOL II: Highlights and Techniques
               James Janossy (John Wiley & Sons, Inc., 1992)

Long live COBOL! ===> Enter full name of source code file to renumber:
Long live COBOL! ===> copyit.cbl

Long live COBOL! ===> Backup file created as COPYIT.BAK
Long live COBOL! ===> Renumbering ended, lines written =        67
Long live COBOL! ===> Renumbered program exists as COPYIT.CBL
Need JCL help?  Check out PRACTICAL MVS JCL EXAMPLES (Janossy/Wiley, 1993)!

C:\RMCOB>
```

Figure 4.11

Using the R Line Renumbering Utility

You can create a backup copy of a COBOL program (named with the file extension .BAK) as well as apply consistent COBOL line numbers using the utility program R. After starting the program, just follow the prompts. The R utility program was itself written in COBOL, and was originally published in *VS COBOL II Highlights and Techniques* by James Janossy (John Wiley & Sons, Inc., 1992). It is included on the diskette that accompanies this guide with the permission of the publisher.

TERMTORM flags excessively long lines both on the screen and within the new source code itself.

COPY Member Usage

RM/COBOL-85 supports the use of the COPY compiler directive. You can house record descriptions or other standard elements of source code in separate files, and copy them in using COPY. For example, if you housed a record description in a file named PAYROLL.CBL you could copy it in by coding:

```
COPY PAYROLL.
```

You do not need to enclose the name of the copied in item in quotes or apostrophes, but make sure you include the period at the end of the sentence. RM/COBOL-85 will assume a file extension of .CBL for items you copy. If the item to be copied is located in a different subdirectory, such as \MYLIB, you can specify the path on the COPY:

```
COPY \MYLIB\PAYROLL.
```

```
C:\RMCOB> termtorm

            ┌─────────────────────────────────────────────────────┐
            │       TERMinal TO RM/Cobol-85 Code Conversion Utility │
            │   Converts VAX COBOL On-Line code to a microcomputer. │
            │   Any coding beyond column 72 is flagged, not converted.│
            │   Copyright 1993 James Janossy (John Wiley & Sons, Inc.)│
            └─────────────────────────────────────────────────────┘

TERMTORM ===> Enter name of VAX file to convert to RM/COBOL (.COB):
TERMTORM ===> calc3.cob

TERMTORM ===> Reading CALC3.COB and creating CALC3.CBL
TERMTORM ===> Conversion ended, lines written =      96
TERMTORM ===> Converted program exists as CALC3.CBL

C:\RMCOB>
```

Figure 4.12

Converting a VAX COBOL Program to RM/COBOL-85 Using the TERMTORM Utility

VAX COBOL uses unique coding named "terminal format" in which COBOL statements begin in column 1 rather than columns 7 or 8. You can convert VAX COBOL programs to ANSI standard format, and replace most VAX-specific reserved words with RM/COBOL-85 syntax, using the TERMTORM ("TERMinal TO RM") utility. This utility was written in COBOL and was published in *VAX COBOL On-Line* by James Janossy (John Wiley & Sons, Inc., 1992) and is included on the diskette that accompanies this guide, with the permission of the publisher. TERMTORM also detects and flags source code lines longer than 72 bytes, which are permitted by VAX COBOL.

RM/CO* recognizes copy library members as having the file extension .CPY instead of .CBL. If you plan on using RM/CO* you should name your copy library members with .CPY instead of .CBL and code your copy statements this way (again, don't forget the period at the end of this sentence):

```
COPY \MYLIB\PAYROLL.CPY.
```

You can nest COPY compiler directives up to five levels deep. That is, an item that you copy into a program using COPY can itself contain the COPY directive. Unless you compile the program with the C option, the copied-in lines will be printed in the source code listing produced by the L or P options, as shown in Figure 4.13. Copied-in lines are identified by the symbols +n+ at their start, where n is a number from 1 to 5 indicating the level of COPY nesting. The C option suppresses printing of copied-in lines in your source code listing.

```
RM/COBOL-85 (Version 5.24.00) for DOS 2.00+   10-05-93  14:52:54   Page 1
Source file: COPYDEMO                    Options: L

LINE  DEBUG   PG/LN -A 1 B..+....2....+....3....+....4....+....5....+....6....+....7..IDENTFCN

  1   000100  ID DIVISION.
  2   000200  PROGRAM-ID.  COPYIT.
  3   000300  AUTHOR.  JIM JANOSSY, DEPAUL UNIVERSITY, CHICAGO.
  4   000400
  5   000500*****************************************************************
  6   000600* This program is originally appeared in Practical MVS JCL     *
  7   000700* Examples by Jim Janossy (John Wiley & Sons Inc. 1993) and    *
  8   000800* is reprinted here by permission of the publisher.            *
  9   000900* This program reads a file of records named WORKERS.DAT       *
 10   001000* and prints a simple report to demonstrate file handling      *
 11   001100* using RM/COBOL-85 Version 5.24.      J. Janossy, July 1993   *
 12   001200*****************************************************************
 13   001300
 14   001400  ENVIRONMENT DIVISION.
 15   001500  INPUT-OUTPUT SECTION.
 16   001600  FILE-CONTROL.
 17   001700      SELECT INPUT-FILE     ASSIGN TO DISK 'WORKERS.DAT'
 18   001800          ORGANIZATION IS LINE SEQUENTIAL.
 19   001900      SELECT OUTPUT-FILE    ASSIGN TO DISK 'WORKERS.REP'
 20   002000          ORGANIZATION IS LINE SEQUENTIAL.
 21   002100
 22   002200  COPY THING1.CPY.
 23   +1     *****************************************************************
 24   +1     * COPY MEMBER THING1.CPY                                       *
 25   +1     * I copied in this item from a copy member.  While this is a   *
 26   +1     * comment COPY is handiest for record layouts and other        *
 27   +1     * types of code that should be standardized.  Notice that      *
 28   +1     * I can nest copies and how nested copies are reported.        *
 29   +1     *****************************************************************
 30   +1
 31   +1
 32   +1     COPY THING2.CPY.
 33   +2     *****************************************************************
 34   +2     * COPY MEMBER THING2.CPY                                       *
 35   +2     * Here is a second copy member.  I copied it in using a COPY   *
 36   +2     * statement in copy member THING1.CPY.  It is unusual to       *
 37   +2     * nest COPY statements in this way, but you can do it up to    *
 38   +2     * 5 levels deep in RM/COBOL-85.                                *
 39   +2     *****************************************************************
 40   +2
 41   +2
 42   002300  DATA DIVISION.
 43   002400  FILE SECTION.
 44   002500  FILE SECTION.
```

Figure 4.13

How COPY Affects Your Source Code Listing

You can use the compiler directive COPY to bring in lines of source code from other files at compile time. Lines brought in by the compiler in response to COPY statements are listed with +n+ where n reflects the level of nesting. RM/COBOL-85 allows you to use COPY within items you copy in, to a nesting level five deep.

Chapter 5

File Input and Output: The SELECT Statement

5.1 Input and Output Using RM/COBOL-85

T he RM/COBOL-85 compiler and runtime system supports the full range of file input/output typical of the COBOL environment, including sequential, relative, and indexed files. In addition, the SELECT statement provides the means to deal with text editor-produced ASCII files, which are commonly used as input data to COBOL programs. You'll find that some of the true power of the microcomputer-based COBOL environment is accessed via the coding variations of the SELECT statement, and we show you several examples in this chapter.

It's important to understand the real significance of the extent of support RM/COBOL-85 provides for your programming. For one thing, you do not need any other software to create or access any of the file types mentioned above. That is, RM/COBOL-85 provides complete support for files even as internally complex as indexed files. In the mainframe environment and with some PC-based language products, you would need additional software in the form of a file manager to work with indexed files. In addition, RM/COBOL-85 adheres to ANSI standards for the handling of relative and indexed files, including the way it uses and supports the File Status field. Programs you develop using RM/COBOL-85 will work the same way on a Digital Equipment Corporation VAX or IBM mainframe, even when they deal with relative and indexed files. This degree of high-level portability is still not available with many other languages.

5.2 The SELECT Statement for Input and Output Files

Programs usually use data files on disk as input and will either create output files on disk or on the printer. PC versions of COBOL such as RM/COBOL-85 read data files from disk and create output files on disk in a manner similar to mainframe versions, but there are a few differences that we will discuss here. The small program in Figure 5.1, named COPYIT, illustrates how RM/COBOL-85 SELECT is coded. COPYIT reads the file named WORKERS.DAT illustrated in Chapter 4 in Figure 4.7 and creates the simple listing of the data shown in Figure 5.2. (The program does no printline formatting since it is mainly a syntax illustration.)

To provide the program-to-operating system interface for an input or output disk file with RM/COBOL-85, you code the SELECT statement in this form:

```
SELECT cobol-file-name ASSIGN TO DISK filename.ext
     ORGANIZATION IS LINE SEQUENTIAL.
```

ORGANIZATION IS LINE SEQUENTIAL is a required clause where one record per disk file appears on each line that is terminated with the line feed/carriage return symbols generated by the *<Enter>* or *<Return>* key. This applies to sequential disk files created using a text editor, which are known as ASCII files, and which are described in Chapter 4. Programs can create "stream" data files in which each record is the same length and no line feed/carriage return symbols are presented at the end of

```
000100 ID DIVISION.
000200 PROGRAM-ID.  COPYIT.
000300 AUTHOR.  JIM JANOSSY, DEPAUL UNIVERSITY, CHICAGO.
000400
000500**********************************************************************
000600*   This program is originally appeared in Practical MVS JCL      *
000700*   Examples by Jim Janossy (John Wiley & Sons, Inc. 1993) and    *
000800*   is reprinted here by permission of the publisher.             *
000900*   This program reads a file of records named WORKERS.DAT        *
001000*   and prints a simple report to demonstrate file handling       *
001100*   using RM/COBOL-85 Version 5.24.        J. Janossy, July 1993  *
001200**********************************************************************
001300
001400 ENVIRONMENT DIVISION.
001500 INPUT-OUTPUT SECTION.
001600 FILE-CONTROL.
001700     SELECT INPUT-FILE          ASSIGN TO DISK 'WORKERS.DAT'
001800         ORGANIZATION IS LINE SEQUENTIAL.
001900     SELECT OUTPUT-FILE         ASSIGN TO DISK 'WORKERS.REP'
002000         ORGANIZATION IS LINE SEQUENTIAL.
002100
002200 DATA DIVISION.
002300 FILE SECTION.
002400 FD  INPUT-FILE
002500     RECORD CONTAINS 60 CHARACTERS.
002600 01  INPUT-RECORD               PIC X(60).
002700
002800 FD  OUTPUT-FILE
002900     RECORD CONTAINS 60 CHARACTERS.
003000 01  OUTPUT-RECORD              PIC X(60).
003100/
003200 WORKING-STORAGE SECTION.
003300 01  WS-FLAG                    PIC X(1)  VALUE 'M'.
003400 01  WS-COUNT                   PIC 9(5)  VALUE 0.
003500 01  WS-COUNT-Z                 PIC ZZ,ZZ9.
003600/
003700 PROCEDURE DIVISION.
003800 0000-MAINLINE.
003900     PERFORM 1000-BEGIN-JOB.
004000     PERFORM 2000-PROCESS-A-RECORD UNTIL WS-FLAG = 'E'.
004100     PERFORM 3000-END-JOB.
004200     STOP RUN.
004300
004400 1000-BEGIN-JOB.
004500     OPEN  INPUT  INPUT-FILE   OUTPUT  OUTPUT-FILE.
004600     MOVE '*** START OF COPYIT LISTING' TO OUTPUT-RECORD.
004700     WRITE OUTPUT-RECORD.
004800     PERFORM 2700-READ-A-RECORD.
004900
005000 2000-PROCESS-A-RECORD.
005100     MOVE INPUT-RECORD TO OUTPUT-RECORD.
005200     WRITE OUTPUT-RECORD.
005300     ADD 1 TO WS-COUNT.
005400     PERFORM 2700-READ-A-RECORD.
005500
005600 2700-READ-A-RECORD.
005700     MOVE SPACES TO INPUT-RECORD.
005800     READ INPUT-FILE
005900         AT END MOVE 'E' TO WS-FLAG.
006000
006100 3000-END-JOB.
006200     MOVE WS-COUNT TO WS-COUNT-Z.
006300     MOVE SPACES TO OUTPUT-RECORD.
006400     STRING '*** END OF LISTING, RECORDS = ', WS-COUNT-Z
006500         DELIMITED BY SIZE  INTO OUTPUT-RECORD.
006600     WRITE OUTPUT-RECORD.
006700     CLOSE  INPUT-FILE  OUTPUT-FILE.
```

SELECT
statements

Figure 5.1

COPYIT Program SELECT Statements

COPYIT reads an ASCII file named WORKERS.DAT, which
is illustrated in Chapter 4 in Figure 4.7. It creates a file of
printlines with the COBOL file name OUTPUT-FILE as a
disk file named WORKERS.REP. The output file is shown in
Figure 5.2.

every record. The SELECT statement for a stream file ordinarily does not contain the ORGANIZATION clause and acts as if it had been coded as ORGANIZATION IS BINARY SEQUENTIAL. (See the discussion of the B and V compiler options in Appendix C, which, if properly set, can make it unnecessary for you to code the ORGANIZATION clause for ASCII files.)

Suppose you have created a customer file named CUST.DAT using a text editor. This file is to be read as input by a program, and is in the same subdirectory as your program and the RM/COBOL-85 runtime system. To use this file as input by your program, you can code this SELECT statement in the program:

```
SELECT CUSTOMER-FILE ASSIGN TO DISK "CUST.DAT"
    ORGANIZATION IS LINE SEQUENTIAL.
```

You could also code this statement using the IBM-style quote, which is the apostrophe:

```
SELECT CUSTOMER-FILE ASSIGN TO DISK 'CUST.DAT'
    ORGANIZATION IS LINE SEQUENTIAL.
```

If the file was is stored in a subdirectory other than the one in which the program and runtime system are located, you code the path name in the statement:

```
SELECT CUSTOMER-FILE ASSIGN TO DISK '\DATA\CUST.DAT'
    ORGANIZATION IS LINE SEQUENTIAL.
```

And if the input file is not on the default disk drive, you include the drive letter as a part of the name:

```
SELECT CUSTOMER-FILE ASSIGN TO DISK 'B:CUST.DAT'
    ORGANIZATION IS LINE SEQUENTIAL.
```

The user-defined COBOL file name CUSTOMER-FILE should be a meaningful name that follows the rules for forming COBOL data names and identifiers. It should be composed of no more than 30 characters, be made up of letters and numbers only, and have hyphens between parts of the name.

The actual disk *filename.ext* is the file name on the microcomputer disk and must conform to the DOS rules for forming file names. Such file names contain one to eight characters with an optional three-character file "extension" separated from the name by a period. We typically use .DAT as a file extension for our input data files. While output files can also be named with the file extension .DAT, they can alternatively be named with a file extension of .OUT to highlight the fact that they are output by a program. The extensions .REP, .RPT or .LST are convenient for print files placed on disk. This guide uses .RLF as a file extension for relative files, and .IXF as a file extension for indexed files.

The clause ORGANIZATION IS LINE SEQUENTIAL is not a part of the COBOL standard, but is present in RM/COBOL-85 to allow convenient processing of ASCII ("DOS" or text) files prepared in the microcomputer environment. If you later upload source code created using RM/COBOL-85 to a larger VAX or IBM system for compilation and execution, you will have to remove or comment out the ORGANIZATION IS LINE SEQUENTIAL clause.

```
*** START OF COPYIT LISTING
21256 NILLY      WILLY      402CASHIERS OFFICE
21257 IPPI       MRS.       378PHOTO DEPARTMENT
21260 MALLOW     MARSHA     390KITCHEN APPLIANCES
21307 WARE       DELLA      246FURNITURE
21310 SHAW       ARKAN      300HARDWARE
21574 AH         GEORGE     400PHOTO DEPARTMENT
21668 ZOORI      MOE        179PLUMBING SUPPLIES
25112 CABOOSE    LUCE       305FURNITURE
25189 HOW        IDA        005SUITCASES AND BAGS
33102 IFORNIA    CAL        200TRAVEL DEPARTMENT
33261 CANNON     LUCE       316TOYS
33377 WHIZ       G.         357PERSONAL COMPUTERS
33480 TOUR       D.         160WOMENS CLOTHING
33483 INA        CAROL      530REMODELING SUPPLIES
39321 ABAMA      AL         420WOMENS CLOTHING
39322 TUCKY      KEN        350HARDWARE
*** END OF LISTING, RECORDS =      16
```

Figure 5.2

Output Printed by the COPYIT Program

The COPYIT program reads a file of ASCII records named WORKERS.DAT and outputs this simple report at WORKERS.REP. You can enhance this program to format the "hours worked" field such as 402, which is actually a PIC 99V9 field, so that it prints with a numeric formatted picture such as PIC ZZ.9. WORKERS.DAT and the source code for the COPYIT program is on your RM/COBOL-85 diskette (Diskette 1).

5.3   The SELECT Statement for Direct Printing

You code the SELECT statement for print files in RM/COBOL-85 in much the same way as you code them for the VAX and IBM mainframe environment. One difference, however, is that you can code the device name PRINTER for files intended to be printed:

```
SELECT REPORT-FILE ASSIGN TO PRINTER 'PRN'.
```

The literal 'PRN' is a special name that DOS uses to reference the printer. Including the word PRINTER in the SELECT statement as the device name automatically makes RM/COBOL-85 recognize that this is a line sequential file. The line feed/carriage returns in a line sequential file supply carriage control to microcomputer printers. You do not need to code ORGANIZATION IS LINE SEQUENTIAL for a file assigned to PRINTER, although you can still code this clause for documentation purposes:

```
SELECT REPORT-FILE ASSIGN TO PRINTER 'PRN'
    ORGANIZATION IS LINE SEQUENTIAL.
```

This form of SELECT statement works best if you are working on a single-user microcomputer with a printer attached. If you work on a microcomputer network in which printers are shared, you should not attempt to send print directly to a printer in this way. Instead, you should code the SELECT assign to send printlines into a disk file that can then be copied (and recopied, if necessary) to the printer.

5.4   The SELECT Statement for Printing to a Disk File

In many computer centers, several PCs may be linked to one printer. When you are running or testing a program that creates printed output, you may need to wait for someone else to finish printing. Since debugging can involve several runs of the program, having to wait for your output can be frustrating. To avoid this situation, you can code your SELECT statements to send printlines to a disk file instead of directly to the printer. Code a SELECT statement this way for a print file:

```
SELECT REPORT-FILE ASSIGN TO DISK 'REPORT1.OUT'
       ORGANIZATION IS LINE SEQUENTIAL.
```

This will cause the output to be directed to a disk file called REPORT1.OUT rather than to the printer. After each program run you can use the DOS TYPE command to bring REPORT1.OUT to the screen, or better still, use your text editor or word processor to view it. When the program has been fully debugged and you are sure that the output is correct, you can copy your print output to the printer using the DOS COPY command, since LPT1 is the DOS designation for the printer:

```
C:> copy  report1.out  lpt1
C:> copy  eject.dat    lpt1
```

To eject the last (and most likely only partially full) page of print from the printer, copy the file named EJECT.DAT to the printer immediately afterwards. (EJECT.DAT contains just a form feed character and is one of the files on your RM/COBOL-85 diskette.) Appendix B provides additional advice on handling print file carriage control and using the DOS SET command to reroute print files without having to change SELECT statement coding.

5.5   Length of Printlines

Many computers use the clause RECORD CONTAINS 132 CHARACTERS for print files and/or specify a PIC of X(132) for print file records. This specification is for 132 character printers that do not have an extra leftmost character for carriage control, which is typical of microcomputer printers. IBM mainframes typically require PIC X(133) for printlines, to allow for an extra carriage control byte at the front of each line.

The maximum record size for the RM/COBOL-85 educational version is 132 characters per record, and you cannot specify printlines longer than this. Many printers for microcomputers print 80 characters per line, and almost all computer screens are this width. As a suggestion, design your printed documents for your student COBOL programs with FD printline definitions of no more than 80 characters. This will fit within the restrictions of the educational version of the compiler and will also avoid line "wraparound" on microcomputer printers and terminals.

5.6   The SELECT Statement for Relative Files

Relative files are the simplest and most machine-efficient form of direct (random) access disk file. In a relative file, the places where records will be stored in a file are identified by number, starting with number 1. You do not have to specify a key value when you load records to such a file, because they will be written to the next highest record number. The system puts the record number in which each record is recorded into the relative key field, which must be an unsigned numeric field in WORKING-STORAGE.

RM/COBOL-85 provides full support for relative files without the need for any additional software. It supports ANS 1985 COBOL standards for relative file SELECT statement coding, File Status, the READ, WRITE, REWRITE, DELETE and START verbs, and relative file sequential, random, and dynamic access.

To create a relative file you code a program that reads records from a sequential file and writes them to the relative file. The relative file is not defined in advance as with IBM's VSAM files. This is the form of SELECT statement you code in an RM/COBOL-85 program that outputs records to create a relative file:

```
SELECT REL-FILE   ASSIGN TO DISK 'WORKERS.RLF'
    ORGANIZATION   IS   RELATIVE
    ACCESS MODE    IS   SEQUENTIAL
    RELATIVE KEY   IS   WS-KEY
    FILE STATUS    IS   WS-STATUS.
```

To retrieve records directly from an existing relative file, you put the record number of the record you want to retrieve into the relative key field and READ the file. This is the format of the SELECT statement for a program that reads a relative file:

```
SELECT REL-FILE   ASSIGN TO DISK 'WORKERS.RLF'
    ORGANIZATION   IS   RELATIVE
    ACCESS MODE    IS   RANDOM
    RELATIVE KEY   IS   WS-KEY
    FILE STATUS    IS   WS-STATUS.
```

The source code you use in RM/COBOL-85 to deal with relative files is identical to the code used in VAX COBOL to deal with RMS files and IBM's VS COBOL II Relative Record Data Set (RRDS) VSAM files. You can readily port source code developed with RM/COBOL-85 to either of these large system environments. Consult your COBOL textbook for additional information about programming with relative files.

5.7   The SELECT Statement for Indexed Files

Indexed files are more complex than relative files for direct access, because they contain a "road map" to data records, called an index. When you create an indexed file using RM/COBOL-85 the index is automatically established. When you add records to an indexed file or delete them from it, the index is automatically updated. Despite the fact that both data and index are stored and manipulated, the SELECT statement for an indexed file refers only to one file.

In an indexed file, there is no physical connection between the value of a record key and the location where it is stored. Indexed files deliver a true symbolic key access capability, so identifiers such as account numbers or social security numbers can be used as record keys. For an indexed file, the key field must be defined within the record as a character or numeric field, not in WORKING-STORAGE as with relative files.

RM/COBOL-85 provides full support for indexed files without the need for any additional software. It supports ANS 1985 COBOL standards for indexed file SELECT statement coding, File Status, the READ, WRITE, REWRITE, DELETE and START verbs, and indexed file sequential, random, and dynamic access.

To create an indexed file you code a program that reads records from a sequential file and writes them to the indexed file. The indexed file is not defined in advance as with IBM's VSAM files. The records to be copied in this way must be in ascending key sequence. Records not in key sequence will not be loaded to the newly created indexed file. This is the form of SELECT statement you code in an RM/COBOL-85 program that outputs records to create an indexed file:

```
SELECT IND-FILE    ASSIGN TO DISK 'WORKERS.IXF'
    ORGANIZATION   IS  INDEXED
    ACCESS MODE    IS  SEQUENTIAL
    RECORD KEY     IS  IR-KEY
    FILE STATUS    IS  WS-STATUS.
```

To retrieve records directly from an existing indexed file, you put the key of the record you want to retrieve into the record key field in the FD and READ the file. This is the format of the SELECT statement for a program that reads an indexed file:

```
SELECT IND-FILE    ASSIGN TO DISK 'WORKERS.IXF'
    ORGANIZATION   IS  INDEXED
    ACCESS MODE    IS  RANDOM
    RECORD KEY     IS  IR-KEY
    FILE STATUS    IS  WS-STATUS.
```

The source code you use in RM/COBOL-85 to deal with indexed files is identical to the code used in VAX COBOL to deal with RMS files and IBM's VS COBOL II Key Sequenced Data Set (KSDS) VSAM files. You can readily port source code developed with RM/COBOL-85 to either of these large system environments. Consult your COBOL textbook for additional information about programming with indexed files.

5.8   Obtaining the DOS File Name Interactively

Hardcoded file names within SELECT statements are inflexible and require you to modify and recompile a program in order to change the names of the files it reads, creates, or updates. Instead of hardcoding DOS file names in SELECT statements, you can instead code a data name at the right side of the SELECT statement. You can then arrange beginning-of-job logic to prompt the user to enter the name of the file to be accessed, as shown in Figure 5.3.

It is possible for a user to enter an invalid, incorrect, or nonexistent file name in response to a prompt. If your program obtains a DOS file name interactively, you should consider including logic to check and validate the name received before attempting to open the file. Validation can include redisplay of the file name entered, and actions involving the INSPECT verb to check it for correct length and content, as illustrated at the end of Chapter 6.

Self-Test

Consider the following SELECT statement in answering the following true/false questions:

```
SELECT PAYROLL-FILE ASSIGN TO DISK "A:PAYROLL.DAT"
    ORGANIZATION IS LINE SEQUENTIAL.
```

1. (T or F) The file defined will be on the hard disk as PAYROLL.DAT.
2. (T or F) The ORGANIZATION IS LINE SEQUENTIAL clause is used to indicate that all records end with line feed/carriage return symbols.
3. (T or F) If the above file is an input file, you may use a text editor to create the file before executing the program.
4. (T or F) If the above file is an output file, each record will be saved to the file when a READ statement directed to it is executed.
5. (T or F) The SELECT statement above is not necessary if the data is to be displayed on the screen.
6. (T or F) If the file in the SELECT statement is to be created on a diskette in the B drive, change "A:PAYROLL.DAT" to "B:PAYROLL.DAT".
7. (T or F) The SELECT statement for an indexed file contains only one file name, even though the file contains both the data and an index to the data.

Solutions

1. False; it will defined on the A drive, which is usually a floppy disk
2. True
3. True
4. False; records are written to a file with the WRITE verb
5. True
6. True
7. True

```
000100 ID DIVISION.
000200 PROGRAM-ID.  COPYIT5.
000300 AUTHOR.   JIM JANOSSY, DEPAUL UNIVERSITY, CHICAGO.
000400
000500***********************************************************
000600*   This program is originally appeared in Practical MVS JCL   *
000700*   Examples by Jim Janossy (John Wiley & Sons, Inc. 1993) and *
000800*   is reprinted here by permission of the publisher.          *
000900*   This program reads a file of records named WORKERS.DAT     *
001000*   and prints a simple report to demonstrate file handling    *
001100*   using RM/COBOL-85 Version 5.24.       J. Janossy, July 1993 *
001200***********************************************************
001300
001400 ENVIRONMENT DIVISION.
001500 INPUT-OUTPUT SECTION.
001600 FILE-CONTROL.
001700
001800     SELECT INPUT-FILE         ASSIGN TO DISK  WS-INPUT-FILE-NAME
001900         ORGANIZATION IS LINE SEQUENTIAL.
002000
002100     SELECT OUTPUT-FILE        ASSIGN TO DISK 'WORKERS.REP'
002200         ORGANIZATION IS LINE SEQUENTIAL.
002300
002400 DATA DIVISION.
002500 FILE SECTION.
002600 FD  INPUT-FILE
002700     RECORD CONTAINS 60 CHARACTERS.
002800 01  INPUT-RECORD                      PIC X(60).
002900
003000 FD  OUTPUT-FILE
003100     RECORD CONTAINS 60 CHARACTERS.
003200 01  OUTPUT-RECORD                     PIC X(60).
003300/
003400 WORKING-STORAGE SECTION.
003500 01  WS-INPUT-FILE-NAME                PIC X(25).
003600 01  WS-FLAG                           PIC X(1)  VALUE 'M'.
003700 01  WS-COUNT                          PIC 9(5)  VALUE 0.
003800 01  WS-COUNT-Z                        PIC ZZ,ZZ9.
003900/
004000 PROCEDURE DIVISION.
004100 0000-MAINLINE.
004200     PERFORM 1000-BEGIN-JOB.
004300     PERFORM 2000-PROCESS-A-RECORD UNTIL WS-FLAG = 'E'.
004400     PERFORM 3000-END-JOB.
004500     STOP RUN.
004600
004700 1000-BEGIN-JOB.
004800
004900     DISPLAY 'ENTER NAME OF FILE TO READ: '.
005000     ACCEPT WS-INPUT-FILE-NAME
005100         NO BEEP  COLUMN 0.
005200
005300     OPEN  INPUT  INPUT-FILE   OUTPUT  OUTPUT-FILE.
  -
  -
  -
```

SELECT statement coded with a data-name rather than a hardcoded DOS file name

Obtaining file name interactively provides flexibility

Figure 5.3

Receiving the DOS File Name Interactively

You can code the SELECT statement as shown here using a data name instead of a hardcoded file name. Arrange for the program to ask the user to enter a file name as a beginning-of-job action. If you do this, you can also include logic to provide a default file name extension and/or logic to validate the data name entered before using it.

Chapter 6

ACCEPT and DISPLAY for Interactive Processing

6.1   ACCEPT and DISPLAY Statements

he ACCEPT and DISPLAY verbs are often discussed near the end of mainframe-oriented COBOL books because mainframes often use other options for interactive programming. On a mainframe you typically use ACCEPT to acquire the date or time from the operating system, and DISPLAY for debugging. COBOL programs on microcomputers and minicomputers, however, rely heavily on ACCEPT and DISPLAY for interactive processing.

ACCEPT and DISPLAY give you the capability to receive data from your microcomputer's keyboard and to send data to the computer's screen. You use these verbs, and enhancements to them called **language extensions**, to create an interactive dialogue between the user and the computer. Unlike the case with file input or output, there is no need for a SELECT statement, FD, OPEN, CLOSE, and READ or WRITE for ACCEPT and DISPLAY for input and output.

In this chapter we explain and demonstrate the various capabilities of RM/COBOL-85 ACCEPT and DISPLAY language extensions to control the position of information on the screen, the color and intensity of displayed information, characteristics such as blinking and reverse video, and an attention-getting beep. We show you how to code an interactive program using terminal input/output, which relies only on ACCEPT and DISPLAY verbs, and how to code the same program using a SCREEN SECTION to consolidate the definition of the appearance and operation of a screen. Finally, we demonstrate interactive update to an indexed file.

6.2   A Simple Interactive Program

You can use COBOL on a microcomputer in a manner similar to BASIC and other languages originally designed for minicomputer and microcomputer use. You can write short, interactive programs to obtain immediate on-screen results. This makes use of ACCEPT and DISPLAY in their simplest forms, which is called terminal input/output.

Program ACCEPT1, shown in Figure 6.1, is a very simple interactive COBOL program. When ACCEPT1 is run, it prompts the computer user to enter a pair of numbers. It then sums the numbers, displays the result, and quits. Figure 6.2 shows you the result of running ACCEPT1 and entering the numbers 25 and 12 for summing.

Program ACCEPT1 in Figure 6.1 uses ACCEPT and DISPLAY with no language extensions. You can see in Figure 6.2 that the screen display produced by ACCEPT1 begins without clearing away the other items already on the screen. In addition, the cursor goes to the start of a new line when each DISPLAY or ACCEPT is processed, but it would be more pleasing to the eye if the entry of the number could be made right after the prompt, such as:

```
ENTER A NUMBER: 25
ANOTHER NUMBER: 12
THE TOTAL IS:   37
```

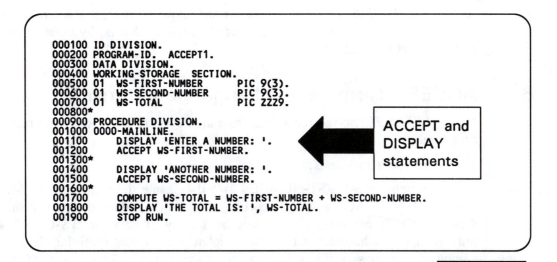

```
000100 ID DIVISION.
000200 PROGRAM-ID.  ACCEPT1.
000300 DATA DIVISION.
000400 WORKING-STORAGE   SECTION.
000500 01  WS-FIRST-NUMBER      PIC 9(3).
000600 01  WS-SECOND-NUMBER     PIC 9(3).
000700 01  WS-TOTAL             PIC ZZZ9.
000800*
000900 PROCEDURE DIVISION.
001000 0000-MAINLINE.
001100      DISPLAY 'ENTER A NUMBER: '.
001200      ACCEPT WS-FIRST-NUMBER.
001300*
001400      DISPLAY 'ANOTHER NUMBER: '.
001500      ACCEPT WS-SECOND-NUMBER.
001600*
001700      COMPUTE WS-TOTAL = WS-FIRST-NUMBER + WS-SECOND-NUMBER.
001800      DISPLAY 'THE TOTAL IS: ', WS-TOTAL.
001900      STOP RUN.
```

ACCEPT and
DISPLAY
statements

Figure 6.1

Interactive ACCEPT and DISPLAY Statements

This simple program asks the computer user to enter one number, then another number. The program then computes the sum of the numbers and displays the answer. Entry of the numbers and computation of a sum represents a *transaction*.

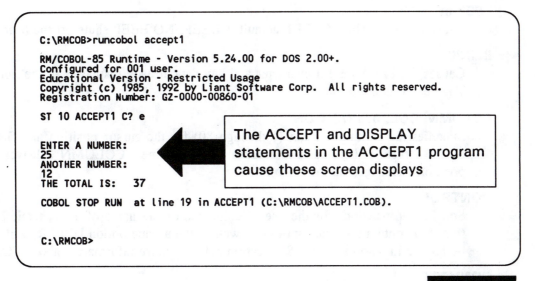

```
C:\RMCOB>runcobol accept1

RM/COBOL-85 Runtime - Version 5.24.00 for DOS 2.00+.
Configured for 001 user.
Educational Version - Restricted Usage
Copyright (c) 1985, 1992 by Liant Software Corp.  All rights reserved.
Registration Number: GZ-0000-00860-01

ST 10 ACCEPT1 C? e


ENTER A NUMBER:
25
ANOTHER NUMBER:
12
THE TOTAL IS:    37

COBOL STOP RUN  at line 19 in ACCEPT1 (C:\RMCOB\ACCEPT1.COB).


C:\RMCOB>
```

The ACCEPT and DISPLAY statements in the ACCEPT1 program cause these screen displays

Figure 6.2

Effect of ACCEPT and DISPLAY Statements

The ACCEPT1 program uses DISPLAY statements to prompt the computer user to enter a pair of numbers, ACCEPT statements to receive the numbers, and the DISPLAY statement to present the sum of the numbers.

ACCEPT and DISPLAY language extensions allow us to clear the screen and control the positioning of the cursor, and to shut off the beep that is, by default, produced by each terminal I/O ACCEPT.

6.3 ACCEPT Terminal I/O Language Extensions

You code ACCEPT to receive a field from the keyboard by specifying a receiving field data name:

```
ACCEPT WS-FIRST-NUMBER.
```

In this example WS-FIRST-NUMBER is a data name defined as a PIC 9(3) field in WORKING-STORAGE and will receive and store the value entered. In this simplest form, ACCEPT continues to seek keyboard entry of data for WS-FIRST-NUMBER until enough data has been entered to completely satisfy the receiving field size, or the computer user presses the *<Enter>* or *<Tab>* key. To use any of the optional language extensions for ACCEPT, you code the options after the receiving field name:

```
ACCEPT WS-FIRST-NUMBER option-1 option-2 option-3 ...
```

The optional language extensions for ACCEPT, and their defaults, are summarized in alphabetical order in the following list. Note that although some of the language extension options for ACCEPT and DISPLAY in terminal input/output mode are similar to options of the SCREEN SECTION, which we discuss in section 6.7, some option coding differences exist between terminal I/O and SCREEN SECTION coding.

BEEP or BELL

Sounds a tone. The ACCEPT default is BEEP; NO BEEP shuts off the beep.

BLINK

Causes the PROMPT fill character and any data already displayed in the field to blink. The default is not to blink.

COLUMN, COL, or POSITION

Specifies the starting column (1 through 80) for the cursor position and field location on the screen. The default is column 1 of next line. COLUMN 0 leaves the cursor position unchanged on the same line.

CONTROL

Specifies instructions for the use of color and/or the name of a "dynamic option list" that may contain the other options as well as the unique option UPPER, which can only be housed in an option list. See section 6.13 for more information about CONTROL.

CONVERT

Causes conversion of the input data to signed numeric form if the receiving field is numeric. The default is for conversion to be in effect. NO CONVERT overrides the default and always causes an alphanumeric move to the receiving field. The UPDATE option also triggers conversion of the data it takes from memory and makes visible on the screen.

CURSOR n

The "n" is an integer from 2 to the limit of the field length. CURSOR causes the cursor to be placed at position n within the field on the screen when the UPDATE option is coded. CURSOR is simply an enhancement of UPDATE. UPDATE allows you to indicate default field contents for modification by the computer user.

ECHO

Causes redisplay of the input data in the field after input of the field is completed, with conversion for display controlled by the UPDATE option or field PIC. If ECHO is not specified, the data as entered remains in the field after completion of entry.

ERASE

ERASE without EOS or EOL causes the entire screen to be erased. ERASE EOS causes screen erasure from the cursor position rightward and downward. By contrast, ERASE EOL erases from just the cursor position to the end of the line on which the cursor is located. Erasure occurs before acceptance of data.

HIGH or HIGHLIGHT

Causes the PROMPT fill character and entered data to be displayed at maximum intensity. This is the default for fields being ACCEPTed.

LOW or LOWLIGHT

Causes the PROMPT fill character and entered data to be displayed at normal intensity.

SECURE or OFF

Causes the PROMPT fill character and entered data to be made invisible.

LINE

Line number (1 through 24) for the field on the screen. The default is the next line. COLUMN 0 coded with ACCEPT leaves the line number unchanged.

PROMPT

Displays "fill" characters on the screen in the field in the positions from which data is to be accepted. The default is for no fill characters to be presented. If you code PROMPT, the fill character used is the underscore. You can code PROMPT 'x' where x is the character to be used as the fill character.

REVERSE or REVERSED or REVERSE-VIDEO

Causes the data entered into the field to be presented as dark characters on a light background.

SIZE

Specifies the size of the screen field. The default is for the system itself to determine the field size based on the coded definition of the receiving field and the optional use of CONVERT and UPDATE.

TAB

Makes it necessary for the computer user to press <Enter> to transmit a field. If TAB is not coded, the cursor leaves the field either when the user presses <Enter> or when the user fills the field. (Note: to get automatic transmission upon filling a field when you use a SCREEN SECTION and ACCEPT a whole screen, you must code AUTO on the field definition. Automatic field transmission is not a default for SCREEN SECTION use.)

UPDATE

Causes the existing value in a field to be displayed the next time an ACCEPT for the field is executed. The value is displayed with conversion to a readable form. The computer user can then modify this value instead of having to completely enter a value, or press *<Enter>* to accept the existing value for the field. UPDATE is not automatically active. If you use the UPDATE option a value coded for the CURSOR option value (if coded) takes effect.

6.4   DISPLAY Terminal I/O Language Extensions

You present a field on the screen by coding the word DISPLAY followed by a literal value, a sending field name, or both:

```
DISPLAY 'THE TOTAL IS: ', WS-TOTAL.
```

Note that with RM/COBOL-85 you can use single quotes or double quotes to delimit a literal. DISPLAY 'THE TOTAL IS: ' produces the same result as DISPLAY "THE TOTAL IS: ". To use any of the optional language extensions for DISPLAY, you code the options after the receiving field name, for example:

```
DISPLAY 'THE TOTAL IS: ', WS-TOTAL   BEEP.
```

The optional language extensions for DISPLAY, and their defaults, are summarized in the following list. (Note that although some of the language extension options for ACCEPT and DISPLAY in terminal input/output mode are similar to options of the SCREEN SECTION, some differences do exist.)

BEEP or BELL

Sounds a tone. The DISPLAY default is for no beep to sound; BEEP produces the tone.

BLINK

Causes the item to be displayed in blinking mode. The default is not to blink.

COLUMN, COL, or POSITION

Starting column (1 through 80) for the field location on the screen. The default is column 1 of next line. COLUMN 0 leaves the cursor position unchanged.

CONTROL

Specifies a "dynamic option list" that may contain the other options; see section 6.11 for more information about the CONTROL option, screen colors, and automatic lowercase to uppercase conversion.

CONVERT

Causes conversion of the sending field data to readable form, including leading zero suppression, sign, and explicit decimal point (period unless DECIMAL-POINT IS

COMMA is coded). If not specified, the movement of the sending field to the screen is treated as an alphanumeric move.

ERASE

ERASE without EOS or EOL causes the entire screen to be erased. ERASE EOS causes screen erasure from the cursor position rightward and downward. By contrast, ERASE EOL erases from just the cursor position to the end of the line on which the cursor is located.

HIGH or HIGHLIGHT

Causes the item to be displayed at maximum intensity. This is the default for fields being displayed.

LOW or LOWLIGHT

Causes the data to be displayed at normal intensity.

LINE

Line number (1 through 24) for the field on the screen. The default is the next line. COLUMN 0 leaves the line number unchanged.

REVERSE or REVERSED or REVERSE-VIDEO

Causes the data to be presented as dark characters on a light background.

6.5 An Example of ACCEPT/DISPLAY Language Extension Usage

Figure 6.3 illustrates how you can code ACCEPT and DISPLAY language extensions to enhance the placement of fields on the screen. The ACCEPT2 program produces the screen shown in Figure 6.4, which removes screen clutter using ERASE EOS and places entered data immediately following the labeling information describing it.

6.6 Practical Choices in ACCEPT/DISPLAY Options

ACCEPT and DISPLAY language extensions provide many options to choose from in creating interactive dialogues. To create convenient and user friendly dialogues, you can select a series of options and use them consistently. In this and the following sections we demonstrate the use of some ACCEPT and DISPLAY terminal input/output options, followed by the same interactive dialogue implemented using a SCREEN SECTION.

Figure 6.5 shows you the screen presented by the CALC3 program. This program might be used by a sales clerk to compute the total cost of a quantity of goods being purchased, the sales tax on the purchase, and the grand total. Figure 6.5 shows how a quantity of 10 of an item, with an individual cost of $2.50, produces a total cost of $25.00, sales tax of $2.00, and a grand total cost of $27.00.

(Text continues on page 109)

```
000100 ID DIVISION.
000200 PROGRAM-ID.  ACCEPT2.
000300 DATA DIVISION.
000400 WORKING-STORAGE   SECTION.
000500 01  WS-FIRST-NUMBER       PIC 9(3).
000600 01  WS-SECOND-NUMBER      PIC 9(3).
000700 01  WS-TOTAL             PIC ZZZ9.
000800*
000900 PROCEDURE DIVISION.
001000 0000-MAINLINE.
001100     DISPLAY ' '                LINE 1 COLUMN 1 ERASE EOS.
001200
001300     DISPLAY 'ENTER A NUMBER: '  LINE 5 COLUMN 1.
001400     ACCEPT WS-FIRST-NUMBER      COLUMN 0  NO BEEP.
001500*
001600     DISPLAY 'ANOTHER NUMBER: '.
001700     ACCEPT WS-SECOND-NUMBER     COLUMN 0  NO BEEP.
001800*
001900     COMPUTE WS-TOTAL = WS-FIRST-NUMBER + WS-SECOND-NUMBER.
002000     DISPLAY 'THE TOTAL IS: ', WS-TOTAL    BEEP.
002100     STOP RUN.
```

ACCEPT and DISPLAY language extensions

Figure 6.3

Erasing the Screen and Positioning the Cursor

The LINE and COLUMN language extensions let you control the position of the cursor, and the ERASE option lets you erase the screen when appropriate. COLUMN 0 with an ACCEPT means "don't start a new line; leave the cursor at its present position." The default for an ACCEPT is for a beep to sound, and the default for DISPLAY is for no beep to sound. You can shut off the beep on an ACCEPT by coding NO BEEP, or activate it with a DISPLAY by coding BEEP.

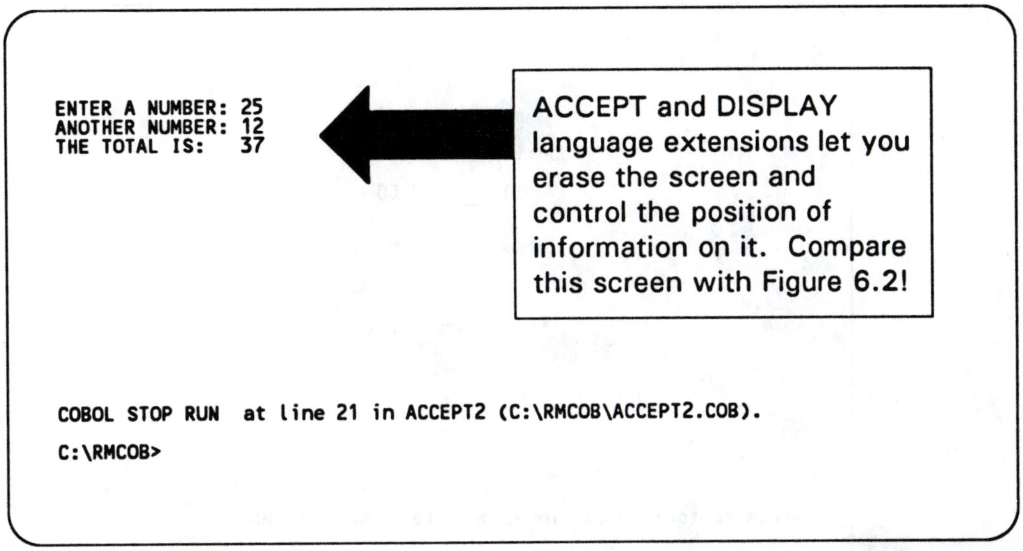

```
ENTER A NUMBER: 25
ANOTHER NUMBER: 12
THE TOTAL IS:   37
```

⬅ ACCEPT and DISPLAY language extensions let you erase the screen and control the position of information on it. Compare this screen with Figure 6.2!

```
COBOL STOP RUN  at line 21 in ACCEPT2 (C:\RMCOB\ACCEPT2.COB).
C:\RMCOB>
```

Figure 6.4

ACCEPT2: ERASE EOS, LINE, and COLUMN

ACCEPT and DISPLAY language extensions provide the capability to format the screen.   Additional language extensions let you control the intensity and color of information presented on the screen, or make it appear in reverse video or blinking.

```
        Quantity    Price              Total
            10       2.50              25.00

                    8% Tax              2.00

                              ==============
                    Grand Total        27.00




    Press <Enter> to continue, or enter "quit" to end          [      ]
```

Figure 6.5

How the CALC3 Screen Appears

The CALC3 program causes this to appear on your screen. You make entries in the Quantity and Price fields. The program computes the Total (the product of quantity and price), 8% Tax, and the Grand Total. The CALC4 and CALC5 programs produce the same screen appearance but use additional RM/COBOL-85 language extensions to give it enhanced treatment. (The CALC3 program originally appeared in *VAX COBOL On-Line* by James Janossy, published in 1992 by John Wiley & Sons, Inc., and is used here by permission of the publisher.)

In the CALC3 program, entering one set of quantity and individual price data, and receiving the three computed values, constitutes a single transaction. Since it is likely that a user will want to process more than one transaction when using the CALC3 program, we have to arranged for the entry and display actions to loop, that is, to be repeated. The source code of the CALC3 program, listed in Figure 6.6, shows you how this is done. CALC3 resembles a batch program reading records from a file. The bottom of the processing loop (the 2000-PROCESS paragraph) obtains more input from the user, in the form of a response to the question "do you want to quit?" When the response to this question is affirmative (the user enters "quit" as a response) the processing loop shuts off and the program ends.

Figure 6.6 shows you how ACCEPT and DISPLAY options have been selected to so that screen labels such as the words PRICE and QUANTITY are brightly highlighted (HIGH), while the entered data appear in normal intensity. Reverse video is used only for the field being entered, setting it off from other fields. Logic is included to format a field and redisplay it after its acceptance, to remove reverse video. The computer user is prompted with a message at the bottom of the screen to guide entry actions.

Try out CALC3 by compiling and executing it. You'll see that it works fine, so long as you enter numeric data when prompted for input. But if you enter non-numeric values at the price and quantity fields, you'll see that they are accepted as zeros. This is not good enough for "real" use, where a computer user may erroneously enter an incorrect value. You could handle this with additional programming using ACCEPT and DISPLAY in terminal input/output mode, but RM/COBOL-85 provides a better way to deal with the problem. The options of the SCREEN SECTION can automatically handle a broad range of potential data entry errors.

6.7 Using a SCREEN SECTION

RM/COBOL-85 provides the ability to code a section in the DATA DIVISION named the SCREEN SECTION, as shown in Figure 6.7 (pages 112-113). You can code entries in the SCREEN SECTION to define the appearance of different screens. Each screen definition appears as a group data-name, and begins with an 01 level name. But a screen name is not an ordinary data name; you can use it only with ACCEPT or DISPLAY. You can code certain options, such as color choices, on the 01 level to apply to the whole screen. You code elementary field entries for the screen under its 01 level, and can code options on fields to control their appearance and treatment. Here is an example from the CALC4 program:

```
SCREEN SECTION.
01  CALC4-LABEL-SCREEN  BACKGROUND IS BLUE
                        FOREGROUND IS WHITE.
    05 BLANK SCREEN.
    05 'Quantity     Price           Total'
       LINE 5   COLUMN 20    HIGHLIGHT.
    05 '8% Tax'
       LINE 10  COLUMN 35    HIGHLIGHT.
    05 '=============='
       LINE 12  COLUMN 43    HIGHLIGHT.
```

(Text continues on page 114)

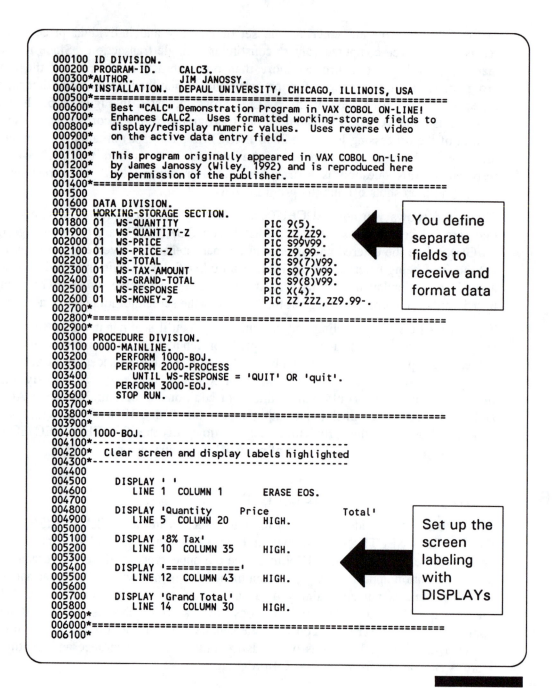

```
000100 ID DIVISION.
000200 PROGRAM-ID.    CALC3.
000300*AUTHOR.         JIM JANOSSY.
000400*INSTALLATION.  DEPAUL UNIVERSITY, CHICAGO, ILLINOIS, USA
000500*===============================================================
000600*    Best "CALC" Demonstration Program in VAX COBOL ON-LINE!
000700*    Enhances CALC2.  Uses formatted working-storage fields to
000800*    display/redisplay numeric values.  Uses reverse video
000900*    on the active data entry field.
001000*
001100*    This program originally appeared in VAX COBOL On-Line
001200*    by James Janossy (Wiley, 1992) and is reproduced here
001300*    by permission of the publisher.
001400*===============================================================
001500
001600 DATA DIVISION.
001700 WORKING-STORAGE SECTION.
001800 01  WS-QUANTITY             PIC 9(5).
001900 01  WS-QUANTITY-Z           PIC ZZ,ZZ9.
002000 01  WS-PRICE                PIC S99V99.
002100 01  WS-PRICE-Z              PIC Z9.99-.
002200 01  WS-TOTAL                PIC S9(7)V99.
002300 01  WS-TAX-AMOUNT           PIC S9(7)V99.
002400 01  WS-GRAND-TOTAL          PIC S9(8)V99.
002500 01  WS-RESPONSE             PIC X(4).
002600 01  WS-MONEY-Z              PIC ZZ,ZZZ,ZZ9.99-.
002700*
002800*===============================================================
002900*
003000 PROCEDURE DIVISION.
003100 0000-MAINLINE.
003200     PERFORM 1000-BOJ.
003300     PERFORM 2000-PROCESS
003400         UNTIL WS-RESPONSE = 'QUIT' OR 'quit'.
003500     PERFORM 3000-EOJ.
003600     STOP RUN.
003700*
003800*===============================================================
003900*
004000 1000-BOJ.
004100*-----------------------------------------------------
004200*  Clear screen and display labels highlighted
004300*-----------------------------------------------------
004400
004500     DISPLAY ' '
004600         LINE 1  COLUMN 1        ERASE EOS.
004700
004800     DISPLAY 'Quantity    Price              Total'
004900         LINE 5  COLUMN 20       HIGH.
005000
005100     DISPLAY '8% Tax'
005200         LINE 10  COLUMN 35      HIGH.
005300
005400     DISPLAY '============'
005500         LINE 12  COLUMN 43      HIGH.
005600
005700     DISPLAY 'Grand Total'
005800         LINE 14  COLUMN 30      HIGH.
005900*
006000*===============================================================
006100*
```

You define separate fields to receive and format data

Set up the screen labeling with DISPLAYs

Figure 6.6

CALC3: A Simple Interactive Program Model
This program uses ACCEPT and DISPLAY to communicate with the keyboard and screen. You can handle all key entry and screen presentation actions this way or you can encode screens using a SCREEN SECTION as shown in programs CALC4 and CALC5.

```
006200 2000-PROCESS.
006300*-----------------------------------------------------------
006400*  Blank out the data fields from a prior transaction
006500*-----------------------------------------------------------
006600
006700     DISPLAY '         '        LINE  7  COLUMN 21.
006800     DISPLAY '         '        LINE  7  COLUMN 33.
006900     DISPLAY '         '        LINE  7  COLUMN 43.
007000     DISPLAY '         '        LINE 10  COLUMN 43.
007100     DISPLAY '         '        LINE 14  COLUMN 43.
007200
007300*---------------------
007400*  Accept the data
007500*---------------------
007600
007700     DISPLAY 'Enter quantity up to 9,999 and press <Enter>'
007800        LINE 24  COLUMN 1
007900        ERASE EOL.
008000     ACCEPT WS-QUANTITY       LINE 7  COLUMN 21
008100        PROMPT ' ' REVERSED  NO BEEP.
008200     MOVE WS-QUANTITY TO WS-QUANTITY-Z.
008300     DISPLAY WS-QUANTITY-Z  LINE 7  COLUMN 21    LOW.
008400*
008500     DISPLAY 'Enter price up to + or - 99.99 and press <Enter>'
008600        LINE 24  COLUMN 1
008700        ERASE EOL.
008800     ACCEPT WS-PRICE          LINE 7  COLUMN 33
008900        PROMPT ' ' REVERSED  NO BEEP.
009000     MOVE WS-PRICE TO WS-PRICE-Z.
009100     DISPLAY WS-PRICE-Z     LINE 7  COLUMN 33    LOW.
009200
009300*-----------------------------------------------------------
009400*  Compute and display the results (end this transaction)
009500*-----------------------------------------------------------
009600
009700     COMPUTE WS-TOTAL = WS-QUANTITY * WS-PRICE.
009800     MOVE WS-TOTAL TO WS-MONEY-Z.
009900     DISPLAY WS-MONEY-Z     LINE 7  COLUMN 43    LOW
010000
010100     COMPUTE WS-TAX-AMOUNT = WS-TOTAL * .08.
010200     MOVE WS-TAX-AMOUNT TO WS-MONEY-Z.
010300     DISPLAY WS-MONEY-Z     LINE 10  COLUMN 43    LOW.
010400
010500     COMPUTE WS-GRAND-TOTAL = WS-TOTAL + WS-TAX-AMOUNT.
010600     MOVE WS-GRAND-TOTAL TO WS-MONEY-Z.
010700     DISPLAY WS-MONEY-Z     LINE 14  COLUMN 43    LOW.
010800
010900*-------------------------------------------
011000*  Ask if user wants to continue or quit
011100*-------------------------------------------
011200
011300     DISPLAY 'Press'         LINE 24  COLUMN 1    LOW.
011400
011500     DISPLAY ' <Enter>'      LINE 24  COLUMN 6    LOW BLINK.
011600
011700     DISPLAY ' to continue, or enter "quit" to end '
011800        LINE 24  COLUMN 14  LOW.
011900
012000     ACCEPT WS-RESPONSE
012100        LINE 24  COLUMN 60
012200        PROMPT ' ' REVERSED  NO BEEP  LOW.
012300*
012400*===========================================================
012500*
012600 3000-EOJ.
012700*-----------------------------------------------------------
012800*  Clear the screen and display sign-off message
012900*-----------------------------------------------------------
013000
013100     DISPLAY 'QUITTING AS REQUESTED'
013200        LINE 1  COLUMN 1    LOW  ERASE EOS.
```

Clear screen fields of old data

One transaction processes each time this loop is executed

Ask: continue?

Figure 6.6 (end)

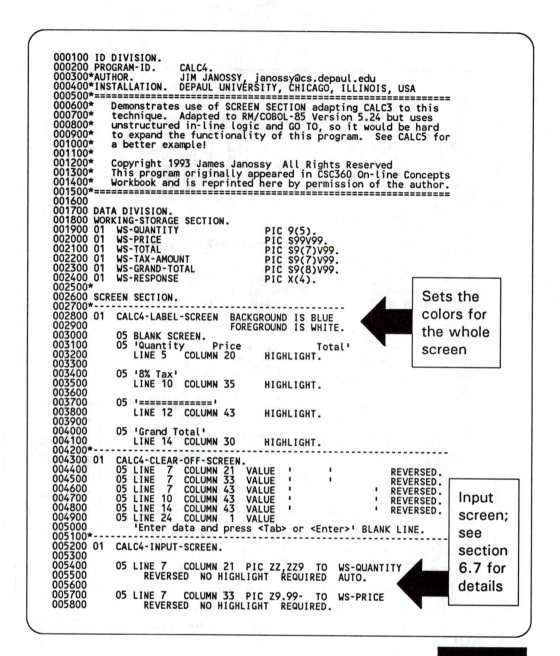

```
000100 ID DIVISION.
000200 PROGRAM-ID.      CALC4.
000300*AUTHOR.          JIM JANOSSY, janossy@cs.depaul.edu
000400*INSTALLATION.    DEPAUL UNIVERSITY, CHICAGO, ILLINOIS, USA
000500*=======================================================================
000600*    Demonstrates use of SCREEN SECTION adapting CALC3 to this
000700*    technique.  Adapted to RM/COBOL-85 Version 5.24 but uses
000800*    unstructured in-line logic and GO TO, so it would be hard
000900*    to expand the functionality of this program.  See CALC5 for
001000*    a better example!
001100*
001200*    Copyright 1993 James Janossy  All Rights Reserved
001300*    This program originally appeared in CSC360 On-line Concepts
001400*    Workbook and is reprinted here by permission of the author.
001500*=======================================================================
001600
001700 DATA DIVISION.
001800 WORKING-STORAGE SECTION.
001900 01  WS-QUANTITY            PIC 9(5).
002000 01  WS-PRICE               PIC S99V99.
002100 01  WS-TOTAL               PIC S9(7)V99.
002200 01  WS-TAX-AMOUNT          PIC S9(7)V99.
002300 01  WS-GRAND-TOTAL         PIC S9(8)V99.
002400 01  WS-RESPONSE            PIC X(4).
002500*
002600 SCREEN SECTION.
002700*-----------------------------------------------
002800 01  CALC4-LABEL-SCREEN     BACKGROUND IS BLUE
002900                            FOREGROUND IS WHITE.
003000     05 BLANK SCREEN.
003100     05 'Quantity      Price              Total'
003200        LINE 5   COLUMN 20    HIGHLIGHT.
003300
003400     05 '8% Tax'
003500        LINE 10  COLUMN 35    HIGHLIGHT.
003600
003700     05 '=============='
003800        LINE 12  COLUMN 43    HIGHLIGHT.
003900
004000     05 'Grand Total'
004100        LINE 14  COLUMN 30    HIGHLIGHT.
004200*-----------------------------------------------
004300 01  CALC4-CLEAR-OFF-SCREEN.
004400     05 LINE  7   COLUMN 21   VALUE '    '        REVERSED.
004500     05 LINE  7   COLUMN 33   VALUE '    '        REVERSED.
004600     05 LINE  7   COLUMN 43   VALUE '          '  REVERSED.
004700     05 LINE 10   COLUMN 43   VALUE '          '  REVERSED.
004800     05 LINE 14   COLUMN 43   VALUE '          '  REVERSED.
004900     05 LINE 24   COLUMN  1   VALUE
005000        'Enter data and press <Tab> or <Enter>' BLANK LINE.
005100*-----------------------------------------------
005200 01  CALC4-INPUT-SCREEN.
005300
005400     05 LINE 7    COLUMN 21 PIC ZZ,ZZ9  TO  WS-QUANTITY
005500        REVERSED  NO HIGHLIGHT  REQUIRED  AUTO.
005600
005700     05 LINE 7    COLUMN 33 PIC Z9.99-  TO  WS-PRICE
005800        REVERSED  NO HIGHLIGHT  REQUIRED.
```

Sets the colors for the whole screen

Input screen; see section 6.7 for details

Figure 6.7

CALC4: SCREEN SECTION, In-Line Logic

The CALC4 program does processing similar to that of CALC3, but uses a SCREEN SECTION to define most screens. The screens defined include labels to identify field contents, a screen to blank out field contents, an input screen, an output screen, and final ending screen. We provide CALC4 only to familiarize you with "in-line" logic. *We do not recommend this older style of coding since GO TO logic is out of keeping with modern structured programming.* See CALC5 for a better version of this program.

```
005900*----------------------------------------------------------
006000 01  CALC4-OUTPUT-SCREEN.
006100
006200     05 LINE 7   COLUMN 21 PIC ZZ,ZZ9          FROM WS-QUANTITY
006300        REVERSED.
006400
006500     05 LINE 7   COLUMN 33 PIC ZZ.99-          FROM WS-PRICE
006600        REVERSED.
006700
006800     05 LINE 7   COLUMN 43 PIC ZZ,ZZZ,ZZ9.99-  FROM WS-TOTAL
006900        REVERSED.
007000
007100     05 LINE 10  COLUMN 43 PIC ZZ,ZZZ,ZZ9.99-  FROM WS-TAX-AMOUNT
007200        REVERSED.
007300
007400     05 LINE 14  COLUMN 43 PIC ZZ,ZZZ,ZZ9.99-
007500        FROM WS-GRAND-TOTAL  REVERSED.
007600
007700     05 LINE 24  COLUMN 1  VALUE
007800        'Press <Enter> to continue or "quit" to end' BLANK LINE.
007900*----------------------------------------------------------
008000 01  CALC4-ENDING-SCREEN  BACKGROUND IS BLACK
008100                          FOREGROUND IS BLUE.
008200     05 BLANK SCREEN.
008300     05 LINE  7   COLUMN  10
008400        VALUE '*****************************'.
008500     05 LINE  8   COLUMN  10
008600        VALUE '*                           *'.
008700     05 LINE  9   COLUMN  10
008800        VALUE '*                           *'.
008900     05 LINE  10  COLUMN  10
009000        VALUE '*                           *'.
009100     05 LINE  11  COLUMN  10
009200        VALUE '*****************************'.
009300*==========================================================
009400*
       PROCEDURE DIVISION.
       BEGIN-PROGRAM.
           DISPLAY CALC4-LABEL-SCREEN.

       START-A-TRANSACTION.
           DISPLAY CALC4-CLEAR-OFF-SCREEN.

      *---------------------------------------------------------
      * Accept the data, do computations, present results
      *---------------------------------------------------------
           ACCEPT CALC4-INPUT-SCREEN.
           COMPUTE WS-TOTAL       = WS-QUANTITY * WS-PRICE.
           COMPUTE WS-TAX-AMOUNT  = WS-TOTAL * .08.
           COMPUTE WS-GRAND-TOTAL = WS-TOTAL + WS-TAX-AMOUNT.
           DISPLAY CALC4-OUTPUT-SCREEN.

      *---------------------------------------------------------
      * Ask if user wants to continue or quit, branch
      * back to start if he/she wants to continue
      *---------------------------------------------------------
           ACCEPT WS-RESPONSE
               LINE 24  COLUMN 60
               PROMPT '_'  REVERSED  NO BEEP  LOW.

           IF WS-RESPONSE(1:1) NOT = 'Q' AND 'q'
               GO TO START-A-TRANSACTION.
012100
012200 END-OF-PROGRAM.
012300*---------------------------------------------------------
012400* Clear the screen, display sign-off message, and
012500* leave the system set to normal screen colors
012600*---------------------------------------------------------
012700     DISPLAY CALC4-ENDING-SCREEN.
012800     DISPLAY 'CALC4 ENDED AS REQUESTED'
012900         LINE 9  COLUMN 14
013000         BLINK
013100         CONTROL "FCOLOR=RED".
013200     DISPLAY ' '
013300         LINE 1 COLUMN 1
013400         CONTROL "FCOLOR=WHITE".
013500     STOP RUN.
```

You ACCEPT or DISPLAY whole screens

You can still ACCEPT or DISPLAY individual fields if a SCREEN SECTION is used

Individual field ACCEPT and DISPLAY syntax differs from SCREEN SECTION coding for color

Figure 6.7 *(end)*

Our discussion of the SCREEN SECTION will use the CALC4 program as a full-scale example. This program is listed in Figure 6.7, and the screen it produces is shown in Figure 6.8. We'll discuss parts of its SCREEN SECTION coding in the next section.

Run the CALC4 program now, to get an idea of how it operates. Running it and seeing what it does will make the following discussion much more meaningful to you. Compare CALC4 with CALC5, which uses structured logic instead of instream logic, and serves as a better base for your programming efforts.

6.8 SCREEN SECTION Automatic Data Validation

RM/COBOL-85 provide several types of data validation automatically when you use a SCREEN SECTION. These validations are especially convenient and important for numeric fields, and their presence frees you from much tedium in program coding. The automatic data validations produce messages on line 25 of the screen. If you use line 24 for your messages (prompts) to the computer user, both your messages and the automatic RM/COBOL-85 messages can coexist.

The CALC4 program in Figure 6.7 demonstrates the use of a SCREEN SECTION for definition of the computer screens. Figure 6.8 gives you an example of the type of messages produced when you ACCEPT a screen and data inconsistent with the screen field PIC is entered. Nonnumeric data is clearly reported, and the cursor remains in the affected field until a valid entry is made. Other automatic tests are made for the presence of too large a value for the receiving field, the presence of too many decimal points, or the entry of a sign when the receiving field is not signed.

6.9 In-Line versus Structured Program Logic

The CALC4 program demonstrates poor logic structuring in its PROCEDURE DIVISION. *We provide CALC4 not as a model for you to follow, but to illustrate functionally the processing action of a transaction-oriented program.* The logic of CALC4 is called "in-line" because control flows directly downward without the use of PERFORMs invoking modules of code such as beginning of job, process, and end of job. In-line logic forces you to use a GO TO to branch backward to the start of each new transaction, and as such, violates modern concepts of structured programming. This coding style is more difficult to deal with as programs become more complex or are modified. Many older interactive minicomputer and mainframe applications were coded with in-line techniques, and we include this illustration only to help you understand the meaning of the term "in-line."

The CALC5 program shown in Figure 6.9 (pages 116-117) uses the same SCREEN SECTION coding as CALC4, but uses a contemporary structured arrangement of its logic in the PROCEDURE DIVISION. *We strongly suggest that you use structured rather than in-line logic for your interactive programming.*

(Text continues on page 118)

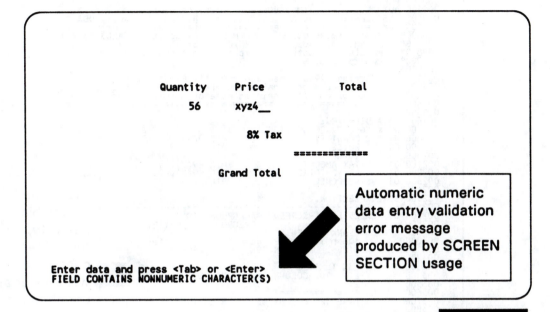

Figure 6.8

Automatic Data Validation with SCREEN SECTION

One of the benefits of using a SCREEN SECTION entry defining input fields is that RM/COBOL-85 gives you automatic numeric data validation, complete with error messages. It uses line 25 on the microcomputer screen for its error messages, as you can see here. This screen is produced by the CALC4 and CALC5 programs.

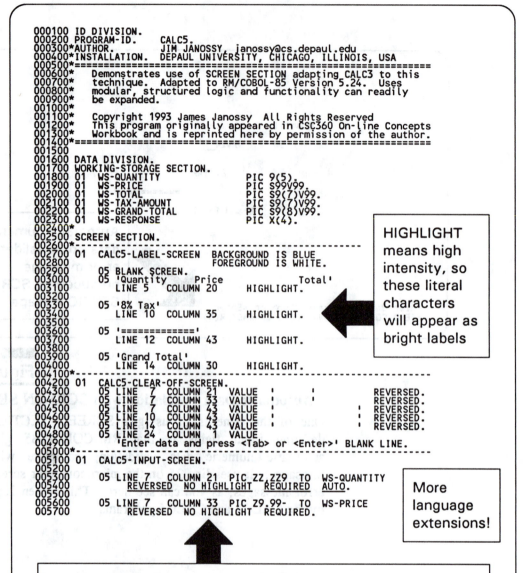

```
000100 ID DIVISION.
000200 PROGRAM-ID.      CALC5.
000300*AUTHOR.          JIM JANOSSY, janossy@cs.depaul.edu
000400*INSTALLATION.    DEPAUL UNIVERSITY, CHICAGO, ILLINOIS, USA
000500*=====================================================================
000600*    Demonstrates use of SCREEN SECTION adapting CALC3 to this
000700*    technique.  Adapted to RM/COBOL-85 Version 5.24.  Uses
000800*    modular, structured logic and functionality can readily
000900*    be expanded.
001000*
001100*    Copyright 1993 James Janossy  All Rights Reserved
001200*    This program originally appeared in CSC360 On-line Concepts
001300*    Workbook and is reprinted here by permission of the author.
001400*=====================================================================
001500
001600 DATA DIVISION.
001700 WORKING-STORAGE SECTION.
001800 01  WS-QUANTITY                    PIC 9(5).
001900 01  WS-PRICE                       PIC S99V99.
002000 01  WS-TOTAL                       PIC S9(7)V99.
002100 01  WS-TAX-AMOUNT                  PIC S9(7)V99.
002200 01  WS-GRAND-TOTAL                 PIC S9(8)V99.
002300 01  WS-RESPONSE                    PIC X(4).
002400*
002500 SCREEN SECTION.
002600*--------------------------------------------------------------------
002700 01  CALC5-LABEL-SCREEN    BACKGROUND IS BLUE
002800                           FOREGROUND IS WHITE.
002900     05 BLANK SCREEN.
003000     05 'Quantity    Price             Total'
003100        LINE 5   COLUMN 20      HIGHLIGHT.
003200
003300     05 '8% Tax'
003400        LINE 10  COLUMN 35      HIGHLIGHT.
003500
003600     05 '============='
003700        LINE 12  COLUMN 43      HIGHLIGHT.
003800
003900     05 'Grand Total'
004000        LINE 14  COLUMN 30      HIGHLIGHT.
004100*--------------------------------------------------------------------
004200 01  CALC5-CLEAR-OFF-SCREEN.
004300     05 LINE  7   COLUMN 21  VALUE '   '          REVERSED.
004400     05 LINE  7   COLUMN 33  VALUE '   '          REVERSED.
004500     05 LINE  7   COLUMN 43  VALUE '          '   REVERSED.
004600     05 LINE 10   COLUMN 43  VALUE '          '   REVERSED.
004700     05 LINE 14   COLUMN 43  VALUE '          '   REVERSED.
004800     05 LINE 24   COLUMN  1  VALUE
004900        'Enter data and press <Tab> or <Enter>' BLANK LINE.
005000*--------------------------------------------------------------------
005100 01  CALC5-INPUT-SCREEN.
005200
005300     05 LINE 7   COLUMN 21 PIC ZZ,ZZ9  TO  WS-QUANTITY
005400        REVERSED  NO HIGHLIGHT  REQUIRED  AUTO.
005500
005600     05 LINE 7   COLUMN 33 PIC Z9.99-  TO  WS-PRICE
005700        REVERSED  NO HIGHLIGHT  REQUIRED.
```

HIGHLIGHT means high intensity, so these literal characters will appear as bright labels

More language extensions!

Input fields are treated as if HIGHLIGHT has been coded; to make them appear at normal intensity, code NO HIGHLIGHT. The PIC of each input field determines how many underscore prompting characters appear in it, and how it is automagically redisplayed by RM/COBOL-85. An automatic MOVE with de-editing occurs to the "TO" field.

Figure 6.9

CALC5: SCREEN SECTION, Structured Logic

The CALC5 program uses the same SCREEN SECTION as CALC4, but uses modular, structured logic. *We strongly recommend that you use structured logic rather than in-line coding style for your interactive programs!*

```
005800*------------------------------------------------------
005900 01   CALC5-OUTPUT-SCREEN.
006000
006100      05 LINE 7    COLUMN 21 PIC ZZ,ZZ9          FROM WS-QUANTITY
006200         REVERSED.
006300
006400      05 LINE 7    COLUMN 33 PIC ZZ.99-          FROM WS-PRICE
006500         REVERSED.
006600
006700      05 LINE 7    COLUMN 43 PIC ZZ,ZZZ,ZZ9.99-  FROM WS-TOTAL
006800         REVERSED.
006900
007000      05 LINE 10   COLUMN 43 PIC ZZ,ZZZ,ZZ9.99-  FROM WS-TAX-AMOUNT
007100         REVERSED.
007200
007300      05 LINE 14   COLUMN 43 PIC ZZ,ZZZ,ZZ9.99-
007400         FROM WS-GRAND-TOTAL   REVERSED.
007500
007600      05 LINE 24   COLUMN 1  VALUE
007700         'Press <Enter> to continue or "quit" to end' BLANK LINE.
007800*------------------------------------------------------
007900 01   CALC5-ENDING-SCREEN   BACKGROUND IS BLACK
008000                            FOREGROUND IS BLUE.
008100      05 BLANK SCREEN.
008200      05 LINE 7    COLUMN 10
008300         VALUE  '*****************************'.
008400      05 LINE 8    COLUMN 10
008500         VALUE  '*                          *'.
008600      05 LINE 9    COLUMN 10
008700         VALUE  '*                          *'.
008800      05 LINE 10   COLUMN 10
008900         VALUE  '*                          *'.
009000      05 LINE 11   COLUMN 10
009100         VALUE  '*****************************'.
009200*==================================================
009300*
009400 PROCEDURE DIVISION.
009500 0000-MAINLINE.
009600      PERFORM 1000-BOJ.
009700      PERFORM 2000-PROCESS
009800         UNTIL WS-RESPONSE(1:1) = 'Q' OR 'q'.
009900      PERFORM 3000-EOJ.
010000      STOP RUN.
010100
010200*==================================================
010300
010400 1000-BOJ.
010500*------------------------------------------------------
010600* Clear screen and display labels highlighted
010700*------------------------------------------------------
010800      DISPLAY CALC5-LABEL-SCREEN.
010900
011000*==================================================
011100
011200 2000-PROCESS.
011300*------------------------------------------------------
011400* Blank out the data fields from any prior transaction
011500*------------------------------------------------------
011600      DISPLAY CALC5-CLEAR-OFF-SCREEN.
011700
011800*------------------------------------------------------
011900* Accept the data, do computations, present results
012000*------------------------------------------------------
012100      ACCEPT CALC5-INPUT-SCREEN.
012200      COMPUTE WS-TOTAL       = WS-QUANTITY * WS-PRICE.
012300      COMPUTE WS-TAX-AMOUNT  = WS-TOTAL * .08.
012400      COMPUTE WS-GRAND-TOTAL = WS-TOTAL + WS-TAX-AMOUNT.
012500      DISPLAY CALC5-OUTPUT-SCREEN.
012600
012700*------------------------------------------------------
012800* Ask if user wants to continue or quit
012900*------------------------------------------------------
013000      ACCEPT WS-RESPONSE
013100         LINE 24  COLUMN 60
013200         PROMPT '_'  REVERSED  NO BEEP  LOW.
013300
013400*==================================================
013500
013600 3000-EOJ.
013700*------------------------------------------------------
013800* Clear the screen, display sign-off message, and
013900* leave the system set to normal screen colors
014000*------------------------------------------------------
014100      DISPLAY CALC5-ENDING-SCREEN.
014200      DISPLAY 'CALC5 ENDED AS REQUESTED'
014300         LINE 9  COLUMN 14
014400         BLINK
014500         CONTROL "FCOLOR=RED".
014600      DISPLAY ' '
014700         LINE 1 COLUMN 1
014800         CONTROL "FCOLOR=WHITE".
```

Mainline controls the program

One startup task is to display labels

This is the processing loop. One transaction processes each time this loop executes.

Ending informs the user that the program has terminated

Figure 6.9 *(end)*

6.10 Categories of Screens in the SCREEN SECTION

A few distinct categories of screen exist:

- **Labeling screens,** such as CALC4-LABEL-SCREEN shown in section 6.7. You code these with literal characters, line and column locations, and options such as HIGHLIGHT. Note that PIC does not occur in a labeling screen. These screens produce just field labels, and are DISPLAYed only (you don't use them with the ACCEPT verb), at the start of the program.

- **Input screens,** such as CALC4-INPUT-SCREEN shown below. You code these screens with "screen field" line and column locations, PIC in the format you want to see the information on the screen, and a "TO" field that will receive the entered data. "TO" provides an automatic MOVE from the screen field to the receiving field when valid data (data meeting the requirements of the PIC) has been entered in the field. You can code options that affect screen field appearance and entry actions, such as REVERSED, HIGHLIGHT, REQUIRED and AUTO, among others. When you ACCEPT this form of screen, the lines of your coding are processed in the sequence you have listed them. Here is an example of an input screen:

```
01  CALC4-INPUT-SCREEN.
    05 LINE 7   COLUMN 21 PIC ZZ,ZZ9        TO  WS-QUANTITY
       REVERSED  NO HIGHLIGHT  REQUIRED  AUTO.
    05 LINE 7   COLUMN 33 PIC Z9.99-         TO  WS-PRICE
       REVERSED  NO HIGHLIGHT  REQUIRED.
```

- **Output screens,** such as CALC4-OUTPUT-SCREEN shown below. You code these screens with screen field line and column locations and PIC as with input screens, but with "FROM" and a sending field name. The "FROM" causes an automatic MOVE from the sending field to the screen field as the line is processed. You can code options that affect the field appearance, such as REVERSED. When you DISPLAY this form of screen, the lines of your coding are processed in the sequence you have listed them:

```
01  CALC4-OUTPUT-SCREEN.
    05 LINE 7   COLUMN 21  PIC ZZ,ZZ9        FROM WS-QUANTITY
       REVERSED.
    05 LINE 7   COLUMN 33 PIC ZZ.99-         FROM WS-PRICE
       REVERSED.
    05 LINE 7   COLUMN 43 PIC ZZ,ZZZ,ZZ9.99-  FROM WS-TOTAL
       REVERSED.
    -
    -
```

If you examine the CALC4 program at START-A-TRANSACTION you'll see that the essential logic of the program DISPLAYs the "clear off" screen (a type of labeling screen), ACCEPTs the input screen, does what is necessary to construct the fields to be displayed as output, and DISPLAYs the output screen. This is how a transaction is processed with screens defined in a SCREEN SECTION, no matter how complex the computations, file accesses, and miscellaneous processing actions of the program.

6.11 Overview of SCREEN SECTION Coding Options

You can use the following options at the 01 level in the SCREEN SECTION, where they apply to the entire screen. The options are shown here in the order in which they are commonly coded:

BACKGROUND *color (*)*
FOREGROUND *color (*)*
SIGN IS LEADING or TRAILING (sign is always separate)
AUTO
SECURE (or OFF)
REQUIRED
FULL (applies to elementary fields coded with TO or USING only)

(*) Color can be black, blue, green, cyan, red, magenta, brown, or white.

You can use the following options at the field level within a screen definition. Not all options can be coded together. Note that some coding variations permitted by terminal input/output ACCEPT and DISPLAY, such as HIGH in the place of HIGHLIGHT, are not permitted with SCREEN SECTION coding. The options are shown here in the order in which they are commonly coded:

LINE n or LINE +n
COLUMN n or COLUMN +n
PIC
FROM and/or TO, or USING
USING
VALUE
BACKGROUND color
FOREGROUND color
BEEP (or BELL)
BLANK SCREEN, LINE, or REMAINDER
BLINK
ERASE SCREEN, EOS, EOL
REVERSE (or REVERSED, or REVERSE-VIDEO)
HIGHLIGHT or LOWLIGHT or NO HIGHLIGHT
JUSTIFIED RIGHT (or JUST RIGHT)
AUTO
SECURE
REQUIRED
FULL

These options are described in detail in section 6.12, and many examples of their coding are shown in Figures 6.10 and 6.15.

6.12 SCREEN SECTION Coding Reference

The SCREEN SECTION coding options and their defaults are summarized in alphabetical order in the following list. *Note that some of the same features, such as HIGHLIGHT, have different coding syntax for the SCREEN SECTION than for terminal input/output use of ACCEPT or DISPLAY!*

AUTO

When auto is coded, the cursor leaves an input field either when the user presses <*Enter*> or when the user fills the field. Without AUTO, the computer user must press the <*Enter*> key to leave a field.

BACKGROUND

Sets the background color. Color can be black, blue, green, cyan, red, magenta, brown, or white.

BEEP or BELL

Sounds a tone when an input field coded with it is processed as the screen is accepted.

BLANK

BLANK SCREEN clears the entire screen, BLANK LINE clears the line from the cursor position rightward, BLANK REMAINDER clears the line from the cursor position rightward and all of the lines below the line on which it is coded. BLANK WHEN ZERO works as in ordinary WORKING-STORAGE coding.

BLINK

Causes the item to be displayed in blinking mode. The default is not to blink.

COLUMN or COL

Starting column (1 through 80) for the field location on the screen.

ERASE

ERASE offers capabilities almost identical to BLANK. ERASE SCREEN causes the entire screen to be erased. ERASE EOS causes screen erasure from the cursor position rightward and downward. ERASE EOL erases from just the cursor position to the end of the line on which the cursor is located. Erasure occurs before acceptance of data.

FOREGROUND

Sets the foreground color. Color can be black, blue, green, cyan, red, magenta, brown, or white.

FROM

Causes an automatic MOVE from the named field to the screen field when the screen is DISPLAYed.

FULL

Forces the computer user to either enter a value that is the full length of the field, or to press only the <*Enter*> key to bypass the field. If REQUIRED is also coded, the computer user must enter a value in the field, and cannot bypass it by pressing <*Enter*>.

HIGHLIGHT
Causes the item to be displayed at maximum intensity; default for DISPLAY.

JUSTIFIED RIGHT or JUST RIGHT
Used only with alphanumeric or alphabetic fields, this option causes the FROM field data to be right justified in the screen field instead of left justified. The effect becomes apparent when the screen field is longer than the FROM data field.

LOWLIGHT
Causes the data to be displayed at normal intensity.

LINE
Line number (1 through 24) for the field on the screen. The default is the next line.

PIC or PICTURE
As with WORKING-STORAGE coding, PIC specifies the intended use and processing of a field as alphanumeric or numeric. It governs the way the field is presented on the screen. You code PIC only when you code the FROM, TO, or USING options. The definition of a TO, FROM, or USING field may be qualified or subscripted, but not reference modified.

REQUIRED
Makes it necessary for the computer user to enter at least one character in a field; entry of the field cannot be bypassed by simply pressing the <*Enter*> key.

REVERSE or REVERSED or REVERSE-VIDEO
Causes the data to be presented as dark characters on a light background. Caution: Any of the variations works when coded as a static option in a screen definition, but only REVERSE works as a keyword in a dynamic option list (see CONTROL).

SECURE
Data entered into a field carrying the SECURE option is accepted and stored as usual, but it is not displayed on the screen. Instead, an asterisk is displayed for each character entered. This option is useful for the entry of passwords or other information that must be kept secret.

TO
Causes an automatic MOVE to the named field from the screen field when the screen is ACCEPTed.

USING
Combines the operations the field receives if both FROM and TO are coded with the same data name. An automatic MOVE is made from the named field to the screen field when the screen is DISPLAYed, and an automatic MOVE is made from the screen field to the named field when the screen is ACCEPTed.

VALUE
Provides a value for screen fields active in DISPLAY operations only.

6.13 CONTROL: Terminal I/O Use of Color

Controlling screen color using a SCREEN SECTION is fairly straightforward, as you can see in the main part of program CALC5 in Figure 6.9. Controlling color in using terminal input/output ACCEPT and DISPLAY statements is a bit more involved. An example of this is also contained in CALC5, at its very end:

```
DISPLAY 'CALC5 ENDED AS REQUESTED'
    LINE 9  COLUMN 14
    BLINK
    CONTROL "FCOLOR=RED".
```

You can specify colors for various parts of the computer screen using the CONTROL option and the phrases FCOLOR=*color*, BCOLOR=*color*, and BORDER=*color*, where *color* is one of the colors listed below. FCOLOR stands for "foreground color," the color of the text and symbols your display. BCOLOR stands for "background color," the color of the area behind the text or symbols you display. BORDER stands for "border color," the color of a narrow border surrounding the area you can access with program commands. This area is normally dark (black) but you can set it to whatever color you wish. If you set it to a color different from background color it appears as a box delimiting the screen.

Listed below are the colors you can specify for terminal I/O with FCOLOR, BCOLOR, and BORDER. You can use the specifications FCOLOR, BCOLOR, and BORDER in any combination. If you specify a color in combination with HIGH (or HIGHLIGHT) the color produced on the screen is as shown here, except that not all color screens display yellow or brown in the same way.

COLOR	Displays LOW as:	Displays HIGH as:
BLACK	Black	Gray
BLUE	Blue	Light blue
GREEN	Green	Light green
CYAN	Cyan	Light cyan
RED	Red	Light red
MAGENTA	Magenta	Light magenta
BROWN	Brown	Yellow (on some monitors)
WHITE	White	Bright white

When you use reverse video, the color values of the foreground and background are interchanged. If you set the foreground and background colors to the same value, the text or symbols displayed become invisible, such as blue on blue.

6.14 CONTROL, Dynamic Option Lists, and UPPER

You can use the specifications FCOLOR, BCOLOR, and BORDER in any terminal I/O ACCEPT statement, and house them in a field as a dynamic option list, as shown here and in program ACCEPT3 in Figure 6.10:

in WORKING-STORAGE:

```
01   RED-UPPER              PIC X(36)  VALUE
        'UPPER, FCOLOR=RED, BCOLOR=BLUE'.
```

in the PROCEDURE DIVISION:

```
ACCEPT WS-FIRST-FIELD
   COL  0
   NO BEEP
   CONTROL RED-UPPER.
```

The UPPER option automatically converts lowercase letters like "a" to uppercase (capital) letters such as "A". Standardizing on uppercase letters for key field and other look-up field contents is important for consistency and reliability of data retrieval. But UPPER is unusual in that you can use it with ACCEPT only when it is contained in a dynamic option list as shown above. You cannot code UPPER as part of a CONTROL phrase as a literal value. The ACCEPT3 program in Figure 6.10 demonstrates the use of UPPER; the effect it produces is shown in Figure 6.11.

6.15 Coding Restrictions of Dynamic Option Lists

Several important factors apply to dynamic option lists and their reference by the CONTROL option. A lack of awareness of these factors can cause you much frustration, so we have outlined them here.

- The contents of the dynamic option list (such as RED-UPPER above, and WS-UPPER in the UPDATE1 program shown later in Figure 6.15) are not validated by the COBOL compiler. If you make a spelling error in options in the dynamic option list, they will simply not be recognized and will not apply. You will receive no error about these, either at compile time or at runtime.

- Many of the option coding variations usable with ACCEPT are not recognized when they are housed in a CONTROL data name. For example, of the variations REVERSE, REVERSED, and REVERSE-VIDEO, only REVERSE is recognized when housed in a dynamic option list. Similarly, only HIGH, and not HIGHLIGHT, is recognized. As noted in the last point below, the unrecognized variations are not detected as errors, and are simply ignored! Here are the only codings that are recognized in a dynamic option list referenced by CONTROL:

(Text continues on page 126)

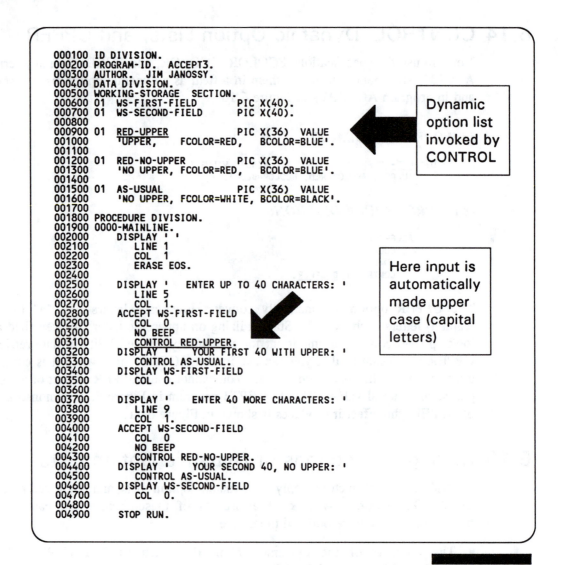

```
000100 ID DIVISION.
000200 PROGRAM-ID.  ACCEPT3.
000300 AUTHOR.   JIM JANOSSY.
000400 DATA DIVISION.
000500 WORKING-STORAGE  SECTION.
000600 01  WS-FIRST-FIELD        PIC X(40).
000700 01  WS-SECOND-FIELD       PIC X(40).
000800
000900 01  RED-UPPER             PIC X(36)  VALUE
001000     'UPPER,   FCOLOR=RED,    BCOLOR=BLUE'.
001100
001200 01  RED-NO-UPPER          PIC X(36)  VALUE
001300     'NO UPPER, FCOLOR=RED,    BCOLOR=BLUE'.
001400
001500 01  AS-USUAL              PIC X(36)  VALUE
001600     'NO UPPER, FCOLOR=WHITE, BCOLOR=BLACK'.
001700
001800 PROCEDURE DIVISION.
001900 0000-MAINLINE.
002000     DISPLAY ' '
002100         LINE 1
002200         COL  1
002300         ERASE EOS.
002400
002500     DISPLAY '   ENTER UP TO 40 CHARACTERS: '
002600         LINE 5
002700         COL  1.
002800     ACCEPT WS-FIRST-FIELD
002900         COL  0
003000         NO BEEP
003100         CONTROL RED-UPPER.
003200     DISPLAY '    YOUR FIRST 40 WITH UPPER: '
003300         CONTROL AS-USUAL.
003400     DISPLAY WS-FIRST-FIELD
003500         COL  0.
003600
003700     DISPLAY '   ENTER 40 MORE CHARACTERS: '
003800         LINE 9
003900         COL  1.
004000     ACCEPT WS-SECOND-FIELD
004100         COL  0
004200         NO BEEP
004300         CONTROL RED-NO-UPPER.
004400     DISPLAY '   YOUR SECOND 40, NO UPPER: '
004500         CONTROL AS-USUAL.
004600     DISPLAY WS-SECOND-FIELD
004700         COL  0.
004800
004900     STOP RUN.
```

Dynamic option list invoked by CONTROL

Here input is automatically made upper case (capital letters)

Figure 6.10

ACCEPT3: Dynamic Option List with CONTROL

You can put several of the controlling options for terminal input/output ACCEPT and DISPLAY into a character string stored in a data name, such as RED-UPPER. This allows you to use the option UPPER to automatically convert input alphabetic characters to capital letters. The CONTROL feature makes it possible to consolidate some of your ACCEPT and DISPLAY coding for consistency and compactness if you choose not you use a SCREEN SECTION. UPPER is the only RM/COBOL-85 option that *can't* be coded directly with ACCEPT, but must be housed in a dynamic option list.

```
    ENTER UP TO 40 CHARACTERS: The time has come, the walrus said,
    YOUR FIRST 40 WITH UPPER: THE TIME HAS COME, THE WALRUS SAID,
```

```
    ENTER 40 MORE CHARACTERS: To talk of many things.
    YOUR SECOND 40, NO UPPER: To talk of many things.
```

> The UPPER option automatically converts lowercase letters to uppercase (capital) letters

```
COBOL STOP RUN  at line 45 in ACCEPT3 (C:\RMCOB\ACCEPT3.COB).

C:\RMCOB>
```

Figure 6.11

Effect of the UPPER Option Used with CONTROL

The ACCEPT3 program accepts two 40-character lines of text entry. It uses UPPER on the first ACCEPT, but not the second. Here you see the effect of UPPER on the first entry. If you run the ACCEPT3 program on a microcomputer with a color screen you will also see the effect of the FCOLOR (foreground color) and BCOLOR (background color) options.

BEEP or NO BEEP
BLINK or NO BLINK
CONVERT or NO CONVERT
ECHO or NO ECHO
ERASE or NO ERASE
ERASE EOL
ERASE EOS
HIGH or LOW or OFF
PROMPT or NO PROMPT
REVERSE or NO REVERSE
TAB or NO TAB
UPDATE or NO UPDATE
UPPER

- A dynamic option list, CONTROL, and UPPER apply only to terminal input/output ACCEPT statements, not for SCREEN SECTION use. To gain field conversion to uppercase when you use a screen section, you can use the INSPECT verb with the CONVERTING option, as shown in line 19300 in the UPDATE1 program in Figure 6.15 (see also lines 3300 and 3400 in that program).

6.16 Putting it Together: An Interactive File Update Example

ACCEPT and DISPLAY provide so many potential coding variations that it's easy to get lost in their variations. As a final demonstration of interactive programming we present a comprehensive example here. This example, called UPDATE1, updates the records in an indexed file. The file to be updated contains one record for each part sold by the Chicago Widget Corporation. The records appear as shown in Figure 6.12, and contain fields for part id, description, unit cost (cost each) and quantity on hand.

Figure 6.13 illustrates a screen design for the UPDATE1 program. This design was prepared on a grid form similar to a printer spacing chart, to plan how the labels and data fields would be placed on the screen.

In order to test the UPDATE1 program after developing it, the indexed file needs to be present. The easiest way to prepare such a file is to place the records shown in Figure 6.12 into a sequential ASCII file, such as you can prepare using RM/CO* or a word processor. You can use a simple program like PARTLOAD, shown in Figure 6.14, to read the records from the sequential file and write them into an indexed file. PARTLOAD reads the parts records from a sequential file named PARTS.DAT and creates an indexed file named PARTS.IXF.

The source code of the UPDATE1 program is listed in Figure 6.15. Since the annotations explaining parts of this program are too extensive to be housed in boxes on the program itself, we have listed the program on right-hand pages, and annotations on left hand pages. You will see that the interactive programming features described and

Note: The records in the PARTS.DAT file should be sorted into ascending key sequence as shown here for successful loading of all records. *In your PARTS.DAT file on Diskette 1, however, the record with key C300 is not in proper sequence, to demonstrate the error handling built into the PARTLOAD indexed file loading program.* Your loading will work, but your record C300 will not be loaded to the indexed file.

A100	MICROWIDGET	0110018	1500
B200	MINIWIDGET	0147562	1283
C300	WIDGET	0206835	8736
D400	BIG WIDGET	0295075	2874
E500	JUMBO WIDGET	0477052	1960

Figure 6.12

Contents of the PARTS Master File

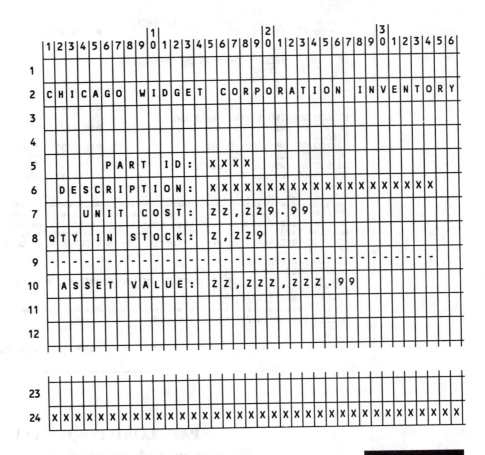

Figure 6.13

Screen Design for the UPDATE1 Interactive Program

```
000100 ID DIVISION.
000200 PROGRAM-ID.      PARTLOAD.
000300*AUTHOR.          J JANOSSY, INTERNET: JANOSSY@CS.DEPAUL.EDU
000400*INSTALLATION.  DEPAUL UNIVERSITY, CHICAGO ILLINOIS, USA
000500*    PROGRAM TO LOAD AN INDEXED FILE
000600
000700 ENVIRONMENT DIVISION.
000800 INPUT-OUTPUT SECTION.
000900 FILE-CONTROL.
001000*------------------------------------------------------------
001100     SELECT SEQ-FILE            ASSIGN TO DISK 'PARTS.DAT'
001200         ORGANIZATION IS  LINE SEQUENTIAL.
001300
001400     SELECT IDX-FILE            ASSIGN TO DISK 'PARTS.IXF'
001500         ORGANIZATION  IS  INDEXED
001600         ACCESS MODE   IS  SEQUENTIAL
001700         RECORD KEY    IS  IDX-KEY
001800         FILE STATUS   IS  WS-STATUS.
001900*------------------------------------------------------------
002000 DATA DIVISION.
002100 FILE SECTION.
002200*
002300 FD  SEQ-FILE
002400     RECORD CONTAINS 30 CHARACTERS.
002500 01  SEQ-RECORD                  PIC X(30).
002600*
002700 FD  IDX-FILE
002800     RECORD CONTAINS 30 CHARACTERS.
002900 01  IDX-RECORD.
003000     05 IDX-KEY                   PIC X(4).
003100     05 FILLER                    PIC X(26).
003200/
003300*------------------------------------------------------------
003400 WORKING-STORAGE SECTION.
003500 01  WS-STATUS                    PIC X(2).
003600*
003700 01  WS-INPUT-COUNT              PIC 9(5)    VALUE 0.
003800 01  WS-REC-LOADED              PIC 9(5)    VALUE 0.
003900 01  WS-REC-NOT-LOADED         PIC 9(5)    VALUE 0.
004000 01  F1-EOF-FLAG               PIC X(1)    VALUE 'M'.
004100/
004200 PROCEDURE DIVISION.
004300*=============================================================
004400*   In RM/COBOL-85 you need declaratives (even in dummy form) to
004500*   avoid abends even when non-zero File Status values such as
004600*   '23' are received for a key-not-found condition.  Since
004700*   DECLARATIVES are a "section" MAIN-PROGRAM must be a section.
004800*
004900 DECLARATIVES.
005000 0000-ERROR    SECTION.
005100     USE AFTER STANDARD ERROR PROCEDURE ON IDX-FILE.
005200 0000-DUMMY.  EXIT.
005300 END DECLARATIVES.
005400*=============================================================
005500 0000-MAIN-PROGRAM    SECTION.
```

(program continues on next page. . .)

Figure 6.14

PARTLOAD Program to Load an Indexed File
This program reads records from a sequential file and writes them to an indexed file. The information in its SELECT statement for the indexed file (IDX-FILE) tells the RM/COBOL-85 compiler all it needs to know to establish the data and index components of the indexed file, which is written as one file. You can use this program as a model for file-loading programs to create test files for the interactive programs that you develop. This program creates the indexed file updated by the UPDATE1 program in Figure 6.15.

```
005600 0000-MAINLINE.
005700     PERFORM 1000-BOJ.
005800     PERFORM 2000-PROCESS
005900         UNTIL F1-EOF-FLAG = 'E'.
006000     PERFORM 3000-EOJ.
006100     STOP RUN.
006200*
006300 1000-BOJ.
006400     DISPLAY '*** Start of program partload'.
006500     OPEN OUTPUT IDX-FILE.
006600     IF WS-STATUS(1:1) NOT = '0'
006700         DISPLAY '*** Error opening indexed file, program ended'
006800         DISPLAY '    File Status = ', WS-STATUS
006900         STOP RUN.
007000     OPEN  INPUT  SEQ-FILE.
007100     PERFORM 2700-READ.
007200*
007300 2000-PROCESS.
007400     WRITE IDX-RECORD FROM SEQ-RECORD.
007500     IF WS-STATUS(1:1) = '0'
007600         ADD 1 TO WS-REC-LOADED
007700      ELSE
007800     IF WS-STATUS = '21'
007900         DISPLAY '*** Prev rec out of order  File Status = ',
008000             WS-STATUS, ', record not loaded to indexed file!'
008100         DISPLAY ' '
008200         ADD 1 TO WS-REC-NOT-LOADED
008300      ELSE
008400         DISPLAY '*** Loading failed!   File Status = ', WS-STATUS
008500         STOP RUN.
008600     PERFORM 2700-READ.
008700*
008800 2700-READ.
008900     MOVE SPACES TO SEQ-RECORD.
009000     READ SEQ-FILE
009100         AT END
009200             MOVE 'E' TO F1-EOF-FLAG
009300         NOT AT END
009400             ADD 1 TO WS-INPUT-COUNT
009500             DISPLAY SEQ-RECORD.
009600*
009700 3000-EOJ.
009800     DISPLAY ' '.
009900     DISPLAY 'Seq file records read ', WS-INPUT-COUNT.
010000     DISPLAY 'Records loaded         ', WS-REC-LOADED.
010100     DISPLAY 'Records not loaded     ', WS-REC-NOT-LOADED.
010200
010300     CLOSE  SEQ-FILE  IDX-FILE.
010400     IF WS-STATUS(1:1) NOT = '0'
010500         DISPLAY '*** Error closing indexed file, check results'
010600         DISPLAY '    File Status = ', WS-STATUS
010700      ELSE
010800         DISPLAY '*** Program ended normally'.
```

Figure 6.14 *(end)*

explained in this chapter are brought together and used in a consistent and productive way in UPDATE1. The PARTS.DAT file and the source code for the PARTLOAD and UPDATE1 programs are contained on your Diskette 1. We suggest that you take these actions to demonstrate UPDATE1 for yourself:

- Compile and run the PARTLOAD program. This will create the PARTS.IXF indexed file. (Note: the record in the PARTS.DAT sequential file with key C300 is out of sequence, and will not be loaded, to demonstrate error handling.)

- Run the UPDATE1 program, using it to access the records with keys A100, B200, D400, and E500.

6.17 UPDATE1 Program Annotations

a. The SELECT statement in UPDATE1 is coded to obtain random access to the PARTS.IXF indexed file. LINE SEQUENTIAL is not relevant here since we are dealing with an indexed file. WS-STATUS is a two-byte field that receives a value from the indexed file access method indicating the outcome of file open, read, and close actions.

b. WS-LOW and WS-CAP are character strings used by the INSPECT statement at line 19300 to standardize the PR-DESCRIPTION field as uppercase (capital) letters. This is a common 1985 COBOL method for standardizing character string content. (The UPPER option associated with CONTROL works only with terminal I/O in RM/COBOL-85.)

c. WS-UPPER is a dynamic option list used by the ACCEPT at line 21800. This is an RM/COBOL-85 language extension usable only with terminal input/output, not in a SCREEN SECTION.

d. A label screen uses literals, LINE and COLUMN; you do not code PIC.

e. A "clear off" screen is useful to begin each transaction without data lingering from a previous transaction. This is a variation of label screen coding.

```
000100 ID DIVISION.
000200 PROGRAM-ID.    UPDATE1.
000300*AUTHOR.        JIM JANOSSY, janossy@cs.depaul.edu
000400*INSTALLATION. DEPAUL UNIVERSITY, CHICAGO, ILLINOIS, USA
000500*=============================================================
000600*   Demonstrates indexed file update and use of SCREEN SECTION.
000700*   Load the indexed file first using the PARTLOAD program!
000800*   For RM/COBOL-85 version 5.24.
000900*=============================================================
001000 ENVIRONMENT DIVISION.
001100 INPUT-OUTPUT SECTION.
001200 FILE-CONTROL.
001300     SELECT PARTS-FILE     ASSIGN TO DISK 'PARTS.IXF'
001400        ORGANIZATION  IS  INDEXED                          a
001500        ACCESS MODE   IS  RANDOM
001600        RECORD KEY    IS  PR-PART-ID
001700        FILE STATUS   IS  WS-STATUS.
001800*--------------------------------------------------------------
001900 DATA DIVISION.
002000 FILE SECTION.
002100*
002200 FD  PARTS-FILE
002300     RECORD CONTAINS 30 CHARACTERS.
002400 01  PARTS-RECORD.
002500     05  PR-PART-ID              PIC X(4).
002600     05  PR-DESCRIPTION          PIC X(15).
002700     05  PR-UNIT-PRICE           PIC 9(5)V99.
002800     05  PR-QTY-ON-HAND          PIC 9(4).
002900*--------------------------------------------------------------
003000 WORKING-STORAGE SECTION.
003100 01  WS-STATUS                   PIC X(2).
003200
003300 01  WS-LOW  PIC X(26)  VALUE 'abcdefghijklmnopqrstuvwxyz'.   b
003400 01  WS-CAP  PIC X(26)  VALUE 'ABCDEFGHIJKLMNOPQRSTUVWXYZ'.
003500
003600 01  WS-RESPONSE                 PIC X(4).
003700 01  WS-ASSET-VALUE              PIC 9(8)V99.
003800 01  WS-UPPER                    PIC X(55) VALUE            c
003900     'UPPER, PROMPT, REVERSE, NO BEEP, LOW'.
004000*
004100 SCREEN SECTION.
004200*--------------------------------------------------------------
004300 01  LABEL-SCREEN  BACKGROUND IS BLUE
004400                   FOREGROUND IS WHITE.
004500     05  BLANK SCREEN.
004600     05  'CHICAGO WIDGET CORPORATION INVENTORY'
004700         LINE 2   COLUMN 1      HIGHLIGHT.
004800
004900     05  'PART ID:'
005000         LINE 5   COLUMN 6      HIGHLIGHT.
005100
005200     05  'DESCRIPTION:'
005300         LINE 6   COLUMN 2      HIGHLIGHT.            d
005400
005500     05  'UNIT COST:'
005600         LINE 7   COLUMN 4      HIGHLIGHT.
005700
005800     05  'QTY IN STOCK:'
005900         LINE 8   COLUMN 1      HIGHLIGHT.
006000
006100     05  '-----------------------------------'
006200         LINE 9   COLUMN 1      HIGHLIGHT.
006300
006400     05  'ASSET VALUE:'
006500         LINE 10  COLUMN 2      HIGHLIGHT.
006600*--------------------------------------------------------------
006700 01  CLEAR-OFF-SCREEN.
006800     05  LINE  5 COLUMN 15 VALUE '    '           REVERSE.
006900     05  LINE  6 COLUMN 15 VALUE '               ' REVERSE.
007000     05  LINE  7 COLUMN 15 VALUE '        '        REVERSE.   e
007100     05  LINE  8 COLUMN 15 VALUE '    '            REVERSE.
007200     05  LINE 10 COLUMN 15 VALUE '          '      REVERSE.
```

(program continues on next page. . .)

Figure 6.15

UPDATE1, a Complete Indexed File Update Model

UPDATE1 combines many of the features described in this chapter and provides a well-developed model for robust and convenient interactive programming.

UPDATE1 Program Annotations (continued)

f. GET-ID-SCREEN and the three screens that follow are not complete screens, but just variations of the 24th line prompt. These are displayed, as appropriate, just before the paragraph named 2700-GET-USER-RESPONSE is performed.

g. DATA-SCREEN is the main input/output screen. Coding a field with FROM provides an automatic MOVE from the named field to the screen field when the screen is displayed. Coding TO causes an automatic MOVE from the screen field to the named field when the screen is ACCEPTed. You can code both FROM and TO with the same field name for complete access to the field, or code USING, which accomplishes the same thing. The PIC coding on these fields governs how the field will be presented on the screen.

h. ASSET-DISPLAY-SCREEN is separate from DATA-SCREEN because the computed asset value (PR-UNIT-PRICE times PR-QTY-ON-HAND) must be redisplayed after any change.

i. The "ending" screen provides a border of asterisks for the message displayed at end-of-job.

j. DECLARATIVES are necessary, at least in "dummy" form, if you want to use File Status without INVALID KEY. Without declaratives, your program will abnormally end when a nonexistent part id is entered for record retrieval from the indexed file because such an occurrence produces a nonzero File Status. Using INVALID-KEY alone does not require DECLARATIVES, but File Status is useful for error reporting.

```
007300*--------------------------------------------------
007400 01   GET-ID-SCREEN.
007500      05 LINE 24  COLUMN  1 VALUE
007600         'Enter part id, <Enter>, or "Q" to quit '.
007700      05 LINE 24  COLUMN 41  VALUE
007800         '                          ===>          '.
007900*--------------------------------------------------
008000 01   UPDATE-INSTRUCTIONS-SCREEN.
008100      05 LINE 24  COLUMN  1 VALUE
008200         'Change data or press <Enter> to leave da'.
008300      05 LINE 24  COLUMN 41  VALUE
008400         'ta as is                  ===>          '.
008500*--------------------------------------------------
008600 01   UPDATE-DONE-SCREEN.
008700      05 LINE 24  COLUMN  1 VALUE
008800         'Record updated, enter another part id or'.
008900      05 LINE 24  COLUMN 41  VALUE
009000         ' "Q" to quit              ===>          '.
009100*--------------------------------------------------
009200 01   NO-SUCH-RECORD-SCREEN.
009300      05 LINE 24  COLUMN  1 VALUE
009400         'Part id not on file, enter another or "Q'.
009500      05 LINE 24  COLUMN 41  VALUE
009600         '" to quit                 ===>          '.
009700      05 LINE 24  COLUMN 80  BEEP.
009800*--------------------------------------------------
009900 01   DATA-SCREEN.
010000
010100      05 LINE 5   COLUMN 15  PIC X(4)        FROM PR-PART-ID
010200         REVERSE  NO HIGHLIGHT  REQUIRED  AUTO.
010300
010400      05 LINE 6   COLUMN 15  PIC X(15)       USING PR-DESCRIPTION
010500         REVERSE  NO HIGHLIGHT  REQUIRED  AUTO.
010600
010700      05 LINE 7   COLUMN 15  PIC ZZ,ZZ9.99   USING PR-UNIT-PRICE
010800         REVERSE  NO HIGHLIGHT  REQUIRED  AUTO.
010900
011000      05 LINE 8   COLUMN 15  PIC Z,ZZ9       FROM PR-QTY-ON-HAND
011100                                             TO   PR-QTY-ON-HAND
011200         REVERSE  NO HIGHLIGHT  REQUIRED  AUTO.
011300*--------------------------------------------------
011400 01   ASSET-DISPLAY-SCREEN.
011500      05 LINE 10  COLUMN 15  PIC ZZ,ZZZ,ZZ9.99
011600         FROM WS-ASSET-VALUE
011700         REVERSE  NO HIGHLIGHT.
011800*--------------------------------------------------
011900 01   ENDING-SCREEN  BACKGROUND IS BLACK
012000                     FOREGROUND IS BLUE.
012100      05 BLANK SCREEN.
012200      05 LINE  7  COLUMN  10
012300         VALUE '**********************************'.
012400      05 LINE  8  COLUMN  10
012500         VALUE '*                              *'.
012600      05 LINE  9  COLUMN  10
012700         VALUE '*                              *'.
012800      05 LINE 10  COLUMN  10
012900         VALUE '*                              *'.
013000      05 LINE 11  COLUMN  10
013100         VALUE '**********************************'.
013200*==================================================
013300 PROCEDURE DIVISION.
013400
013500*  In RM/COBOL-85 you need declaratives (even in dummy form) to
013600*  avoid abends even when non-zero File Status values such as
013700*  '23' are received for a key-not-found condition.  Since
013800*  DECLARATIVES are a "section" MAIN-PROGRAM must be a section.
013900
014000 DECLARATIVES.
014100 0000-ERROR    SECTION.
014200     USE AFTER STANDARD ERROR PROCEDURE ON PARTS-FILE.
014300 0000-DUMMY.  EXIT.
014400 END DECLARATIVES.
014500*--------------------------------------------------
014600 0000-MAIN-PROGRAM   SECTION.
014700 0000-MAINLINE.
014800     PERFORM 1000-BOJ.
014900     PERFORM 2000-PROCESS
015000        UNTIL WS-RESPONSE(1:1) = 'Q' OR 'q'.
015100     PERFORM 3000-EOJ.
015200     STOP RUN.
015300
```

f **g** **h** **i** **j**

Figure 6.15 *(continued)*

UPDATE1 Program Annotations (continued)

k. File Status is tested after opening the indexed file to make sure that the OPEN succeeded. If the file fails to open, the File Status value will help diagnose what kind of problem exists with the file. (Execute UPDATE1 without the PARTS.IXF indexed file present, and you can see how File Status works.)

l. The heart of UPDATE1 is the 2000-PROCESS paragraph, which is executed once for each update transaction. The indexed file is read to obtain the record with the key entered by the computer operator. If File Status indicates that the record has been obtained (line 18300), DATA-SCREEN is DISPLAYed to present the data from the record (the FROM's are active). DATA-SCREEN is later ACCEPTed to obtain field contents from the keyboard (and the TO's are processed). REWRITE puts the record (changed or unchanged) back into the indexed file.

m. The terminal I/O ACCEPT in the paragraph named 2700-GET-USER-RESPONSE uses CONTROL with the UPPER option to convert letters entered as part of the record key to uppercase. The dynamic option list named WS-UPPER is coded at lines 3800 and 3900. Case variations between entered and stored keys would cause confusing operation.

n. Rather than just stopping, a program should confirm its normal ending. In addition, you should check File Status to make sure that the indexed file closed properly, so that we know it to be uncorrupted and ready for another program to access.

```
015400*=================================================================
015500 1000-BOJ.
015600*-----------------------------------------------------------------
015700*  Clear screen and display labels highlighted
015800*-----------------------------------------------------------------
015900     DISPLAY LABEL-SCREEN.
016000     DISPLAY CLEAR-OFF-SCREEN.
016100     OPEN I-O PARTS-FILE.
016200     IF WS-STATUS(1:1) NOT = '0'
016300        DISPLAY '*** Error opening indexed file, program ended'
016400        DISPLAY '    File Status = ', WS-STATUS
016500        DISPLAY '    RUN STOPPED!'
016600        STOP RUN.
016700     DISPLAY GET-ID-SCREEN.
016800     PERFORM 2700-GET-USER-RESPONSE.
016900
017000*=================================================================
017100 2000-PROCESS.
017200*-----------------------------------------------------------------
017300*  Blank out the data fields from any prior transaction
017400*-----------------------------------------------------------------
017500     DISPLAY CLEAR-OFF-SCREEN.
017600
017700*-----------------------------------------------------------------
017800*  Accept the data, do computations, present results
017900*-----------------------------------------------------------------
018000     MOVE WS-RESPONSE TO PR-PART-ID.
018100     READ PARTS-FILE.
018200
018300     IF WS-STATUS(1:1) = '0'
018400        DISPLAY DATA-SCREEN
018500        DISPLAY UPDATE-INSTRUCTIONS-SCREEN
018600        COMPUTE WS-ASSET-VALUE = PR-UNIT-PRICE * PR-QTY-ON-HAND
018700        DISPLAY ASSET-DISPLAY-SCREEN
018800
018900        ACCEPT DATA-SCREEN
019000        COMPUTE WS-ASSET-VALUE = PR-UNIT-PRICE * PR-QTY-ON-HAND
019100        DISPLAY ASSET-DISPLAY-SCREEN
019200
019300        INSPECT PR-DESCRIPTION CONVERTING WS-LOW TO WS-CAP
019400        DISPLAY DATA-SCREEN
019500
019600        REWRITE PARTS-RECORD
019700        IF WS-STATUS(1:1) NOT = '0'
019800           DISPLAY '*** Error on rewrite, program ended'
019900           DISPLAY '    File Status = ', WS-STATUS
020000           DISPLAY '    RUN STOPPED!'
020100           STOP RUN
020200        END-IF
020300
020400        DISPLAY UPDATE-DONE-SCREEN
020500     ELSE
020600        DISPLAY NO-SUCH-RECORD-SCREEN
020700     END-IF.
020800
020900     PERFORM 2700-GET-USER-RESPONSE.
021000
021100*=================================================================
021200 2700-GET-USER-RESPONSE.
021300*-----------------------------------------------------------------
021400*  Ask if user wants to continue or quit
021500*-----------------------------------------------------------------
021600     ACCEPT WS-RESPONSE
021700        LINE 24  COLUMN 72
021800        CONTROL WS-UPPER.
021900     DISPLAY ' ' LINE 24 COLUMN 1  ERASE EOL.
022000
022100*=================================================================
022200 3000-EOJ.
022300*-----------------------------------------------------------------
022400*  Clear the screen, display sign-off message, and
022500*  leave the system set to normal screen colors
022600*-----------------------------------------------------------------
022700     DISPLAY ENDING-SCREEN.
022800     DISPLAY 'PROGRAM ENDED AS REQUESTED'
022900        LINE 9  COLUMN 13
023000        BLINK
023100        CONTROL "FCOLOR=RED".
023200     DISPLAY ' '
023300        LINE 1 COLUMN 1
023400        CONTROL "FCOLOR=WHITE".
023500
023600     CLOSE  PARTS-FILE.
023700     IF WS-STATUS(1:1) NOT = '0'
023800        DISPLAY '*** Error closing indexed file, check results'
023900        DISPLAY '    File Status = ', WS-STATUS.
```

k

l

m

n

Figure 6.15 *(end)*

6.18 Verifying File Names Using ACCEPT and DISPLAY

An ACCEPT and DISPLAY can be used to verify file names where files are inputted or outputted. Let's say that your disk already has a file on it named PAYROLL.DAT. Suppose that you run a program with the following SELECT statement for an output file:

```
SELECT PAYROLL-FILE ASSIGN TO DISK 'PAYROLL.DAT'
    ORGANIZATION IS LINE SEQUENTIAL.
```

This program inadvertently creates an output file with the same name (PAYROLL.DAT). Once you OPEN OUTPUT PAYROLL-FILE and WRITE a record to it, the existing PAYROLL.DAT file will be or lost. Experienced programmers know that such a situation could result in the loss of important data and that measures should be taken to avoid such potential problems. As students, you may not have too many data files on your disks and may regard precautions against destroying files as unnecessary, but should you ever lose an important file you will quickly change your mind. We recommend that all programs that create output disk files include instructions similar to the following in their beginning of job logic, to be executed prior to opening an output file:

```
DISPLAY 'This program will create an output disk file'
DISPLAY 'named PAYROLL.DAT. If such a file already exists'
DISPLAY 'on your disk and you wish to keep it, terminate'
DISPLAY 'this program so that the filename can be changed.'
DISPLAY 'Do you want to continue (Y/N)?'
ACCEPT WS-RESPONSE.
IF WS-RESPONSE = 'N' OR 'n'
    STOP RUN.
```

Such a routine gives the computer user the opportunity to abort the run if the file to be created will write over an existing file. If a file exists with the same name specified in the program, the program will need to be modified before it can run properly. Type the DOS command DIR at the prompt for a directory of the file names on disk.

You need not hardcode the file name and extension in your programs. Instead, you can prompt for and ACCEPT the name of the file to be accessed when a program begins execution. To do this, code the SELECT statement in this way:

```
SELECT user-file-name ASSIGN TO DISK WS-FILE-NAME
    ORGANIZATION IS ...
    -
    -
    -
------------------------------------------------------------
WORKING-STORAGE SECTION.
01  WS-FILE-NAME            PIC X(25).
```

Request that the user enter the file name when the program begins execution:

```
DISPLAY 'Enter an input filename (be sure that the name'.
DISPLAY 'selected matches an existing filename'.
ACCEPT WS-FILE-NAME.
OPEN I/O user-file-name.
```

See section 5.8 for a more complete example of this technique, which you can combine with verification of the file name before your OPEN for the file.

Appendix A

A Microcomputer Primer for Newcomers

A.1 An Overview of PC Hardware

I n this section, we consider the most common components of a microcomputer, as known as a personal computer, PC, or "micro." We focus on the IBM family of personal computers. If you have an IBM-compatible machine you will find that your equipment is similar to the equipment shown in Figure A.1. Note that RM/COBOL-85 is designed to run on IBM PC or equivalent compatible equipment. RM/COBOL-85 will not run on Apple MacIntosh computers.

In the modern environment, most microcomputers are configured with these devices:

- Keyboard
- Monitor
- At least one hard disk drive and one or two floppies
- Printer
- Microprocessor (central processing unit)

We will examine each of these devices in the following sections of this appendix, beginning with the two varieties of keyboards commonly associated with IBM and IBM-compatible microcomputers.

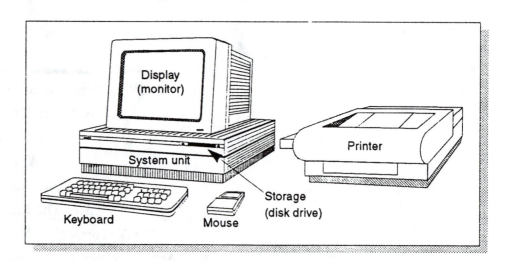

Figure A.1

The IBM Personal System/2 Model 30

A.2 Using the Keyboard

Keyboards are not always identical, but most keyboards include the basic keys in roughly the same positions. Figure A.2 illustrates the basic keyboard that originated in 1981 with the first model of IBM PC in 1981, while Figure A.3 illustrates the enhanced keyboard introduced in 1987 by IBM. We provide a brief introduction to some of the more important keys on the keyboard.

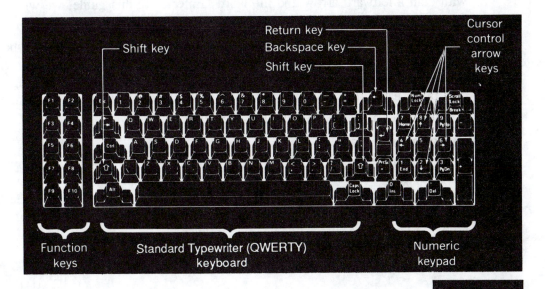

Figure A.2

The Original IBM PC 83-Key Keyboard (1981)

Figure A.3

The IBM PC 101-Key Keyboard (1987)

<Enter> Key

One of the most important keys on the keyboard is the <*Enter*> key. Keystrokes you make at the keyboard are received by the computer system and in most cases displayed on the screen and stored, but not acted upon, until you press <*Enter*>. <*Enter*> might also be labeled the <*Return*> key. It is similar to a carriage return key on a typewriter. On an IBM PC the <*Enter*> key is marked with a leftward arrow. Figure A.3 illustrates how this key appears on an enhanced keyboard, which labels it with both a leftward arrow and the word "Enter." In this guide, we will call this key the <*Enter*> key.

You type DOS commands and instructions and enter data using your keyboard as if it were a typewriter. When you are ready to send a line to the computer, press the <*Enter*> key. While data is received by the computer's screen handling software as you press each key, no data, instruction, or system command is transmitted to the computer for execution until you press <*Enter*>.

<Backspace> Key

You can make changes to an entry before pressing <*Enter*> by using the <*Backspace*> key. The <*Backspace*> key is usually marked with a straight left arrow; it's above the <*Enter*> key as shown in Figures A.2 and A.3. Each time you press <*Backspace*> the computer will delete one character to the left of your cursor point, and move the cursor one position leftward.

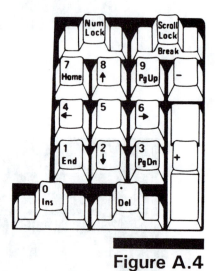

Figure A.4

The Numeric Keypad

Numeric Keypad

The numeric keypad is typically located at the right side of the keyboard and is shown in Figure A.4. The numeric keypad allows you to enter numbers with your right hand, without the need to use the numerals on the top row of the keyboard, when the <*NumLock*> key is pressed. When <*NumLock*> is off, the 2, 4, 6,and 8 keys act as cursor movement keys.

Cursor Control <Arrow> Keys

Cursor control *<Arrow>* keys such as *<Left>*, *<Right>*, *<Up>*, *<Down>*, *<Home>*, *<End>*, *<PgUp>*, and *<PgDn>* are used for positioning the cursor at a desired point on the screen. These either share the numeric keypad with numbers, as in Figure A.3, or may be on a separate dedicated group of keys, as in Figure A.4. Many programs use cursor arrow keys to highlight the commands you want to execute. You also use these keys for text editing when keying in or revising a program.

If there are cursor control characters on your numeric keypad, you can access them when *<NumLock>* is off. When the *<NumLock>* light is on, the keypad keys generate numbers rather than cursor control signals. You turn *<NumLock>* on and off by pressing the *<NumLock>* key. How is *<NumLock>* set when your microcomputer starts operation? This varies with different machines. IBM PS/2s and some compatibles with enhanced keyboards will be in "number" mode initially and you must press the *<NumLock>* key once to get into "cursor" mode.

<CapsLock> Key

The *<CapsLock>* key is on the lower right side of the 83 key keyboard but is on the lefthand side of the enhanced 101-key keyboard, as shown in Figures A.2 and A.3. *<CapsLock>*, like *<NumLock>*, is a toggle key. If you do not press it at all, lowercase letters are transmitted when the alphabetic keys are pressed. If you press the *<Capslock>* key once, each letter you subsequently enter will be transmitted as an uppercase letter. If you press the *<CapsLock>* key again, you get lowercase letters again. A light usually appears on the keyboard if you have toggled *<CapsLock>* on. *<CapsLock>* affects only letters. It has no effect on the numbers and special symbols on the top line of the keyboard. For example, to transmit the asterisk * above the number 8 on the top row of the keyboard, you must use the *<Shift Key>*, which is marked with an upward-pointing arrow, even if the *<CapsLock>* key is on.

We recommend that you enter your program using uppercase letters, with *<CapsLock>* on. Data files should also be entered using uppercase letters unless you are instructed to do otherwise. Note that if your program tests for an 'M' in a data field and you have entered a lowercase 'm', these characters will not be considered equal when the comparison is performed. This is one reason why using all uppercase letters for data may help you to avoid errors.

<Shift> Key

The *<Shift>* and *<CapsLock>* keys function just as they do on a typewriter. To continuously enter data or instructions in uppercase mode press the *<CapsLock>* key. To enter only some data or instructions in uppercase, and others in lowercase, use the *<Shift>* key to control the case. There are two identical *<Shift>* keys on the keyboards, one on the lower right side of the central keyboard and one on the lower left. The *<Shift>* keys make all the special characters above the numbers on the basic keyboard available. The *<Shift>* key is not a toggle key because it must be held down or pressed for each special character or uppercase letter desired. *<CapsLock>*, on the other hand, need only be pressed once to transmit all uppercase letters.

<Page Down> and <Page Up> Keys

When using the RM/COBOL-85 text editor for entering program and data files and with many other types of text editors, the *<PgDn>* key on the numeric keypad will scroll, or move, one page (screen) down in a program or file. *<PgUp>* will scroll one page up in a program or file. If you press the *<Ctrl>* key and the *<Home>* key at the same time, the cursor will move to the beginning of the file. Pressing *<Ctrl>* and *<End>* will bring the cursor to the end of a file.

Function Keys

Function keys appear to the left of the main keyboard on the original 83-key keyboard, as shown in Figure A.2. On 101-key enhanced keyboards, function keys appear above the main keyboard, as shown in Figure A.3. Function keys are typically numbered *<F1>* through *<F10>* or *<F1>* through *<F12>*. These keys have specific meanings for each software product that you run. In RM/COBOL-85, for example, when using the RM/CO* editor, the *<F1>* function key is used to display a context-sensitive "help" screen.

A.3   The Monitor

When you enter data using a keyboard, or when the computer responds to you, the keyed data and computer response are displayed on the monitor. Other names for the monitor are screen, cathode ray tube (CRT), and video display. Some monitors have a special "on" switch separate from the computer's on switch. If there is a switch or knob on the monitor marked "on/off", turn it on before getting started.

Older monitors are monochrome monitors, which means they are white and black, green and black, or amber and black. Most modern monitors provide color screens, which can display graphics as well as text. Monochrome monitors are adequate for use with RM/COBOL-85. We recommend, however, that you use a color monitor with the RM/CO* text editor to get the full benefit of its ability to trace the execution of your programs, which it does using contrasting colors.

Monitors usually come with a knob for adjusting the screen's color and/or brightness. You can make adjustments to suit your tastes. Most monitors can display 25 lines of output and 80 characters per line.

A.4   The Printer

Printers are used to obtain a written or "hard" copy of programs, data, or output. All printers can print letters, digits, and special symbols in black ink but some can also print in color and can print graphics and characters as well.

Modern printers take the form of dot-matrix, ink jet, or laser printers. While many dot-matrix printers produce near-letter-quality output, ink jet and laser printers are faster, quieter, and produce higher quality print. Most printers print 80 characters per line but some can print 100 to 120 characters per line as well. Printers are controlled by a power switch separate from the computer power switch.

Access to a printer is important for COBOL programming work on a microcomputer for several reasons. First, of course, you will want to be able to take a listing of your source code for a program away from the computer, to be able to study it, and, eventually, to be able to submit it for grading. Secondly, some of your programs will create reports as output, which are designed to be printed. But, at any point in your computer work, you might also want to obtain a printed copy of a screen display. To get a screen print with either DOS or the RM/CO* text editor, press the <*Shift*> key on the left side of the keyboard and the <*PrtSc*> key on the right side of the keyboard. With PS/2 microcomputers and some compatibles, pressing <*PrtSc*> alone will produce a screen print.

A.5   Diskette and Disk Drives

In order to be run (executed), a program file (machine language) must first be loaded into the microprocessor. Similarly, data files to be processed into reports or updated must be available as machine readable input before they can be processed. These machine language and data files must be stored externally to memory, which is volatile and resumes a random bit pattern when power is removed. Disk storage is called **auxiliary storage** or **secondary storage** to distinguish it from the computer's memory, which is called **primary storage.** Bit patterns forming information remain in place on disk when the computer is turned off. We usually store data and programs as files on disks so that they can be used again without having to rekey them on the keyboard.

Microcomputers use two types of disks: floppy diskettes and hard disks. Floppy disks are called "floppy" because they use a thin, removable, flexible medium with a magnetic surface on which data is recorded. We use the term "floppy disk" and "diskette" interchangeably. "Hard" disks use rigid, nonremovable aluminum plates coated with a magnetic surface, and are encased in a sealed unit.

Floppy disk-only systems typically use two floppy disk drives for auxiliary storage although computers with just a single floppy disk drive are available. But since the price of hard disk computer systems has fallen dramatically since 1990, floppy-only systems are obsolescent. In addition, floppy-only systems are much more awkward to use with modern software, which often requires frequent access to disk storage.

Hard disk systems typically have a hard disk and either one or two floppy disk drives. The most common type of diskette drive now is the 3-1/2 inch size. Many computer systems are configured with two diskette drives to facilitate copying and backup. Floppy disk drives are usually labeled A for the left or upper drive and B for the right or lower drive, if there is one. The hard drive is typically referred to as the C drive. Your system may also have hard drive designations of D, E, and so forth.

Floppy Diskettes

Floppy disk drives may be built in as part of the microcomputer or they may be units housed in separate units from the computer. The photo in Figure A.1 shows the floppy

Figure A.5

3-1/2 Inch Floppies Are Replacing 5-1/4 Inch Floppies

disk in an IBM PS/2 labeled as the "disk drive." Floppy disks for most IBM PCs are 5-1/4 inch; newer computers, laptops, and notebook computers use 3-1/2 inch diskettes, as shown in Figure A.5. Despite its size, a 3-1/2 inch disk has a larger storage capacity than a 5-1/4 inch disk.

Standard double-sided double-density (DSDD) 5-1/4 inch disks can store approximately 360,000 bytes of data, while double-sided high-density diskettes (DSHD) can store about 1.2 megabytes (million bytes). While a high-density floppy diskette drive can read a standard (low) density diskette, a low-density diskette drive cannot read a high-density disk.

Double-sided double-density 3-1/2 inch floppy diskettes are labeled 2DD and can store approximately 720,000 bytes, twice as much as 5-1/4 inch diskettes. High-density 3-1/2 inch diskettes are labeled 2HD and can store 1.44 megabytes. As with 5-1/4 inch floppies, higher-density 3-1/2 inch diskette drives can read and process both capacities of 3-1/2 inch floppy, but lower-density diskette drives are limited to reading and writing lower-density diskettes. Technology has advanced and made it possible to store two to four megabytes on some special types of 3-1/2 inch diskettes. As yet, neither diskettes for this purpose nor diskette drives to handle them are commonly used.

The smaller, 3-1/2 inch disks have a number of advantages over the older 5-1/4 inch size. They have a hard plastic casing, rather than a thin flexible sleeve, and are more resistant to damage. In addition, 3-1/2 inch disks have a metal cover over the magnetic media, which automatically slides away to reveal an opening to the disk when it is read or written. Whereas 5-1/4 inch disks use stick-on write protect tabs for write protection, which can fall off, each 3-1/2 inch disk has a built-in plastic tab to prevent writing. Instead of attaching a gummed tape, you slide the tab to write protect the disk (the position closest to the edge is the write-protected position).

Hard Disks

The hard disk is a much more versatile storage device than either 3-1/2 inch or 5-1/4 inch floppy diskettes. A modern hard disk has a capacity of 40 to 320 or more megabytes. In addition to a much larger storage capacity than floppy diskettes, hard disks access data ten or more times as fast as floppy diskette. Hard disks are used to permanently store both programs and data and eliminate the need to "swap" floppy disks in and out of diskette drives to process large programs or files. But hard disks are vulnerable to damage from mechanical or electrical shock. *Do not move, carry, jar, or drop a microcomputer that has a hard disk when the machine is on.* Unless the hard disk is shock-mounted and designed to accommodate movement during operation (as with many laptops) it can easily be damaged by such movement while it is running. Floppies are commonly used to make copies, or "backups," of files and programs stored on hard disk, to preserve data in case of hard disk damage or failure.

Handling Floppy Disks

Diskettes are relatively durable but they do not tolerate physical abuse very well. Always handle diskettes by their protective outer covering, taking care not to touch the metallic portion. Keep all diskettes away from magnetic fields such as those associated with televisions, telephones, microwaves, and other electrical devices. Do not bend 5-1/4 inch diskettes. Store diskettes in the envelopes that are supplied with them. Contrary to popular misconception, diskettes are not usually affected by the magnetic security scanning gates employed at airports, and we have not encountered problems with either floppies or hard disks in laptops in carry-on luggage that has been scanned.

Blank diskettes are provided with adhesive labels that you, yourself, attach to label them. Write on the label before you attach the label to the diskette. Use only a felt tip pen to mark on the label after it has been attached to the diskette.

To insert a disk in the A or B floppy disk drive, the drive door must be open. On some drives you must press a release to open it. Similarly, most drives must be closed before they can be used. A disk drive is active when the small light on its face is on. Do not insert a disk in a drive when the light is on because you could damage the mechanism that reads and writes data, and you might damage the diskette itself.

To protect a 5-1/4 inch diskette from being written on by accident, put an adhesive write-protect tab over the square notch on its right side. To protect a 3-1/2 inch diskette from being written on by accident, slide the small plastic tab at its top to the position closest to the edge.

A.6   The Microprocessor

A microprocessor is the "brains" or processing unit of the system and performs all processing. It is referred to as the central processing unit (CPU). It is mounted on a circuit board inside the main unit, and consists of a chip that contains millions of integrated circuits, as shown in Figure A.6. The original IBM PCs of the early 1980s used the 8088 chip, manufactured by Intel Corporation. Modern PCs and compatibles use the faster 80386 and 80486 chips, or the Intel Pentium processor. (The Pentium

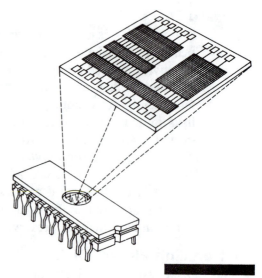

Figure A.6

The Microprocessor "Chip" Contains Millions of Circuits

was to be named the 80586 until Intel decided to use a name for it that could be trademarked. Numbers can't be registered as trademarks in the United States.)

The microprocessor stores data and processes all instructions. It uses two types of memory. Read-only memory (ROM) is electronic storage that is "prewired" to perform system functions. ROM is installed by the computer manufacturer and cannot be changed by the user. Random access memory (RAM) is changeable and stores programs and data loaded from external sources, such as floppy and hard disks.

On most microcomputers, the capacity of RAM is typically measured in megabytes (MB). A megabyte is approximately one million bytes. Two to sixteen megabytes of RAM is a common range for modern microcomputers.

Most modern software depends on access to several megabytes of RAM (memory) in your microcomputer, so one of the most important considerations you face when selecting a microcomputer is its memory capacity. A second consideration is hard disk capacity. We suggest that you acquire at least 80 to 100 megabytes or more of hard disk capacity in any microcomputer you buy. Thirdly, you should realize that much of the present generation of software is designed to run best on machines using 80486 chips. The 80386 chip is still popular, but earlier chips, such as the 80286, are not capable of supporting much modern software.

A.7   Turning on Your Computer

You will typically have several devices to turn on when you want to activate your computer. You should turn on your monitor and printer before turning on your computer. The power switches on these devices will vary in location, and you must become familiar with your own equipment complement.

Before actually turning on the microcomputer, determine whether or not you have a hard disk drive. For diskette systems with no hard drive, place a DOS operating diskette in the A drive before you turn on the computer. For computers with hard disks, the operating system is automatically loaded directly from the hard disk, and no diskette should be in any diskette drive. *Caution! One way that a destructive virus can enter a computer system is via an "infected" floppy that is present in a diskette drive when you turn on the power.* If a floppy is present, the microcomputer attempts to load the operating system from it before seeking this from the hard disk. *On a system with a hard disk, do not leave floppies in your diskette drives when you turn on power.*

Most operating systems automatically perform a diagnostic hardware test to ensure that hardware components are working properly. If there is a hardware problem, you will be advised of it. If everything is okay, the computer will transmit a message and you will be given some form of prompt on the screen, which is a request for a user response.

A.8   Activating the DOS Operating System

Most modern microcomputers have an internal clock that automatically keeps track of the date and time. If yours has one, your system is probably configured to omit any request to you to enter the date and time. In this case you will receive a prompt that looks like:

> `C:>`   *(for hard disk systems)*

This means that the computer is ready for you to begin work. Whenever an A:> or C:> prompt appears, whatever you type in will be processed by the DOS operating system. Starting up the computer in this way is referred to as "booting" the system. If you arrive automatically at this prompt, you may bypass the following discussion, and skip to section A.9 now.

If your computer system does not have an internal clock, you will most likely be asked to supply the date and time with this prompt:

> `Current date is Tuesday 1-01-1980`
> `Enter new date:    [    ]`

The form of the date entry is *mm-dd-yy*, where *mm* is a two-digit month, *dd* is a two-digit day, and *yy* is a two-digit year. Thus you would enter 05-27-94 for May 27, 1994. If the system prompts you to enter a new time you may enter the time as *hh:mm.ss* where *hh* is hours, *mm* is minutes, and *ss* is seconds (optional). DOS assumes a 24-hour clock. 1:00 AM to noon is 01 to 12, and 1:00 PM becomes 13, 2 PM is 14, and so on. For example, you can enter 1:06 PM as 13:06. Remember to press the <*Enter*> key after entering the date and also after the time has been entered. The DOS message displayed following the date and time may vary, depending on your computer and the version of DOS you are using.

You can ignore the DOS request for date and time by pressing the <*Enter*> key when "Enter new date:" and "Enter new time:" are displayed. It is, however, useful to make these entries because the date and time will be recorded for each program you create or change. In this way, your directory of programs will include the date and time each was created or changed. This can also help distinguish between copies of programs that you have created earlier that are now obsolete.

A.9   Rebooting or Restarting the Computer

Restarting your computer after it has been turned on and booted up is called "rebooting." This is necessary only if software you are executing fails and "locks up" (freezes) the system, making it impossible for you to control the machine. To reboot, you press the <*Ctrl*>, <*Alt*> and <*Del*> keys together. Some computers have a reset switch or button that functions like <*Ctrl*> + <*Alt*> + <*Del*>.

You can always restart your computer by turning the machine off, waiting a few seconds, and then turning the computer back on again. For diskette systems, make certain that your operating system is in the A drive. For hard disk systems, make sure there is no diskette in the A drive (the hard disk already contains the operating system). Restarting a computer by turning it off and on again is called a **cold start** as opposed to pressing <*Ctrl*>, <*Alt*> and <*Del*>, which is called a **warm start**. Cold starts take longer because you must wait a few seconds before turning the machine on again, and more hardware tests need to be performed during booting.

A.10 Summary of DOS Commands

You enter DOS operating system commands at the C:> prompt to cause the microcomputer to take specific actions. Listed below is a summary of the most common DOS commands. In this listing, <*Enter*> means that you press the <*Enter*> or <*Return*> key, and *filename.ext* means the name of the file you want to manipulate. The file name may be up to eight characters, followed by a period, and this followed by an "extension" of the name of up to three characters. Source code files for the RM/COBOL-85 compiler should be named with up to eight characters, followed by a period, followed by the letters CBL. The compiler creates object files using the source code file name followed by the extension .COB.

C:> dir

Lists all of the files in the current directory, as well as their size in bytes and the date and time each was last changed. The file names will be roughly in the order in which you created the files. An exception occurs when you have erased any files, and later created new ones. You will see some of the newer file names occupying the same place in the listing of file names as was previously occupied by an erased file. To see the list of file names in the directory in sorted sequence, use the command:

```
C:> dir|sort <Enter>
```

You can use the asterisk symbol (*) as a "wild card" to form filters to access only certain files in a directory listing or copy command. The * takes the place of any other one or more characters. For example, the command

    C:> dir *.cbl <Enter>

will list the names of any files that end with the file name extension .CBL. The command

    C:> dir test1.* <Enter>

will list the names of any files that have TEST1 as the file name and any extension.

If the subdirectory in which you are working contains more than about 20 file names, you will want to use the directory command followed by /p such as:

    C:> dir/p <Enter>

The /p tells the system to pause after showing a full screen ("page") of the directory. You can see the next screen by pressing the <Enter> key.

C:> type *filename.ext*

Shows the contents of the file named *filename.ext*. Note that the system will direct this to the screen very quickly, and if the file has more than a few hundred bytes in it, the beginning will quickly scroll off the screen. To pause at each full screen of a file you are displaying on the screen, use the type command with a pipe to the MORE function:

    C:> type *filename.ext* | more <Enter>

C:> copy *filename1.ext filename2.ext*

Copies the first file named to a new file. If the file named at *filename2.ext* already exists, it is overwritten but you are given a warning message or chance to cancel the copy action.

C:> rename *filename1.ext   filename2.ext*

Change the name of the file named *filename1.ext* to the name *filename2.ext*. If *filename1.ext* does not exist, or *filename2.ext* already exists, an error message is produced.

C:> erase *filename.ext*

Eliminates *filename.ext* from the directory. The file remains on disk, but cannot be accessed. Some types of utility programs give you the ability to "unerase" a file erased by mistake, but only if you have caused no other disk activity since the erasure.

C:> cd *dirname*

Changes the "current" directory to the name specified. If you have executed the directive prompt pg either at the keyboard or by placing it into your AUTOEXEC.BAT file, you will see the directory in which you are active at the prompt. Directories are used to group and organize information instead of having all files housed in one large heap. The directory indicated by just the backslash (\) with no name is the "root directory." It should contain only a few important system files and the names of all of the other directories on the system. Technically, all directories but the root directory are known as subdirectories.

C:> md *subdir*

Creates a subdirectory named *subdir*. Subdirectory names can be up to eight characters long. The subdirectory is housed within the directory in which you are "current" when you take this action.

C:> rd *subdir*

Eliminates a subdirectory if it is empty (contains no files), otherwise an error message is issued. In order to eliminate a subdirectory you have to:

- Erase all of the files within the subdirectory

- Be within the directory in which it is housed and issue the rd command.

A.11 Using an AUTOEXEC.BAT File with RM/COBOL-85

AUTOEXEC.BAT is a special file name. If a file of this name is contained in the root directory, DOS reads it and executes any commands in it as a part of the system startup process. You can create and put commands into AUTOEXEC.BAT using any text editor capable of creating ASCII files. You can use the RM/CO* editor to do this.

One handy command that you should put into your AUTOEXEC.BAT file is:

```
prompt p$g$
```

This command tells DOS to display the name of the directory and subdirectory in which you are current, as a part of the normal system prompt. For example, if the prompt pg command has been invoked, and you are in the \RMCOB subdirectory, the prompt will look like this:

```
C:\RMCOB>
```

RM/COBOL-85 does not require any special system setup or features in order for you to use it. But your RM/COBOL-85 files are housed in the subdirectory named \RMCOB if you used the installation procedure described in Chapter 2 of this guide. You will therefore need to change to the \RMCOB subdirectory before using the system. You can do this by issuing the command cd \rmcob at the DOS C:> prompt. You can store this "change directory" command in your AUTOEXEC.BAT file if you wish to go directly to the \RMCOB subdirectory as a part of normal system startup:

```
cd \RMCOB  <Enter>
```

If you do not use an AUTOEXEC.BAT file, the system will prompt you for the entry of date and time. To eliminate these prompts create an AUTOEXEC.BAT file and put at least this command into it:

```
ECHO OFF
```

A.12 Deactivating the NUMLOCK Key

Some computer systems such as the IBM PS/2 start up as if the <*NumLock*> key had been pressed, to make the numeric keypad ready for the entry of numbers in a "data entry" mode. On such a machine, the "NumLock" light will be on when you start the computer system. Press <*NumLock*> once to shut off the NumLock light and make the numeric keypad arrow keys work as you expect them to.

Self-Test

Assess your comprehension of basic microcomputer knowledge by taking this self test. The correct answer to each question is provided on the next page.

1. "Micro" is an abbreviation for _____ .

2. Another term used to describe a "micro" is _____ .

3. The main hard disk drive of a micro is typically called the _____ drive.

4. Before turning on a microcomputer, you should have a _____ diskette in the main drive unless you have a hard disk.

5. (T or F) There are usually two sets of keys on a keyboard that can be used for entering numbers.

6. Before data is transmitted to a program, the _____ key must be depressed.

7. The most common operating system for an IBM microcomputer is called _____ .

8. DOS begins by asking for the _____ and the _____ unless you have an _____ _____ .

9. The danger posed by leaving a diskette in a microcomputer with a hard disk when you turn on (boot up) the system is that a _____ may enter the system from an infected diskette.

10. Disk storage is also called _____ storage or _____ storage.

11. RAM stands for _____ _____ _____ .

12. You write-protect a 3-1/2 inch floppy diskette by moving the write protect tab to the _____ edge.

13. ROM stands for _____ _____ _____ and is not alterable by a computer user.

14. When you start using your computer, you should turn on your _____ and _____ first, then your _____ .

15. Turning off the power to a computer, waiting a few seconds, and turning it on again is known as a _____ start.

16. (T or F) When you copy one file to another using the DOS COPY command, and the file you are copying to already exists, you do not get a warning message but the existing file is overwritten.

Solutions

1. microcomputer
2. personal computer
3. C
4. DOS
5. T (true); the top row of the main keyboard and the numeric keypad can both be used to enter numbers.
6. *<Enter>* or *<Return>*
7. DOS
8. date, time; internal clock
9. virus
10. auxiliary, secondary
11. random access memory
12. outer
13. read only memory
14. monitor, printer, computer
15. cold
16. T (true); COPY replaces an existing file with the one you indicated should be copied to it.

Appendix B

RM/COBOL-85 Enhancements to the ANS COBOL 1985 Standard

B.1 Delimiting Literal Characters

In RM/COBOL-85, as in 1985 COBOL in general, literals can be delimited by single or double quotation marks. You need not specify any compiler option to use " or ' to delimit character values, but you must be consistent within the same sentence. That is, if you begin a literal character values with " you must mark the end of it with ". You can mix usage of the delimiters within the same program.

B.2 LINAGE Clause of the FD

Since paper lengths and printers used to print output on a microcomputer vary widely, you might want to incorporate precise specifications into your program to indicate the lines on which printing is to occur. You can accomplish this with a LINAGE clause coded as part of the FD for a print file. Use of the LINAGE clause is illustrated in the program in Figure B.1.

LINAGE specifies the number of lines of program output to be written to a page of print. The total length of the paper to be printed on should be the sum of LINES AT TOP, LINAGE, and LINES AT BOTTOM. FOOTING identifies a line number within the linage area where a "hot zone" begins. When you write enough printlines to reach this hot zone, an END-OF-PAGE condition is triggered, which you can detect with an optional phrase of the WRITE verb, as shown in Figure B.1. The combination of LINAGE clause and WRITE verb END-OF-PAGE detection provides an ability to adequately handle page control when a printer does not support standard COBOL form feed carriage control.

You can code the LINAGE clause only with a LINE SEQUENTIAL file such as a print file. ORGANIZATION IS LINE SEQUENTIAL is assumed when a SELECT is coded ASSIGN TO PRINTER. You can code LINE SEQUENTIAL as documentation in a SELECT that carries the designation PRINTER.

B.3 Length of Nonnumeric Literals

With RM/COBOL-85 non-numeric literals in the PROCEDURE DIVISION can be up to 2,047 characters long. This is shorter than nonnumeric literals on IBM mainframes using VS COBOL II, which can handle nonnumeric literals of 4,096 bytes, but it is still quite adequate.

B.4 Internal Sorting (SORT) and Abandoning SECTIONs

RM/COBOL-85 supports use of the SORT verb without any need for a separate supplementary sorting utility. You need not house input and output procedures for an internal sort in SECTIONs; 1985 COBOL allows input and output procedures to be ordinary paragraphs. When using the SORT verb, you must request additional memory

```
000100 ID DIVISION.
000200 PROGRAM-ID.  COPYIT2.
000300 AUTHOR.  JIM JANOSSY, DEPAUL UNIVERSITY, CHICAGO.
000400
000500**********************************************************************
000600*   Adaptation of the original COPYIT program to demonstrate     *
000700*   the LINEAGE clause of the FD and the AT END-OF-PAGE          *
000800*   feature of of the WRITE verb.                                *
000900*   Uses RM/COBOL-85 Version 5.24.         J. Janossy  9/23/93   *
001000**********************************************************************
001100
001200 ENVIRONMENT DIVISION.
001300 INPUT-OUTPUT SECTION.
001400 FILE-CONTROL.
001500     SELECT INPUT-FILE          ASSIGN TO DISK 'WORKERS.DAT'
001600         ORGANIZATION IS LINE SEQUENTIAL.
001700     SELECT OUTPUT-FILE         ASSIGN TO PRINTER 'WORKERS.REP'.
001800
001900 DATA DIVISION.
002000 FILE SECTION.
002100 FD  INPUT-FILE
002200     RECORD CONTAINS 80 CHARACTERS.
002300 01  INPUT-RECORD                   PIC X(80).
002400
002500 FD  OUTPUT-FILE
002600     RECORD CONTAINS 80 CHARACTERS
002700     LINAGE IS 11 WITH FOOTING AT 6
002800         LINES AT TOP 2
002900         LINES AT BOTTOM 3.
003000 01  OUTPUT-RECORD                  PIC X(80).
003100/
003200 WORKING-STORAGE SECTION.
003300 01  WS-FLAG                        PIC X(1)  VALUE 'M'.
003400 01  WS-COUNT                       PIC 9(5)  VALUE 0.
003500 01  WS-COUNT-Z                     PIC ZZ,ZZ9.
003600 01  WS-HEADING  PIC X(50) VALUE '*** THIS IS PAGE HEADING ***'.
003700/
003800 PROCEDURE DIVISION.
003900 0000-MAINLINE.
004000     PERFORM 1000-BEGIN-JOB.
004100     PERFORM 2000-PROCESS-A-RECORD UNTIL WS-FLAG = 'E'.
004200     PERFORM 3000-END-JOB.
004300     STOP RUN.
004400
004500 1000-BEGIN-JOB.
004600     OPEN INPUT INPUT-FILE  OUTPUT  OUTPUT-FILE.
004700     WRITE OUTPUT-RECORD FROM WS-HEADING
004800         AFTER ADVANCING 0 LINES.
004900     PERFORM 2700-READ-A-RECORD.
005000
005100 2000-PROCESS-A-RECORD.
005200     MOVE INPUT-RECORD TO OUTPUT-RECORD.
005300     WRITE OUTPUT-RECORD AFTER ADVANCING 1 LINES
005400         AT END-OF-PAGE
005500             WRITE OUTPUT-RECORD FROM WS-HEADING
005600                 AFTER ADVANCING PAGE.
005700     ADD 1 TO WS-COUNT.
005800     PERFORM 2700-READ-A-RECORD.
005900
006000 2700-READ-A-RECORD.
006100     MOVE SPACES TO INPUT-RECORD.
006200     READ INPUT-FILE
006300         AT END MOVE 'E' TO WS-FLAG.
006400
006500 3000-END-JOB.
006600     MOVE WS-COUNT TO WS-COUNT-Z.
006700     MOVE SPACES TO OUTPUT-RECORD.
006800     STRING '*** END OF LISTING, RECORDS = ', WS-COUNT-Z
006900         DELIMITED BY SIZE  INTO OUTPUT-RECORD.
007000     WRITE OUTPUT-RECORD.
007100     CLOSE INPUT-FILE  OUTPUT-FILE.
```

The LINAGE clause describes the number of printlines to be used for printing

END-OF-PAGE detects when print has reached the FOOTER area

Figure B.1

LINAGE and WRITE ... AT END-OF-PAGE

The FD for a print file can include the LINAGE clause to describe the size and vertical margins of the printed page. The length of the page in printlines equals the sum of LINES AT TOP, LINAGE, and LINES AT BOTTOM.

for running the program unless you are sorting a trivial amount of data. Code a runtime option using the letter T, such as

```
c:> runcobol first1 t=20000
```

This entry requests 20,000 bytes for the sort. The area specified must be large enough to hold all records being sorted. Thus if 200 records are being sorted, each with a length of 100 characters, T=20000 is required.

B.5   Setting Flag Values (Switches)

In COBOL various fields can be used as switches. A switch is a data field that, depending on its content, will cause one of two or more courses of action to be selected. The most commonly used switch is the one that signals an end-of-job, as shown in Figure B.2. The value "Y" in ARE-THERE-MORE-RECORDS causes repeated execution of 2000-PROCESS-A-RECORD, while the value "N" terminates execution of this loop. This field is used as a switch, and to change its logical state you would previously have had to MOVE the value "N" to it. RM/COBOL-85 allows you to change the value of an 88-level condition name used as a switch in a more natural way. You can now use the SET verb to set the logical condition of the switch without having to worry about what specific data value makes the condition true.

B.6   Signed Numbers

Signed numbers may be entered on a keyboard with a leading sign. That is, suppose we have a field called AMT1 with PIC S99. In response to ACCEPT AMT1, you may enter -12. You may also enter such a value with the negative sign trailing, as 12-. Chapter 6 of this guide shows you many other facets of interactive programming using RM/COBOL-85, including the entry of signed numbers.

B.7   IF-THEN-ELSE

You can use a NEXT SENTENCE clause in conjunction with an END-IF, for example:

```
IF WS-VALUE > 13
   NEXT SENTENCE
 ELSE
   PERFORM 123-ADD-ROUTINE
END-IF.
```

B.8   Extensions to the COBOL 1985 Standard

RM/COBOL-85 is in full conformance with the ANS COBOL 85 specifications. In addition, it provides numerous enhancements that make it even more flexible. We specify only the most significant ones in the following list:

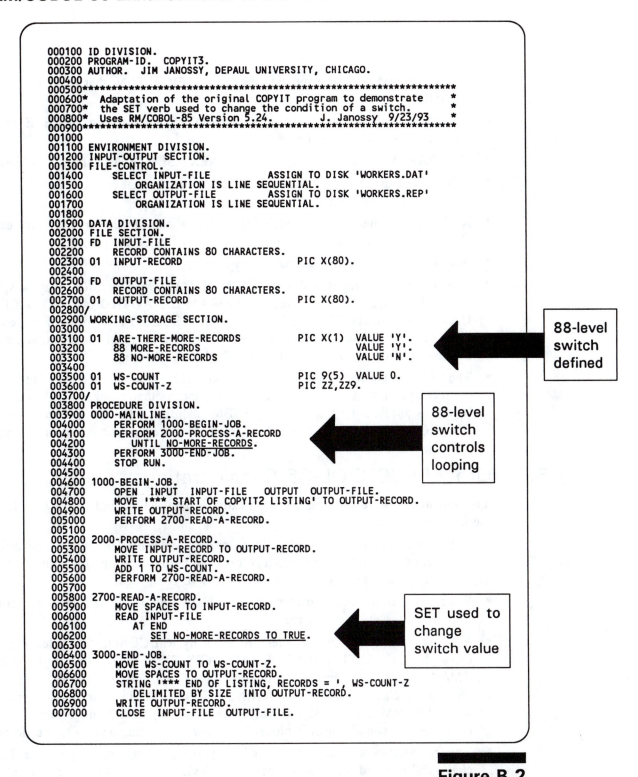

```
000100 ID DIVISION.
000200 PROGRAM-ID.  COPYIT3.
000300 AUTHOR.  JIM JANOSSY, DEPAUL UNIVERSITY, CHICAGO.
000400
000500****************************************************************
000600*  Adaptation of the original COPYIT program to demonstrate   *
000700*  the SET verb used to change the condition of a switch.      *
000800*  Uses RM/COBOL-85 Version 5.24.        J. Janossy 9/23/93    *
000900****************************************************************
001000
001100 ENVIRONMENT DIVISION.
001200 INPUT-OUTPUT SECTION.
001300 FILE-CONTROL.
001400     SELECT INPUT-FILE          ASSIGN TO DISK 'WORKERS.DAT'
001500         ORGANIZATION IS LINE SEQUENTIAL.
001600     SELECT OUTPUT-FILE         ASSIGN TO DISK 'WORKERS.REP'
001700         ORGANIZATION IS LINE SEQUENTIAL.
001800
001900 DATA DIVISION.
002000 FILE SECTION.
002100 FD  INPUT-FILE
002200     RECORD CONTAINS 80 CHARACTERS.
002300 01  INPUT-RECORD              PIC X(80).
002400
002500 FD  OUTPUT-FILE
002600     RECORD CONTAINS 80 CHARACTERS.
002700 01  OUTPUT-RECORD             PIC X(80).
002800/
002900 WORKING-STORAGE SECTION.
003000
003100 01  ARE-THERE-MORE-RECORDS    PIC X(1)  VALUE 'Y'.
003200     88 MORE-RECORDS                     VALUE 'Y'.
003300     88 NO-MORE-RECORDS                  VALUE 'N'.
003400
003500 01  WS-COUNT                  PIC 9(5)  VALUE 0.
003600 01  WS-COUNT-Z                PIC ZZ,ZZ9.
003700/
003800 PROCEDURE DIVISION.
003900 0000-MAINLINE.
004000     PERFORM 1000-BEGIN-JOB.
004100     PERFORM 2000-PROCESS-A-RECORD
004200        UNTIL NO-MORE-RECORDS.
004300     PERFORM 3000-END-JOB.
004400     STOP RUN.
004500
004600 1000-BEGIN-JOB.
004700     OPEN  INPUT  INPUT-FILE   OUTPUT  OUTPUT-FILE.
004800     MOVE '*** START OF COPYIT2 LISTING' TO OUTPUT-RECORD.
004900     WRITE OUTPUT-RECORD.
005000     PERFORM 2700-READ-A-RECORD.
005100
005200 2000-PROCESS-A-RECORD.
005300     MOVE INPUT-RECORD TO OUTPUT-RECORD.
005400     WRITE OUTPUT-RECORD.
005500     ADD 1 TO WS-COUNT.
005600     PERFORM 2700-READ-A-RECORD.
005700
005800 2700-READ-A-RECORD.
005900     MOVE SPACES TO INPUT-RECORD.
006000     READ INPUT-FILE
006100        AT END
006200           SET NO-MORE-RECORDS TO TRUE.
006300
006400 3000-END-JOB.
006500     MOVE WS-COUNT TO WS-COUNT-Z.
006600     MOVE SPACES TO OUTPUT-RECORD.
006700     STRING '*** END OF LISTING, RECORDS = ', WS-COUNT-Z
006800        DELIMITED BY SIZE  INTO OUTPUT-RECORD.
006900     WRITE OUTPUT-RECORD.
007000     CLOSE INPUT-FILE  OUTPUT-FILE.
```

88-level switch defined

88-level switch controls looping

SET used to change switch value

Figure B.2

Using SET with 88-Level Condition Names

The 1985 COBOL standards define new capabilities for the SET verb. You can now use SET to change the value of a switch based on an 88-level condition name, without having to directly manipulate the specific data values involved.

- ID may be used as an abbreviation for IDENTIFICATION, that is, you can code ID DIVISION.

- The DELETE FILE statement is available to make use of the DELETE verb with relative and indexed files clearer.

- The SEARCH statement can specify both NEXT SENTENCE and END-SEARCH.

- OCCURS clauses can be nested to any desired depth; that is, more than seven levels of subscripting are permitted.

- A COPY statement may be included within a copied file, that is, you can nest COPY statements. You can do this to a level of five deep.

- A user-defined word may end with a hyphen.

- The optional paragraphs within the IDENTIFICATION DIVISION may be specified in any sequence. These include PROGRAM-ID, AUTHOR, DATE-WRITTEN, DATE-COMPILED, INSTALLATION, and SECURITY. (Note that except for PROGRAM-ID these are now regarded as obsolete language elements, scheduled to be removed from the ANS COBOL standard in the future.)

- The ASCII collating sequence is used with this as well as many other microcomputer versions of COBOL. This means that numbers will come before letters in an ascending sort. On an IBM mainframe (which is encoded with the EBCDIC encoding scheme) the letters sort before the numbers in an ascending sort.

B.9 Other RM/COBOL-85 Considerations

You should be aware of several other factors in connection with RM/COBOL-85 and the DOS environment:

- If you move a field with PIC Xs to a field with PIC 9s it can can affect the alignment of the data in the output record. Note that moving alphanumeric fields to numeric fields can cause errors with all COBOL compilers.

- When using comments, consider leaving a blank line before and after each comment to make your code easier to read.

- You can simplify the FD for files processed by RM/COBOL-85 by leaving out the extra phrases LABEL RECORDS and DATA RECORDS. But if you are using RM/COBOL-85 to construct programs to be uploaded to an IBM mainframe, include the clause BLOCK CONTAINS 0 RECORDS in your FDs. This will be ignored by RM/COBOL-85 but will be necessary on an IBM mainframe in order to read files that contain records blocked together for reading and writing efficiency.

- You can specify a symbolic external-file-name for input or output in a SELECT clause and then redirect it to a specific I/O device with a DOS SET command (not to be confused with the COBOL SET statement). Consider the following:

```
SELECT REPORT-FILE ASSIGN TO 'W4'
   ORGANIZATION IS LINE SEQUENTIAL.
```

This will ordinarily create a disk file named W4 (with no file extension) with printlines in it. To redirect the output directly to the printer enter this at the DOS prompt before you run the program:

```
SET W4=LPT1
```

The format for the DOS SET command is:

```
SET external-file-name = [parameter]
```

In the SELECT statement above, W4 is the *external-file-name*. To redirect the output in that SELECT so that it puts the emerging printlines into a disk file named W4REP.DAT in the subdirectory \REPOUTS on the C drive, enter the following before running the program:

```
SET W4=C:\REPOUTS\W4REP.DAT
```

The DOS SET command places entries into a table maintained by DOS that is used to direct output. With the DOS SET command, you can avoid having to change a program and recompile it when you want to have it operate on different input or output files.

- You can use the DOS RENAME command to rename the RM/COBOL-85 compiler from the name RMCOBOL.EXE to a name that makes it easier to use it at the DOS prompt for compiling a program. Renaming the compiler to be COB.EXE, for example, will let you compile programs with the same command used on the VAX:

```
C:> cob first1
```

You can also rename the runtime system from RUNCOBOL.EXE to a name such as RUN.EXE, so that you can run a compiled program from the DOS prompt by entering:

```
C:> run first1
```

If you rename the compiler and runtime system in this way, include the following two SET statements in your AUTOEXEC.BAT file, so that RM/CO* will become aware of the new names for these programs. Note that the "@" symbols are necessary in the SET statements for RM/COBOL-85:

```
SET @RMCOBOL=COB.EXE
SET @RUNCOBOL=RUN.EXE
```

- You can code variable length records with RM/COBOL-85 as with other COBOL compilers on minicomputers and mainframes by coding multiple 01 levels in the FD for a file or by using the clause RECORD VARYING nnn to nnn CHARACTERS in the FD for a file and the OCCURS DEPENDING ON clause:

```
DATA DIVISION.
FILE SECTION.
FD  DATA-FILE
    BLOCK CONTAINS 0 RECORDS
    RECORD CONTAINS 20 TO 55 CHARACTERS.
01  DR-FORMAT-1          PIC X(14).
01  DR-FORMAT-2          PIC X(32).
01  DR-FORMAT-3          PIC X(55).
```

```
000100 ID DIVISION.
000200 PROGRAM-ID.    VARY1.
000300*AUTHOR.        JIM JANOSSY, janossy@cs.depaul.edu
000400*INSTALLATION.  DEPAUL UNIVERSITY, CHICAGO, ILLINOIS, USA
000500*=====================================================================
000600*    Demonstrates simple variable length records in RM/COBOL-85.
000700*=====================================================================
000800 ENVIRONMENT DIVISION.
000900 INPUT-OUTPUT SECTION.
001000 FILE-CONTROL.
001100     SELECT DATA-FILE    ASSIGN TO  DISK 'VAROUT.DAT'
001200        ORGANIZATION IS LINE SEQUENTIAL.
001300*
001400 DATA DIVISION.
001500 FILE SECTION.
001600*
001700 FD  DATA-FILE
001800     BLOCK CONTAINS 0 RECORDS
001900     RECORD CONTAINS 20 TO 55 CHARACTERS.
002000 01  DR-FORMAT-1            PIC X(14).
002100 01  DR-FORMAT-2            PIC X(32).
002200 01  DR-FORMAT-3            PIC X(55).
002300/
002400 WORKING-STORAGE SECTION.
002500 01  WS-LINE-OF-HYPHENS     PIC X(100)  VALUE ALL 'a'.
002600/
002700 PROCEDURE DIVISION.
002800 0000-MAINLINE.
002900     OPEN  OUTPUT  DATA-FILE.
003000     WRITE DR-FORMAT-1 FROM WS-LINE-OF-HYPHENS.
003100     WRITE DR-FORMAT-2 FROM WS-LINE-OF-HYPHENS.
003200     WRITE DR-FORMAT-3 FROM WS-LINE-OF-HYPHENS.
003300     WRITE DR-FORMAT-2 FROM WS-LINE-OF-HYPHENS.
003400     WRITE DR-FORMAT-1 FROM WS-LINE-OF-HYPHENS.
003500     CLOSE DATA-FILE.
003600     STOP RUN.
```

Figure B.3

Program VARY1: Creating Variable Length Records

or

```
       DATA DIVISION.
       FILE SECTION.
       FD  DATA-FILE
           RECORD VARYING 28 TO 118 CHARACTERS.
       01  DATA-REC.
           05 DR-ROOT.
              10 DR-CUST-ID           PIC X(10).
              10 DR-ORDER-COUNT       PIC 9(3).
           05 DR-ORDERS        OCCURS 1 TO 7 TIMES
                               DEPENDING ON DR-ORDER-COUNT.
              10 DR-ORDER-DATE        PIC 9(6).
              10 DR-ORDER-AMOUNT      PIC 9(7)V99.
```

RM/COBOL-85 supports both methods of defining a variable length record file. Program VARY1 in Figure B.3 demonstrates the use of the first method. You can experiment with it and use it to create a file named VAROUT.DAT. Use the DOS DEBUG utility, as described in Chapter 4, section 4.15 of this guide (pages 80-83), to examine the contents of this file. You can see how variable length record ASCII files are simply streams of characters delimited by the carriage return (hex '0D') and line feed (hex '0A') characters. On an IBM mainframe, variable length record files are stored in a more complex format, with system-generated and interpreted prefacing bytes indicating the length of each record and block (group of records) as described in Chapter 13 (page 227) of *Practical MVS JCL Examples* by James Janossy, published by John Wiley & Sons, Inc., in 1993, and in *Advanced MVS/ESA JCL Examples* by James Janossy (John Wiley & Sons, Inc., 1994).

Appendix C

Compiler and Runtime Options

C.1 Compiler Options Overview

Compiler options allow you to request special services from the RM/COBOL-85 compiler, such as a source code listing of a program or a sorted cross-reference of data names. If you are using RM/CO*, you set your option choices interactively using a menu. If you execute the RM/COBOL-85 compiler from the DOS prompt, you request options by placing one or more letter codes at the end of your compile command. For example, this compile command requests that a source code listing file be produced (L) and that the listing be followed by an allocation map (A) showing the attributes of each data item, and a cross-reference of data and paragraph names (X):

```
C:> rmcobol first1 L,A,X
```

You can specify different combinations of compiler options each time you compile a program. You can enter the option letter codes shown below in any sequence after the program name, using capital or lowercase letters. Separate a series of options with either a space or comma between each.

The compiler options you use to compile a program are printed for information purposes at the top of each page of the source code listing. If you enclose the options within parentheses you can also include a comment after them. The comment will appear at the top of every page of the source code listing as documentation:

```
C:> cob first1 (L,A,X)  this is a source code listing comment
```

The educational version of the RM/COBOL-85 compiler has access to a subset of the options available in the commercial version. You can access these 23 options with the educational version (the ones you'll find most useful are printed in **bold** type);

A **Produces an "allocation listing" useful for debugging**
B Makes the default data file type BINARY-SEQUENTIAL
C Suppresses listing of text copied in using COPY
D **Compiles lines marked with "D" in column 7**
E Prints only lines with syntax errors and error messages
F Flags usage of obsolete or extended language features
K Suppresses the RM/COBOL-85 "banner" text for a compile
L **Causes a source code listing to be written to disk with extension .LST**
M Suppresses automatic de-editing (conversion) on ACCEPT
N Suppresses creation of an object file
O Specifies the path name for placement of the object file
P Causes a source code listing to be sent to the printer
Q Eliminates debugging information from the object file
R Puts sequential line numbers on the source code listing
S Makes separate numeric sign the default, not a last-byte "zoned" sign for input data
T Causes the complete source code listing to be sent to the screen (ordinarily, only the lines with errors and the associated error messages are sent to the screen)
U Changes interpretation of COMP numeric field definitions

V Makes the default data file type LINE SEQUENTIAL

X Generates a cross-reference of data names, in alphabetical sequence

Y Makes data name display and trapping possible in debugging

Z Limits the object file to an earlier RM/COBOL-85 version

2 Compiles according to the version 2 RM/COBOL-85 compiler

7 Compiles according to 1974 COBOL standards

C.2 Compiler Options Documentation

The information that follows focuses on the options you might, as a student, find especially useful in your work with RM/COBOL-85.

A Allocation Listing (by default off)

Produces an "allocation listing" that documents the type, address, size, and descriptive debugging term used to refer to every SPECIAL-NAME field and memory field defined in the program. Figure C.1 illustrates the allocation map for the COPYIT program. To use this option, you have to also specify either the L or P option which causes a source code listing to be generated. The allocation map is produced at the end of the listing. While it was formerly needed for debugging, the Y option makes it less necessary. Figure C.2 lists the data type codes used in the allocation map, and their meanings.

B Binary-Sequential Files (by default on)

If you do not specify ORGANIZATION IS LINE SEQUENTIAL for a file, this option treats the file as if you had specified BINARY SEQUENTIAL. This is the default. BINARY-SEQUENTIAL files do not have line feed/carriage returns at the end of records. (See also option V.)

C COPY Text Suppression (by default off)

Text you copy in with the COPY compiler directive is ordinarily included in your source code listing. If you use option C, you tell the compiler not to include the copied-in text in the source code listing.

D Debugging Lines Activated (by default off)

Lines coded with "D" in column 7 are ordinarily treated as comments. If you use option D, you tell the compiler to treat them as ordinary, active lines of code. This option is the same as coding WITH DEBUGGING MODE in a program. To activate "D" lines with program coding instead of with option D, code this line in your CONFIGURATION SECTION:

```
ENVIRONMENT DIVISION.
CONFIGURATION SECTION.
SOURCE-COMPUTER.  IBM-PC WITH DEBUGGING MODE.
OBJECT-COMPUTER.  IBM-PC.
```

You can include DISPLAY statements and other actions on such lines and activate them whenever you wish by compiling with the D option or by using the WITH DEBUGGING MODE phrase. The option is a much easier way to do this.

```
RM/COBOL-85 (Version 5.24.00) for DOS 2.00+   10-09-93   16:17:03    Page 1
Source file: COPYIT                Options: L A X Y

LINE   DEBUG    PG/LN -A 1 B..+....2....+....3....+....4....+....5....+....6....+....7..IDENTFCN

  1             000100 ID DIVISION.
  2             000200 PROGRAM-ID. COPYIT.
  3             000300 AUTHOR.   JIM JANOSSY, DEPAUL UNIVERSITY, CHICAGO.
  4             000400
  5             000500**************************************************
  6             000600*   This program is originally appeared in Practical MVS JCL  *
  7             000700*   Examples by Jim Janossy (John Wiley & Sons, Inc. 1993) and *
  8             000800*   is reprinted here by permission of the publisher.          *
  9             000900*   This program reads a file of records named WORKERS.DAT     *
 10             001000*   and prints a simple report to demonstrate file handling    *
 11             001100*   using RM/COBOL-85 Version 5.24.     J. Janossy July 1993   *
 12             001200**************************************************
 13             001300
 14             001400 ENVIRONMENT DIVISION.
 15             001500 INPUT-OUTPUT SECTION.
 16             001600 FILE-CONTROL.
 17             001700     SELECT INPUT-FILE      ASSIGN TO DISK 'WORKERS.DAT'
 18             001800        ORGANIZATION IS LINE SEQUENTIAL.
 19             001900     SELECT OUTPUT-FILE     ASSIGN TO DISK 'WORKERS.REP'
 20             002000        ORGANIZATION IS LINE SEQUENTIAL.
 21             002100
 22             002200 DATA DIVISION.
 23             002300 FILE SECTION.
 24             002400 FD  INPUT-FILE
 25             002500     RECORD CONTAINS 60 CHARACTERS.
 26             002600 01  INPUT-RECORD             PIC X(60).
 27             002700
 28             002800 FD  OUTPUT-FILE
 29             002900     RECORD CONTAINS 60 CHARACTERS.
 30             003000 01  OUTPUT-RECORD            PIC X(60).
 31             003100*
 32             003200 WORKING-STORAGE SECTION.
 33             003300 01  WS-FLAG                  PIC X(1)  VALUE 'M'.
 34             003400 01  WS-COUNT                 PIC 9(5)  VALUE 0.
 35             003500 01  WS-COUNT-Z               PIC ZZ,ZZ9.
 36             003600*
```

Figure C.1

COPYIT Source Code Listing with L,A,X,Y Options

Compiling a program with the "L" option produces a source code listing file named with the extension .LST. The A and X options add an allocation map and sorted cross-reference to the end of the source code listing, making it handier to work with. You can see the effect of the A and X options at the end of this multipage listing.

```
37 003700 PROCEDURE DIVISION.
38 003600 0000-MAINLINE.
39 003900     PERFORM 1000-BEGIN-JOB.
40 004000     PERFORM 2000-PROCESS-A-RECORD UNTIL WS-FLAG = 'E'.
41 004100     PERFORM 3000-END-JOB.
42 004200     STOP RUN.
43 004300
44 004400 1000-BEGIN-JOB.
45 004500     OPEN INPUT INPUT-FILE OUTPUT OUTPUT-FILE.
46 004600     MOVE '*** START OF COPYIT LISTING' TO OUTPUT-RECORD.
47 004700     WRITE OUTPUT-RECORD.
48 004600     PERFORM 2700-READ-A-RECORD.
49 004900
50 005000 2000-PROCESS-A-RECORD.
51 005100     MOVE INPUT-RECORD TO OUTPUT-RECORD.
52 005200     WRITE OUTPUT-RECORD.
53 005300     ADD 1 TO WS-COUNT.
54 005400     PERFORM 2700-READ-A-RECORD.
55 005500
56 005600 2700-READ-A-RECORD.
57 005700     MOVE SPACES TO INPUT-RECORD.
58 005600     READ INPUT-FILE
59 005900         AT END MOVE 'E' TO WS-FLAG.
60 006000
61 006100 3000-END-JOB.
62 006200     MOVE WS-COUNT TO WS-COUNT-Z.
63 006300     MOVE SPACES TO OUTPUT-RECORD.
64 006400     STRING '*** END OF LISTING, RECORDS = ' WS-COUNT-Z
65 006500         DELIMITED BY SIZE INTO OUTPUT-RECORD.
66 006600     WRITE OUTPUT-RECORD.
67 006700     CLOSE INPUT-FILE OUTPUT-FILE.
```

```
RM/COBOL-85 (Version 5.24.00) for DOS 2.00+    10-09-93   16:17:03    Page 4
Source file: COPYIT                          Options: L A X Y

Allocation Map
File Section for program COPYIT
```

Address	Size	Debug Order	Type	Name
8		Fixed	File Seq/Seq	INPUT-FILE
	60	ANS	Alphanumeric	INPUT-RECORD
76		Fixed	File Seq/Seq	OUTPUT-FILE
	60	ANS	Alphanumeric	OUTPUT-RECORD

```
Working-Storage Section for program COPYIT
```

Address	Size	Debug Order	Type	Name
140	1	ANS	Alphanumeric	WS-FLAG
142	5	NSU	Numeric unsigned	WS-COUNT
148	6	NSE	Numeric edited	WS-COUNT-Z

Allocation Map

The compiler "A" option produces this allocation map, which shows the displacement in memory of each data field buffer (FD) and data field, and the size of each in bytes. The data type abbreviations are unique to RM/COBOL-85 and are listed for your convenience in Figure C.2.

```
RM/COBOL-85 (Version 5.24.00) for DOS 2.00+   10-09-93  16:17:03     Page 5
Source file: COPYIT                             Options: L A X Y

Cross Reference                      /Declaration/  *Destination*

INPUT-FILE               /0017/  0024   0045      0058   0067
INPUT-RECORD             /0026/  0051  *0057*
OUTPUT-FILE              /0019/  0028   0045      0067
OUTPUT-RECORD           *0030/ *0046* *0047*    *0051* *0052* *0063* *0065* *0066*
WS-COUNT                *0034/ *0053*  0062
WS-COUNT-Z               /0035/ *0062*  0064
WS-FLAG                  /0033/  0040  *0059*
0000-MAINLINE            /0038/
1000-BEGIN-JOB            0039  /0044/
2000-PROCESS-A-RECORD     0040  /0050/
2700-READ-A-RECORD        0048   0054   /0056/
3000-END-JOB              0041  /0061/
```

Sorted Cross-Reference

The compiler "X" option produces a sorted cross-reference of data names and paragraph names. The line numbers within slashes following each name indicate where the data name is a receiving field and is potentially modified. Line numbers without slashes or asterisks indicate where a data name is referenced but cannot be modified, and where a paragraph is PERFORMed.

```
RM/COBOL-85 (Version 5.24.00) for DOS 2.00+   10-09-93  16:17:03     Page 6
Source file: COPYIT                             Options: L A X Y

Program Summary Statistics

Read only size:                      614 (X"00000266") bytes
Read/write size:                     464 (X"000001D0") bytes
Overlayable segment size:              0 (X"00000000") bytes

Total generated object size:        1078 (X"00000436") bytes

Errors: 0, Warnings: 0, Lines: 67 for program COPYIT.

Object version level: 6

Options in effect:
   A - Allocation map listing
   X - Cross reference listing
   Y - Symbol table output to object file
```

Figure C.1 *(end)*

COPYIT Source Code Listing with L,A,X,Y Options

Code   Data Type

Code	Data Type
ABS	Alphabetic
ABSE	Alphabetic edited
ANS	Alphanumeric
ANSE	Alphanumeric edited
GRP	Group
HEX	Hexadecimal
IXN	Index-name
NBS	Binary signed
NBU	Binary unsigned index data item
NCS	Numeric unpacked signed
NCU	Numeric unpacked unsigned
NLC	Numeric display signed, leading combined
NLS	Numeric display signed, leading separate
NPP	Packed unsigned
NPS	Packed signed
NPU	Packed unsigned
NSE	Numeric edited
NSU	Numeric display unsigned
NTC	Numeric display signed, trailing combined
NTS	Numeric display signed, trailing separate

Figure C.2

RM/COBOL-85 Data Type Codes

RM/COBOL-85 uses these 20 codes in its allocation map (see page 165), produced by the "A" compiler option. Each code denotes a different memory field declaration type and usage. You will also see these codes in the prompt line of the interactive debugger.

E   Error Line Printing Only (by default off)

The source code listing produced by the L or P options usually includes the correct lines of a program as well as the lines with errors. If you use option E, the listing contains only source code lines that cause compiler messages to be generated, and their associated messages.

F   Flag Obsolete or Extended Coding (by default off)

American National Standard COBOL X3.23-1985 defines the specifications for several levels of COBOL implementation. You can code the F option with any of these keywords to have the compiler flag lines that contain various codings not in the standard: EXTENSION, OBSOLETE, INTERMEDIATE, HIGH, COM1, COM2, SEG1, and/or SEG2. You code the F option differently depending on whether you specify one or multiple keywords:

One keyword:

        F=OBSOLETE

Multiple keywords:

        F=(EXTENSION,OBSOLETE)

If you use the F=EXTENSION option you can see the enhancements that RM/COBOL-85 adds to the COBOL standard. We suggest that you compile programs with the F=OBSOLETE option as a means of learning modern coding practices. This will identify coding that you should avoid, because the verbs or syntax flagged as obsolete will eventually be eliminated from the language.

K   Suppress RM/COBOL-85 "Banner" (by default off)

If you compile with the K option you will see approximately 10 lines less on the screen when the compiler begins operation. This option tells the compiler not to display its version and serial number and the other lines that identify it. For a successfully compiled program, you will receive only the summary message about a successful compile.

L   Produce Source Code Listing (by default off)

If you specify the L option the compiler will produce a source code listing containing all compiler messages, housing it in a file with the same file name and the extension .LST. The listing file will be written into the same subdirectory in which the source code is located. If you want the listing file to be written into a different subdirectory or disk drive, you can specify the path by coding L=*path*, such as L=\COBLIST. (Regardless of whether or not you code a path for the listing file, it will always be named with the same file name as the source code and the extension .LST.)

O   Path for Object File (by default same as source code)

The RM/COBOL-85 compiler will ordinarily create its object file in the same subdirectory on the same disk drive as the source code file. You can specify a different location for it by specifying O=*path*, such as O=\RMOBJ. The object file will always have the same file name as the source code file, and the extension .COB.

P Send Source Code Listing to Printer (by default off)

Option P is similar to option L in that it causes the compiler to generate a source code listing. Whereas option L writes this listing to a file, option P sends the listing directly to the printer. If you work on a computer system directly attached to a printer, the P option will work. But if you work in a computer lab in which your printers are accessed via a network, you should use the L option rather than the P option to obtain a source code listing.

V Line-Sequential Files (by default off)

If you do not specify ORGANIZATION IS LINE SEQUENTIAL for a file, it is ordinarily assumed to be BINARY SEQUENTIAL. If you code option V the default is taken to be LINE SEQUENTIAL. Using this option makes it unnecessary to change your SELECT statements if and when you later upload your source code to a VAX or IBM mainframe computer system.

X Create a Data Name Cross-Reference (by default off)

By specifying option X you tell the compiler to print a sorted cross-reference of data names defined in the program being compiled, as illustrated in Figure C.1. The cross-reference indicates the line number where each data name and procedure (paragraph) is defined, and all of the lines in the program where each data name and procedure is referenced. It also shows lines at which each data name is potentially modified.

Y Put Symbol Table in Object File (by default off)

Use option Y if you plan on using the interactive debugger. It makes it possible for you to request the display of data name contents by data name rather than by the address of the data name. This is a considerable convenience and spares you the need to find and use data name addresses and storage abbreviations produced by the "A" allocation map option. *RM/CO* automatically sets this option on.*

C.3   Runtime Options Overview

Runtime options let you tell the RM/COBOL-85 runtime system to do special processing when you execute a program, or provide more memory to it. The commercial implementation of RM/COBOL-85 provides 12 runtime options. Only four of these are relevant to the educational version of RM/COBOL-85. You specify runtime options when you execute a program:

```
C:> runcobol first1 k
```

These runtime options are available for the educational version of RM/COBOL-85:

A Passes an argument of up to 100 bytes into a program
K Suppresses the RM/COBOL-85 "banner" text for the run
T Specifies the amount of memory available for internal sorting
L Specifies the subdirectory and "library" file containing subprograms that will be invoked in a run

C.4 Runtime Options Documentation

Runtime options are less numerous than compiler options, but you may find them useful. We provide documentation here covering each of the options available in the educational version of RM/COBOL-85.

A Pass an Argument to a Program

You can code a program with a LINKAGE SECTION so that it can receive a parameter from the runtime system when you execute it. The program is coded as shown in Figure C.3. You pass the argument by entering the RUNCOBOL or RUN command in this way:

```
C:> runcobol parmtest a='abc123'
```

The program receiving this value can use it to label reports or affect its operation. Option A serves the same purpose for RM/COBOL-85 that the PARM parameter of the EXEC statement does for IBM mainframe job control language. For additional examples of parameter use in COBOL programs, see Chapter 7 of *Practical MVS JCL Examples* by James Janossy (John Wiley & Sons, Inc., 1993).

K Suppress RM/COBOL-85 "Banner" Text

If you execute a program with the K option the first thing you will see is the debugging prompt. Without the K option (the default) you will first see displayed messages identifying the RM/COBOL-85 version number and copyright notice.

T Specify the Amount of Sort Work Space

This option requests that additional memory be allocated by DOS to house the data to be sorted by a program that uses the SORT verb. If a program sorts more than a small amount of data, you may have to code this option as T=nnnnn, for example, T=20000, where nnnnn specifies the number of bytes of memory to be used for sort work space. You can compute this number by multiplying the record length by the number of records to be sorted.

L Specify a Subprogram Library

While it is not a necessity, you can organize all of your subprograms into one source code file, separating each program from the others with the program delimiter statement END PROGRAM *programname* as shown in Figure C.4. This will allow you to compile all subprograms at once, and create one object file that RM/COBOL-85 regards as a "library." This is advantageous because it eliminates the need to have several separate object files scattered in your working subdirectory. When you execute a main program that will CALL subprograms in such a library, code the L option at runtime:

```
C:> runcobol first1 L=\otherlib\lotsa
```

```
000100 ID DIVISION.
000200 PROGRAM-ID. PARMTEST.
000300*----------------------------------------------------------
000400* COPYRIGHT 1993 JAMES G. JANOSSY
000500* THIS PROGRAM IS PART OF A TRAINING COURSE ENTITLED
000600* "SOFTWARE ENGINEERING IN COBOL" DISTRIBUTED BY
000700* CALIBER DATA TRAINING, INC., CHICAGO, ILLINOIS.
000800* IT IS REPRODUCED HERE BY PERMISSION OF THE AUTHOR
000900*----------------------------------------------------------
001000 DATA DIVISION.
001100 WORKING-STORAGE SECTION.
001200 01  WS-LENGTH-F                    PIC Z,ZZ9.
001300 LINKAGE SECTION.
001400 01  USER-PARM.
001500     05 UP-LENGTH                   PIC S9(4) BINARY.
001600     05 UP-DATA.
001700        10 UP-DATA-BYTE  OCCURS 1 TO 100 TIMES
001800                         DEPENDING ON UP-LENGTH
001900                         PIC X(1).
002000/
002100 PROCEDURE DIVISION USING USER-PARM.
002200 0000-MAINLINE.
002300     DISPLAY 'PARMTEST PROGRAM STARTING'.
002400     MOVE UP-LENGTH TO WS-LENGTH-F.
002500     IF UP-LENGTH = 0
002600        DISPLAY 'TUT TUT! YOU DID NOT ENTER ANY PARM DATA!'
002700      ELSE
002800        DISPLAY 'PARM LENGTH = ', WS-LENGTH-F, ' CHARACTERS'
002900        DISPLAY 'PARM = ', UP-DATA.
003000     STOP RUN.
```

> LINKAGE SECTION is coded to receive a value at runtime

Figure C.3

LINKAGE SECTION to Receive a Runtime Value

The "A" runtime option (different from the "A" compile option!) lets you pass up to 100 characters to the RM/COBOL-85 program being executed. To be able to receive the value passed to it, you need to code a LINKAGE SECTION as shown here. The UP-LENGTH field will carry 0 if no value was passed to the program, or a number representing the number of characters passed to the program. The "A" runtime option works exactly like the PARM option of mainframe IBM MVS/ESA job control language. VS COBOL II program coding, to receive a runtime parameter on IBM mainframes, is identical to that shown here.

In this case "otherlib" is a subdirectory and "lotsa" represents that name of an object file library named LOTSA.COB. If you execute subprograms from a library file, you need to use the L runtime option even if the library file such as LOTSA.COB is in the same subdirectory in which you are attempting the program execution:

```
C:> runcobol first1 L=lotsa
```

Without specification of the "L" runtime option, the runtime system doesn't know which object file to treat as a subprogram library.

The source code for subprograms E1 and E2 in Figure C.4 are housed in a file named ELIB.CBL. When ELIB.CBL is compiled using the command

```
C:> rmcobol elib
```

the object library ELIB.COB is created, housing the object code for both subprograms. Figure C.5 shows you an actual example of a program that CALLs subprograms in an object library. This program, named E1, CALLs the two subprograms E2 and E3 shown in Figure C.4. Once E1 has been compiled (producing an object file named E1.COB) it is executed with the command:

```
C:> runcobol e1 l=elib
```

```
000100***********************************************************
000200 ID DIVISION.
000300 PROGRAM-ID.  E2.
000400*REMARKS.  DEMONSTRATES USE OF "EXTERNAL" ATTRIBUTE
000500*-----------------------------------------------------------
000600* COPYRIGHT 1993 JAMES G. JANOSSY
000700* THIS PROGRAM IS PART OF A TRAINING COURSE ENTITLED
000800* "SOFTWARE ENGINEERING IN COBOL" DISTRIBUTED BY
000900* CALIBER DATA TRAINING, INC., CHICAGO, ILLINOIS
001000* IT IS REPRODUCED HERE BY PERMISSION OF THE AUTHOR
001100*-----------------------------------------------------------
001200 DATA DIVISION.
001300 WORKING-STORAGE SECTION.
001400 01  WS-COUNT        PIC 9(7)  EXTERNAL.
001500*
001600 PROCEDURE DIVISION.
001700 0000-MAINLINE.
001800     ADD 1 TO WS-COUNT.
001900     DISPLAY 'THIS IS DISPLAYED BY PROGRAM E2: COUNT= ', WS-COUNT.
002000     GOBACK.
002100 END PROGRAM E2.
002200********************
002300 ID DIVISION.
002400 PROGRAM-ID.  E3.
002500*REMARKS.  DEMONSTRATES USE OF "EXTERNAL" ATTRIBUTE
002600*-----------------------------------------------------------
002700* COPYRIGHT 1993 JAMES G. JANOSSY
002800* THIS PROGRAM IS PART OF A TRAINING COURSE ENTITLED
002900* "SOFTWARE ENGINEERING IN COBOL" DISTRIBUTED BY
003000* CALIBER DATA TRAINING, INC., CHICAGO, ILLINOIS
003100* IT IS REPRODUCED HERE BY PERMISSION OF THE AUTHOR
003200*-----------------------------------------------------------
003300 DATA DIVISION.
003400 WORKING-STORAGE SECTION.
003500 01  WS-COUNT        PIC 9(7)  EXTERNAL.
003600*
003700 PROCEDURE DIVISION.
003800 0000-MAINLINE.
003900     ADD 1 TO WS-COUNT.
004000     DISPLAY 'THIS IS DISPLAYED BY PROGRAM E3: COUNT= ', WS-COUNT.
004100     GOBACK.
004200 END PROGRAM E3.
004300********************           ****************************
```

END PROGRAM statement marks the end of one subprogram

Figure C.4

Creating a Subprogram Library (ELIB.COB)

You can physically combine the source code for more than one subprogram using END PROGRAM statements. These two subprograms, named E1 and E2, are both housed in a file named ELIB.CBL. When you compile this "library" of subprograms only one .COB object file is created, named in this case ELIB.COB, containing a separate object program for each subprogram. You use the "L" runtime option as shown in Figure C.5 to tell the runtime environment the name of the subprogram object library.

```
000100 ID DIVISION.
000200 PROGRAM-ID.  E1.
000300*REMARKS.  DEMONSTRATES CALL TO E2, E3 USING "EXTERNAL"
000400*-------------------------------------------------------
000500* COPYRIGHT 1993 JAMES G. JANOSSY
000600* THIS PROGRAM IS PART OF A TRAINING COURSE ENTITLED
000700* "SOFTWARE ENGINEERING IN COBOL" DISTRIBUTED BY
000800* CALIBER DATA TRAINING, INC., CHICAGO, ILLINOIS
000900* IT IS REPRODUCED HERE BY PERMISSION OF THE AUTHOR
001000*-------------------------------------------------------
001100 DATA DIVISION.
001200 WORKING-STORAGE SECTION.
001300 01  WS-COUNT               PIC 9(7)  EXTERNAL.
001400
001500 PROCEDURE DIVISION.
001600 0000-MAINLINE.
001700     MOVE 0 TO WS-COUNT.
001800     ADD 1 TO WS-COUNT.
001900     DISPLAY 'THIS IS DISPLAYED BY PROGRAM E1: COUNT= ', WS-COUNT.
002000
002100     CALL 'E2'.
002200
002300     CALL 'E3'.
002400
002500     DISPLAY 'THIS IS DISPLAYED BY PROGRAM E1: COUNT= ', WS-COUNT.
002600     STOP RUN.
```

Figure C.5

Program that CALLs Subprograms from a Library

The E1 main program CALLs subprograms E2 and E3, the object files of which are in a library named ELIB.COB. This program is no different because the subprograms are housed in a library, but you must execute it using the "L" runtime option coded with the name of the subprogram object library, such as

```
C:\RMCOB> runcobol e1 l=elib
```

If you do not use the "L" option when you run this program the runtime environment will not be able to locate the subprograms.

Appendix D

Using the Interactive Debugger

D.1 What Is an Interactive Debugger?

n interactive debugger is software that helps you understand what a program is actually doing as it executes. The term "interactive" means that a debugger lets you interact with your program and control its execution, rather than simply running it outright from beginning to end. An interactive debugger is not limited to working with interactive (that is, "on-line") programs. An interactive debugger lets you take these actions for all programs, both batch and interactive:

- Execute a program step by step, so that you can see the flow of control as control passes from one instruction to the next

- Set breakpoints, which are points at which you want it to stop executing so that you can view the contents of variables

- Set traps, so that the program will automatically stop and show you the contents of data names when they change

- Resume operation after stopping for a breakpoint or trap

When execution of the program is stopped at a breakpoint or trap, a debugger lets you:

- Display the contents of variables (data names)

- Change (modify) the contents of variables

- Clear (remove) breakpoints and/or data traps

The interactive debugger included with RM/COBOL-85 is particularly easy to learn and use. In this appendix we show you what its commands are, how to enter them, and how to interpret the results it produces.

D.2 Compiling with the "Y" Option

To make your use of the RM/COBOL-85 interactive debugger as convenient as possible, you should compile a program to be debugged with the Y compiler option. The Y option includes the "symbol table" developed by the compiler in the object file created from your program, which makes it possible for you to access data items within your program through the debugger by data name. (While you can debug a program that has been compiled without the Y option, you will be limited to accessing data names based on their addresses within the program. Access by address is considerably more error prone and tedious than access by data name.)

You can specify the Y option alone or in combination with other options when you compile a program, as the following commands illustrate. In this appendix we will use the debugger to execute and explore the operation of the the COPYIT.CBL program listed in Chapter 5 in Figure 5.1. COPYIT copies records from a data file named

WORKERS.DAT to a file named WORKERS.REP. To compile COPYIT.CBL with the Y option for debugging, you can enter any of the following commands:

```
c:> rmcobol copyit y          y option alone
```

or

```
c:> rmcobol copyit l,a,x,y    several options, including y
```

Appendix C describes the compiler options in detail. The L, A, and X options produce a source code listing file complete with allocation map and data name cross-reference. While it is not essential to have available such a printed listing when you debug a program, it can be helpful. *RM/CO* automatically sets the Y option on for all program compiles.*

D.3 Same Debugger for RM/CO* and DOS Compiling

The RM/COBOL-85 interactive debugger is built into the runtime system. The same runtime system is invoked by the RM/CO* environment as is used when you enter RUNCOBOL to execute a program. For this reason, the discussion and illustrations that follow apply to use of the debugger both with RM/CO* or direct program execution.

Figure D.1 illustrates a brief debugging session involving the COPYIT.CBL program. While this begins at the DOS prompt, and not within RM/CO*, you will see the same progression of messages at the bottom of the RM/CO* screen when you use it for debugging, as depicted in Figure D.2. RM/CO* uses the top part of the screen to display a portion of the actual source code of the program, and dynamically highlights that next line to be executed.

D.4 The Debugger Prompt

Using the interactive debugger is automatic with the educational version of the RM/COBOL-85 compiler, because your programs always begin execution in debugging mode. If you look at Figure D.1, you'll see that the top part of it shows you the typical "ST" message you get when you begin running a program. The prompt from the debugger carries one of five two-letters codes, indicating the status of debugging, and why program execution has been stopped. The prompt looks like this:

```
ST 38 COPYIT C?
```

The two-letters codes you'll see in this prompt line include:

ST   Programming stepping is active
B   Breakpoint has occurred
DT   Data trap (trap command) has occurred
ER   Runtime error has occurred
SR   Program has executed a STOP RUN instruction

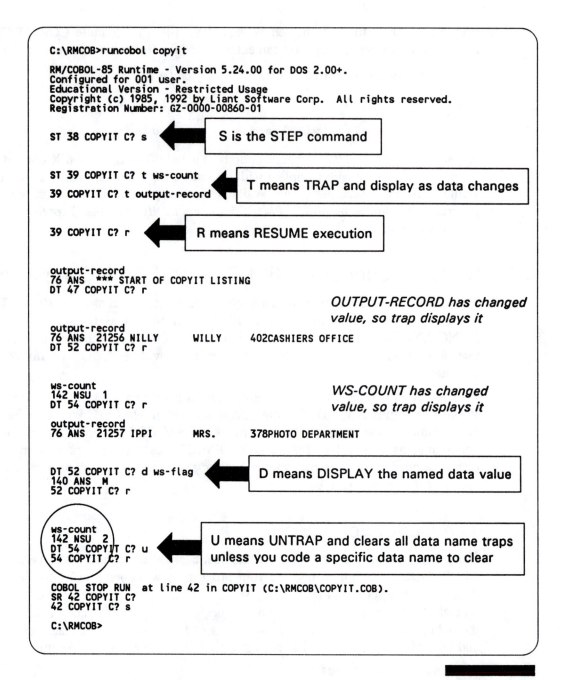

```
C:\RMCOB>runcobol copyit

RM/COBOL-85 Runtime - Version 5.24.00 for DOS 2.00+.
Configured for 001 user.
Educational Version - Restricted Usage
Copyright (c) 1985, 1992 by Liant Software Corp.  All rights reserved.
Registration Number: GZ-0000-00860-01

ST 38 COPYIT C? s                      S is the STEP command

ST 39 COPYIT C? t ws-count
                                       T means TRAP and display as data changes
39 COPYIT C? t output-record

39 COPYIT C? r                         R means RESUME execution

output-record
76 ANS  *** START OF COPYIT LISTING
DT 47 COPYIT C? r
                                                OUTPUT-RECORD has changed
                                                value, so trap displays it
output-record
76 ANS  21256 NILLY      WILLY       402CASHIERS OFFICE
DT 52 COPYIT C? r


ws-count                                        WS-COUNT has changed
142 NSU  1
DT 54 COPYIT C? r                               value, so trap displays it

output-record
76 ANS  21257 IPPI       MRS.        378PHOTO DEPARTMENT


DT 52 COPYIT C? d ws-flag              D means DISPLAY the named data value
140 ANS  M
52 COPYIT C? r


ws-count
142 NSU  2                            U means UNTRAP and clears all data name traps
DT 54 COPYIT C? u                     unless you code a specific data name to clear
54 COPYIT C? r

COBOL STOP RUN  at line 42 in COPYIT (C:\RMCOB\COPYIT.COB).
SR 42 COPYIT C?
42 COPYIT C? s

C:\RMCOB>
```

Figure D.1

RM/COBOL-85 Debugger Commands and Displays

The debugger identifies each data item with a number that indicates its "address" (memory displacement) in the program, such as 142, and its data type, such as "NSU." It then displays the contents of the data item. Neither the address or data type is especially informative, but the data item contents provide insight into what the logic of the program is doing.

```
┌─────────────────────────────────────────────────────────────────────────┐
│                                                                           │
│   JIM1: COPYIT.CBL        | LISTING |     |     |     |       | 01,01     │
│  ═════════════════════════════════════════════════════════════════════   │
│   0034 003400 01  WS-COUNT                    PIC 9(5)  VALUE 0.           │
│   0035 003500 01  WS-COUNT-Z                  PIC ZZ,ZZ9.                  │
│   0036 003600/                                                            │
│   0037 003700 PROCEDURE DIVISION.                                         │
│   0038 003800 0000-MAINLINE.                                              │
│   0039 003900     PERFORM 1000-BEGIN-JOB.                                 │
│   0040 004000     PERFORM 2000-PROCESS-A-RECORD UNTIL WS-FLAG = 'E'.      │
│   0041 004100     PERFORM 3000-END-JOB.                                   │
│   0042 004200     STOP RUN.                                               │
│   0043 004300                                                             │
│   0044 004400 1000-BEGIN-JOB.                                             │
│   0045 004500     OPEN  INPUT  INPUT-FILE   OUTPUT  OUTPUT-FILE.          │
│   0046 004600     MOVE '*** START OF COPYIT LISTING' TO OUTPUT-RECORD.    │
│  ┌────────────────────────────────────────────────────────────────────┐ │
│  │0047 004700     WRITE OUTPUT-RECORD.                                  │ │
│  └────────────────────────────────────────────────────────────────────┘ │
│   0048 004800     PERFORM 2700-READ-A-RECORD.                             │
│   0049 004900                                                             │
│   0050 005000 2000-PROCESS-A-RECORD.                                      │
│  ═════════════════════════════════════════════════════════════════════   │
│                                                                           │
│   39 COPYIT C? t output-record                                            │
│   39 COPYIT C? r                                                          │
│   output-record                                                           │
│   76 ANS  *** START OF COPYIT LISTING                                     │
│   DT 47 COPYIT C?                                                         │
│                                                                           │
│   At line 47 in Program COPYIT Keys: [F9]=Edit [F10]=Show Run             │
│                                                                           │
└─────────────────────────────────────────────────────────────────────────┘
```

Figure D.2

A Debugging Session within RM/CO*

The RM/COBOL-85 interactive debugger is built into the runtime system and you can access it either at the DOS prompt or through RM/CO*. In RM/CO*, you see the line of source code at which the debugger has stopped, and the debugger output at the bottom of the screen. The highlighted line is the next line to be executed.

The debugger prompt tells you what line number will be executed next, and the name of the program. (The name of the program may seem redundant, since you have already indicated which you want to run. But when you execute a program that CALLs a subprogram, the program name in the debugger prompt will change to show you in what subprogram control resides.) The C? is the debugger's way of asking you to enter a letter command. I have entered the "S" command to indicate "step" to the next instruction:"

```
ST 38 COPYIT C? s
```

The "S" step command is one of 12 commands that you can enter to control the debugger. We have demonstrated some of these commands in Figure D.1, and we'll discuss all of them here.

D.5   Overview of Debugging Commands

The commands to control the RM/COBOL-85 interactive debugger are straightforward and easy to use, since they usually consist of the single letter that starts a related word. Listed here are the debugger commands and their syntax.

A *nnn*

This is an "address stop" command. You might think about it as an "advance to" command. It advances program execution to the line number *nnn,* and pauses program execution. Execution stops just before line number *nnn.* For example, this debugging command stops execution at line 60, then resumes normal execution:

    a 60

The full format of the "A" command is:

    a *line,programname,count*

You need not enter the second field, *programname,* unless you are executing a main program and wish to specify a breakpoint in a subprogram that will be called. The third field is a *count.* The breakpoint will become effective immediately before the line number executes the count number of times. For example, this breakpoint will cause execution to stop just before line 102 executes for the fifth time in program ABCD1234, and the breakpoint is then automatically removed:

    a 102,abcd1234,5

To enter a *count* without entering *programname,* code the comma that follows the programname field. This debugging command stops the main program just before the fifth execution of line 102; the "R" command then resumes execution:

    a 102,,5

B *nnn*

The "breakpoint" command sets a breakpoint at a line *nnn* or (if no *nnn*) displays a list of all currently active breakpoints. Breakpoints are places at which you want program execution to pause. For example, this debugging command stops execution at line 60:

    b 60

The full format of this command is:

    b *line,programname,count*

You need not enter the second field, *programname,* unless you are executing a main program and wish to specify a breakpoint in a subprogram that will be called. The third value is a *count.* The breakpoint will become effective immediately before the line number executes the *count* number of times. For example, this breakpoint will cause execution to stop just before line 102 executes for the fifth time in program ABCD1234:

    b 102,abcd1234,5

To enter a *count* without entering *programname*, code the comma that follows the programname field. This debugging command stops the main program just before the fifth execution of line 102; enter the "R" command to resume execution:

```
b 102,,5
```

C *nnn*

Clears the breakpoint at line *nnn* or, if you don't enter any value for *nnn*, clears (removes) all breakpoints.

D *data-name*

Displays the value of a specified data name. For example, this command displays the contents of WS-COUNT:

```
d ws-count
```

E Ends debugging and resumes nondebugging program operation

L *nn*

Specifies the single screen line number *nn* (1 through 25) on which all debugging prompt lines will appear, useful if you are debugging an interactive program outside of the RM/CO* environment. Use the command L 1 to place the debugging prompt at the top of the screen.

M *name, vvv*

Modifies the content of a *data-name*, replacing the current value with *vvv*. For example, this command replaces the current value of WS-COUNT with 17:

```
m ws-count, 17
```

Q Quits the debugger and terminates program execution.

R *nnn*

Resumes program operation at line nnn; if you do not enter a line number, execution resumes at the line number in the debugger prompt. Execution will again pause at the next breakpoint encountered.

S Executes the next program instruction. If you enter SP instead of S, the program executes the next paragraph. Entering SS executes the next section of the program.

T *data-name*

Sets a data trap, so that program execution will pause when the value of the specified data name changes. If you do not enter a data name, the "T" commmand lists all currently active data traps.

U *data-name*

Untraps (clears) a data trap for data name; if you do not enter *data-name*, the "U" command clears all data traps.

D.6   A Sample Debugging Session

Throughout your prior work with RM/COBOL-85, you have been entering "E" in response to the debugger's prompt when you run a program. This command ends debugging mode and simply executes the program to completion. But at the top of Figure D.1 you see the entry of two data trap commands:

```
ST 39 COPYIT C? t ws-count
ST 39 COPYIT C? t output-record
```

These commands tell the debugger to stop when the value of WS-COUNT or OUTPUT-RECORD changes. Notice that the line number 39 remains the same in the debugger prompt as these commands entries are made. The third debugger instruction in Figure D.1 is "resume":

```
ST 39 COPYIT C? r
```

Immediately following this "resume" instruction you see the result of one of the data trap commands. Instructions in the program have been executed until this occurrence. The value of OUTPUT RECORD has changed as a result of the MOVE instruction at line 46 in the program. The program has stopped execution before executing line 47:

```
output-record
76 ANS  *** START of COPYIT LISTING
DT 47 COPYIT C? r
```

The "76 ANS" in this debugger prompt line is information about the data item being displayed, OUTPUT-RECORD. The "76" is the memory displacement of the field in the program. "ANS" is the data type of field, according to the codes of the allocation map, which you can produce with the "A" option when you compile the program. Figure C.2 in Appendix C lists all of the data type codes and shows an allocation map. Neither of these pieces of information is critical to the debugging process. The values "*** START of COPYIT LISTING" represent the contents of OUTPUT-RECORD. You can see that the "resume" command has been entered again at the C? prompt to have the program continue operation, and it next stops at line 52 where the value of OUTPUT-RECORD has again changed:

```
output-record
76 ANS  21256 NILLY        WILLY        402CASHIERS OFFICE
DT 52 COPYIT C? r
```

After another resume command, the program stops at a different data trap, when WS-COUNT changes:

```
ws-count
142 NSU  1
DT 54 COPYIT C? r
```

Follow Figure D.1 through to its conclusion and you will see how a few other debugging commands have been used in this example.

Appendix E

RM/COBOL-85 Compiler and Runtime Messages

E.1   Compiler Messages

Unless your program source code is completely free of syntax errors, you will see one or more informational, warning, and/or error messages appear on the screen when you compile a program. These error messages will also appear within your program source code listing file if you have compiled with the "L" listing option. Figure E.1 illustrates typical RM/COBOL-85 compiler messages.

- **RM/COBOL-85 compiler messages followed by "I" are <u>informational</u> only.** The compiler uses informational messages to tell you about assumptions it has made in interpreting your code, or about a nonstandard coding practice it has found and accommodated in the program source code. The occurrence has not caused an error in processing.

- **Compiler messages followed by "W" are <u>warning</u> messages.** These indicate potential problems, but the compiler has continued to process your source code into executable form by making an assumption about what your code means. You should examine the source of any warning messages since inaccurate results, such as truncation of numbers, may result from them. Other messages, pointing out a more serious problem, may also be associated with the program statement coding that caused the "W" message.

- **Compiler messages followed by "E" are <u>severe</u> (fatal) error messages.** These indicate serious problems with your syntax. The compilation of a program with one or more "E" level messages produces a flawed object file that will not execute properly. You must examine the origin of any severe error messages since these have prevented your program from compiling successfully.

You can often figure out the nature of each problem identified by a message using the message text imbedded in the source code listing and the "$" markers inserted by the compiler. The "$" markers are placed under the offending word or character. In Figure E.1, for example, you see a $ under the period within the name WS-FIRST.NUMBER. The period is a mistake, because periods are not allowed in COBOL data names. This single coding error causes a warning message and an error message, followed by an informational message.

Compiler messages start with five asterisks and are designed to be self-explanatory. All compiler messages carry four digit numbers. The suffix letter, I, W, or E after the message number indicates the severity of the message. RM/COBOL-85 intermingles information, warning, and error message numbers. *RM/COBOL-85 refers to data names as "identifiers."* "Scan resumed" is not an error, but simply indicates the point, after detecting an error, at which the compiler has again started to analyze your program source code.

```
C:\RMCOB> rmcobol color1

RM/COBOL-85 Compiler - Version 5.24.00 for    2.00+.
Configured for 001 user.
Educational Version - Restricted Usage
Copyright (c) 1985, 1992 by Liant Software Corp.  All rights reserved.
Registration number: GY-0000-00860-01
    13              001300 01  WS-FIRST.NUMBER            PIC 9(3)  VALUE 0.
                                       $                      $
*****  1) 0052: W Space separator expected.
*****  1) 0137: E Data description entry has wrong format. (scan suppressed).
*****  2) 0005: I Scan resumed.

    27   000041  002700      ACCEPT WS-FIRST-NUMBER
                                    $
*****  1) 0263: E Identifier is not defined. (scan suppressed).
*****Previous diagnostic message occurred at line 13.

    30           003000      CONTROL "FCOLOR=RED".
                                               $
*****  1) 0005: I Scan resumed.
*****Previous diagnostic message occurred at line 27.

    39   000075  003900      COMPUTE WS-TOTAL = WS-FIRST-NUMBER + WS-SECOND-NUM
                                                       $
*****  1) 0263: E Identifier is not defined. (scan suppressed).
*****  2) 0005: I Scan resumed.
*****Previous diagnostic message occurred at line 30.


Total generated object size:      594 (X"00000252") bytes

Errors: 3, Warnings: 1, Lines: 45 for program COLOR1.

Previous diagnostic message occurred at line 39.

Compilation complete -- Programs: 1, Errors: 3, Warnings: 1.
```

Figure E.1

Typical RM/COBOL-85 Compiler Messages

Compiler messages are marked W for warnings, E for errors, and I for informational. In this program only one error exists, a period between FIRST and NUMBER at line 13 rather than a hyphen. This single error generates several messages, but the location of the error is clearly marked with the "$" directly under it. RM/COBOL-85 is very much like IBM's VS COBOL II in regard to its error flagging.

```
C:\RMCOB> runcobol copyit x

RM/COBOL-85 Runtime - Version 5.24.00 for DOS 2.00+.
Configured for 001 user.
Educational Version - Restricted Usage
Copyright (c) 1985, 1992 by Liant Software Corp.  All rights reserved.
Registration Number: GZ-0000-00860-01


X option not valid.

C:\RMCOB>
```

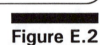

Figure E.2

Runtime Initialization Error Messages

If the RM/COBOL-85 runtime environment detects an error, such as entry of an incorrect runtime option, you'll receive a message like this. Other types of errors detected at runtime produce an error code in the form of a number, the meaning of which you can look up in this appendix.

E.2   Runtime Messages

If your program has compiled successfully, you subsequently execute it using the RUNCOBOL command. Here is how you would execute the demonstration program named FIRST1:

        c:> RUNCOBOL first1

When you do this, the runtime environment assumes control and executes your processed program. During its initialization (preparation to run) the runtime environment may issue several messages, some of which are error diagnostics and some of which are informational.

E.3   Runtime Initialization Error Messages

You can activate various options at runtime using codes as described in Appendix C. If the runtime system detects an unknown option letter in your execution command, a known option letter in error or an option not terminated with a space or comma, you'll get an error message as illustrated in Figure E.2. You must correct your runtime option specification(s).

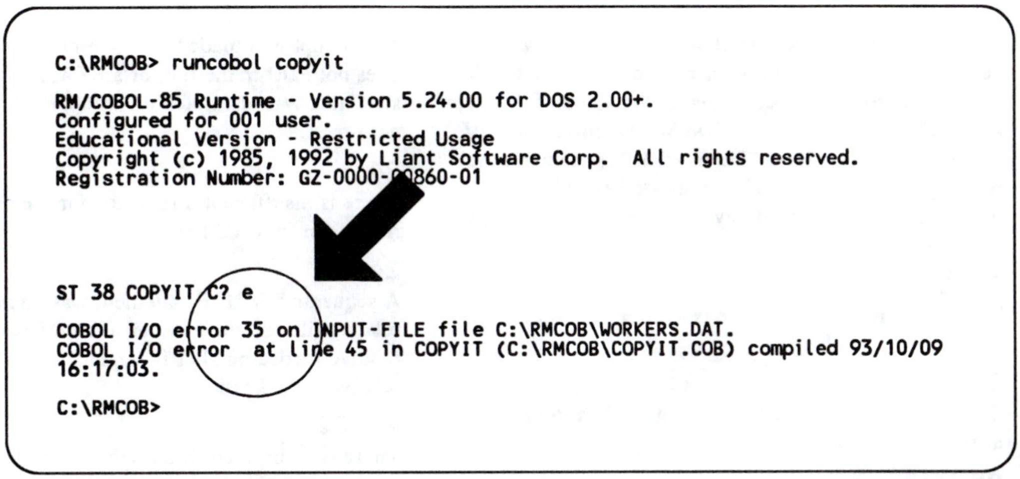

```
C:\RMCOB> runcobol copyit

RM/COBOL-85 Runtime - Version 5.24.00 for DOS 2.00+.
Configured for 001 user.
Educational Version - Restricted Usage
Copyright (c) 1985, 1992 by Liant Software Corp.  All rights reserved.
Registration Number: GZ-0000-00860-01




ST 38 COPYIT/C? e

COBOL I/O error 35 on INPUT-FILE file C:\RMCOB\WORKERS.DAT.
COBOL I/O error  at line 45 in COPYIT (C:\RMCOB\COPYIT.COB) compiled 93/10/09
16:17:03.

C:\RMCOB>
```

Figure E.3

Runtime Error Codes < 100: Input/Output Errors

Input/output errors generate runtime error codes up to value 100. A missing or misnamed data file is one of the most common runtime errors. File input/output errors are reported with File Status values conforming to the ANSI standard. Look up such an error indication in this appendix, which contains all runtime error code values in ascending sequence.

E.4   Abnormal Program Ending Messages

A program that compiles and loads successfully can fail for a variety of reasons, including data reference errors, procedure errors, and file errors. RM/COBOL-85 uses numbers of different formats to document each of these types of errors.

When you encounter an error in running a program you are most interested in finding the error message number and seeing what it means. To make it as easy as possible for you to look up an error number, we have listed the all of the runtime error message numbers in ascending sequence here, regardless of their format as two- or three-digit numbers. For a runtime error, just look up the number here and see what the code means.

In general, the two-digit error codes listed first deal with file input/output problems, and the numbers 100 and above deal with procedure or data reference errors. The first two digits of the codes 00 through 99 are File Status values. For these codes, the second pair of digits provides more specific information on the nature of the error, but is not available in the educational version of RM/COBOL-85. Figure E.3 illustrates the most common input/output error, a missing data file.

02

The operation was successful but a duplicate key was detected. For a READ statement, the key value for the current key of reference is equal to the value of that same key in the next logical record within the current key of reference. For a REWRITE or WRITE statement, the record just written created a duplicate key value for at least one alternate record key for which duplicates are allowed.

04, 05

The record read from the file is shorter than the minimum record length.

04, 06

The record read from the file is longer than the record area.

05

The operation was successful but the file was not present at the time the statement began. For a DELETE FILE statement, the file was not found. For an OPEN statement, the optional file was not found; if the open mode is I-O or EXTEND, the file has been created.

07

The operation was successful. If the operation was a CLOSE statement with a NO REWIND, REEL, UNIT or FOR REMOVAL clause, or if the operation was an OPEN statement with the NO REWIND clause, the file is not on a unit/reel medium.

10

A sequential READ statement was attempted and no text (or previous) logical record exists in the file because the end (or beginning) of the file was reached, or a sequential READ statement was attempted for the first time on an optional input file that is not present.

14

A sequential READ statement was attempted for a relative file and the number of significant digits in the record number is larger than the size of the relative key data item.

21

A sequence error that exists for a sequentially accessed index file. For a REWRITE statement, the prime record key was changed by the program between the execution of the preceding READ statement for the file and the execution of the REWRITE statement, or for a WRITE statement the ascending sequence requirement for successive record key values was violated.

22

The new record value attempts to duplicate an indexed file key that prohibits duplicates, or a relative record number that already exists.

23

An attempt was made to randomly access a record that does not exist in the file, or a START or random READ statement was attempted on an optional input file that is not present.

24

There is insufficient disk space for the operation on a relative or indexed file.

24, 01

A sequential WRITE statement was attempted for a relative file and the number of significant digits in the relative record number is larger than the size of the relative key data item.

24, 02

There is insufficient room left in the file for the operation.

30, nn

I/O error nn occurred, where nn may depend on the device or machine on which the file resides. In general, this is the decimal error number from a DOS function call.

30, 1

This error will occur when running under Microsoft Windows without first installing SHARE.EXE. For correct operation, SHARE.EXE must be loaded before starting Microsoft Windows.

30, 5

This error may occur on a CALL statement to a file with extension .EXE or .DLL which is not marked read-only if two users are loading the same program concurrently. Avoid this by making the .EXE or .DLL file read-only.

34

There is insufficient disk space for the operation on a sequential file.

34, 02

There is insufficient room left in the file for the operation.

35

The file could not be found. The pathname or filename may be misspelled or may not be valid.

37, 01

The file must be mass storage. The device-name specified for the file was DISC, DISK, or RANDOM, but the resultant file access name identifies a file that does not reside on a disk.

37, 07

The requested operation conflicts with the permissions allowed to the run unit for the file. This error can occur under any of the following conditions: a DELETE FILE statement failed because the run unit did not have write permission for the directory containing the file; an OPEN statement with the OUTPUT or EXTEND phrase failed because the run unit does not have run permission for the file; an OPEN statement with the INPUT phrase failed because the run unit does not have read permission for the file; or, an OPEN statement with the I-O phrase failed because the run unit does not have read and write permissions for the file

38

An OPEN or DELETE FILE operation failed because the filename was previously closed WITH LOCK.

39, 01

The file organization specified for the filename does not match the actual file organization of the physical file.

39, 02

The minimum record length specified in the RECORD CONTAINS clause or implied by the record descriptions of the filename does not match the actual minimum record length of the physical file.

39, 03

The maximum record length specified in the RECORD CONTAINS clause or implied by the record descriptions of the filename does not match the actual maximum record length of the physical file.

39, 04

The minimum block length specified in the BLOCK CONTAINS clause for the filename does not match the actual minimum block size of the physical file.

39, 05

The maximum block length specified in the BLOCK CONTAINS clause for the filename does not match the actual maximum block size of the physical file.

39, 06

The record delimiting technique, LINE-SEQUENTIAL or BINARY-SEQUENTIAL, specified for the filename does not match the actual record delimiting technique of the physical file.

39, 07

The CODE-SET specified for the filename does not match the actual character code of the physical file.

39, 08

The COLLATING SEQUENCE specified for the indexed file does not match the actual collating sequence of the physical file.

39, 09

The record type attribute, fixed or variable, specified in the RECORD CONTAINS clause or implied by the record descriptions of the filename does not match the record type attribute of the physical file.

39, 0A

The character specified in the PADDING CHARACTER clause for the filename does not match the actual padding character of the file on the external medium.

39, 5F

The number of keys specified does not match the actual number of keys in the physical file.

41, 01

A duplicate open was rejected by a system which does not allow the physical file to be opened twice.

41, 02

A duplicate open was rejected by a system that does not allow the COBOL filename to be opened twice.

41, 03

A DELETE FILE was rejected because the file was open.

42

A CLOSE or UNLOCK operation was attempted on an unopened file.

43

A DELETE or REWRITE operation was attempted on a file declared to be ACCESS MODE SEQUENTIAL, and the last operation on the file was not a successful READ operation.

44, 03

The length of the record area specified in the WRITE, REWRITE, or RELEASE statement is less than the minimum record length of the file.

44, 04

The length of the record area specified in the WRITE, REWRITE, or RELEASE statement is greater than the maximum record length of the file.

44, 07

A REWRITE statement attempted to change the length of a record in a sequential organization file.

46

No file position is currently defined. A sequential READ operation was attempted, but the last READ or START operation was unsuccessful or returned an at end condition.

47

The requested operation conflicts with the open mode of the file. A START or READ operation was attempted on a file that is not open in the INPUT or I-O mode. A READ or START operation was attempted on an unopened file.

48

This requested operation conflicts with the open mode of the file. This error can occur under the following conditions: a WRITE operation was attempted on a file that is not open in the EXTEND, I-O, or OUTPUT mode; or, a WRITE operation was attempted on a file in the sequential access mode that is open in the I-O mode. A WRITE operation was attempted on an unopened file.

49

The requested operation conflicts with the open mode of the file. A DELETE or REWRITE operation was attempted on a file that is not open in the I-O mode. A DELETE or REWRITE operation was attempted on an unopened file.

90, 01

The requested operation conflicts with the open mode of the file. This error can occur under the following conditions: a READ or START operation was attempted on a file that is not open in the INPUT or I-O mode; a WRITE operation was attempted on a file that is not open in the EXTEND, I-O, or OUTPUT mode or a WRITE operation was attempted on a file in the sequential access mode that is open in the I-O mode; or, a DELETE or REWRITE operation was attempted on a file that is not open in the I-O mode.

90, 02

A DELETE or REWRITE operation was attempted on a file declared to be ACCESS MODE SEQUENTIAL, and the last operation on the file was not a successful READ operation.

90, 03

The requested operation conflicts with the media type. This error can occur under the following conditions: a READ or OPEN INPUT operation was attempted on a file with device-name of OUTPUT, PRINT, or PRINTER; a WRITE, OPEN OUTPUT or EXTEND operation was attempted on a file with a device-name of CARDREADER or INPUT; or a DELETE, REWRITE, START or OPEN I-O operation was attempted on a file with a device-name other than DISC, DISK or RANDOM.

90, 04

The requested operation conflicts with the defined organization. A DELETE or START operation was attempted on an ORGANIZATION SEQUENTIAL file.

90, 05

A file truncate operation conflicts with other users. An OPEN OUTPUT operation was attempted on a physical file that is currently in an open mode.

90, 06

The file access name specified in the OPEN statement indicates that the file is accessed through an alternative access method and the alternative method refused to accept the request by the runtime file system to establish a session.

90, 07

The requested operation conflicts with the permissions allowed to the run unit for the file. This error can occur under the following conditions: a DELETE FILE statement failed because the run unit did not have write permission for the directory containing the file; an OPEN statement with the OUTPUT or EXTEND phrase failed because the run unit does not have write permission for the file; or, an OPEN statement with the INPUT or I-O phrase failed because the run unit does not have read permission for the file.

90, 08

The requested operation is not supported by the alternative access method. A COBOL I/O statement was attempted to a non-RM/COBOL-85 file and the access method for the file does not support the statement.

91

A CLOSE or UNLOCK operation was attempted on an unopened file.

91, 02

A READ, START, WRITE, DELETE, or REWRITE operation was attempted on an unopened file.

92, 01

A duplicate open was rejected by a system that does not allow the physical file to be opened twice.

92, 02

A duplicate open was rejected by a system that does not allow the COBOL filename to be opened twice.

92, 03

A DELETE FILE was rejected because the file was in an open mode.

93, 02

An open was rejected because the file lock conflicts with another user. An OPEN WITH LOCK was attempted on a file that was already open, or an OPEN without lock was attempted and the file is already open WITH LOCK.

93, 03

An OPEN or DELETE FILE operation failed because the filename was previously closed WITH LOCK.

93, 04

The file could not be opened because another file in the same SAME AREA clause is currently open.

93, 05

The file could not be opened because another file in the same MULTIPLE FILE TAPE clause is already open.

93, 06

The file could not be created because a file with the same name already exists.

93, 07

The file could not be opened because a lock table for the requested open mode was full.

94, 01

The file organization specified for the filename does not match the actual file organization of the physical file.

94, 02

The minimum record length specified in the RECORD CONTAINS clause or implied by the record descriptions of the filename does not match the actual minimum record length of the physical file.

94, 03

The maximum record length specified in the RECORD CONTAINS clause or implied by the record descriptions of the filename does not match the actual maximum record length of the physical file.

94, 04

The minimum block length in the BLOCK CONTAINS clause for the filename does not match the actual minimum block size of the physical file.

94, 05

The maximum block length specified in the BLOCK CONTAINS clause for the filename does not match the actual maximum block size of the physical file.

94, 06

The record delimiting technique, LINE-SEQUENTIAL or BINARY-SEQUENTIAL, specified for the filename does not match the actual record delimiting technique of the physical file.

94, 07

The CODE-SET specified for the filename does not match the actual character code of the physical file.

94, 08

The COLLATING SEQUENCE specified for the indexed file does not match the actual collating sequence of the physical file.

94, 09

The record type attribute, fixed or variable, specified in the RECORD CONTAINS clause or implied by the record description of the filename does not match the record type attribute of the physical file.

94, 20

The file is not available because the file identified by the resultant file access name could not be found. The pathname or filename may be misspelled or may not be valid for the operating system. Specifying a pathname or filename that is not a valid name or that is longer than allowed also results in this error.

94, 21

The file organization specified is invalid or unsupported, or the requested open operation is illegal on the specified organization.

94, 22

The minimum record length is invalid. The minimum record length specified in the RECORD CONTAINS clause for the filename exceeds the maximum record length.

94, 23

The maximum record length is invalid. The maximum record length specified in the RECORD CONTAINS clause of the filename exceeds 65280, or the indexed records are not compressed and the maximum record length exceeds the block size.

94, 24

The minimum block size is invalid. The minimum block size specified in the BLOCK CONTAINS clause of the filename exceeds the maximum block size.

94, 25

The maximum block size is invalid. The maximum block size specified in the BLOCK CONTAINS clause of the filename is too large. For indexed organization files, the computed block size is also a function of the maximum record size. In general, if the BLOCK CONTAINS clause is omitted, the runtime system will default to the valid block size that is a multiple of the disk sector size. For files with a very large record size, specifying BLOCK CONTAINS 1 RECORDS will yield the minimum possible block size.

94, 26

The record delimiter is invalid. A record delimiting technique other than LINE-SEQUENTIAL or BINARY-SEQUENTIAL was specified.

94, 27

The code-set specified is invalid or unsupported.

94, 28

The COLLATING SEQUENCE specified for an indexed file is invalid or unsupported.

94, 29

The record type attribute, fixed or variable, specified for the filename is unsupported.

94, 40
More than 254 alternate record keys are specified.

94, 50
The number of specified keys does not match the actual number of keys in the physical file.

94, 60
Insufficient memory to open the file. The amount of memory required to open a file can be reduced by specifying a smaller maximum block size in the BLOCK CONTAINS clause.

94, 61
There is insufficient disk space to create a file.

94, 62
The LINAGE parameters are invalid for an OPEN statement. One or more LINAGE parameters are negative or greater than 32767, LINAGE equals zero. FOOTING equals zero, of FOOTING is greater than LINAGE.

94, 63
An OPEN WITH LOCK was attempted on a system that does not support WITH LOCK.

95, 01
The file must be mass storage. The device-name specified for the file was DISC, DISK, or RANDOM, but the resultant file access name identifies a file that does not reside on a disk.

96
No file position is currently defined. A sequential READ operation was attempted, but the last READ or START operation was unsuccessful or returned an at end condition.

97, 01
One or more characters in the record are illegal in a LINE-SEQUENTIAL file.

97, 02
One or more characters could not be translated from the native character set to the external code-set.

97, 03
The length of the record area specified in the WRITE, REWRITE or RELEASE statement is less than the minimum record length of the file.

97, 04
The length of the record area specified in the WRITE, REWRITE or RELEASE statement is greater than the maximum record length of the file.

97, 05
The record read from the file is shorter than the minimum record length.

97, 06
The record read from the file is longer than the record area.

97, 07
A REWRITE statement attempted to change the length of a record in a sequential organization file.

97, 08
The LINAGE parameters are invalid for a WRITE statement. One or more LINAGE parameters are negative or greater than 32767, LINAGE equals zero, FOOTING equals zero, or FOOTING is greater than LINAGE.

97, 09
The TO LINE value is outside the page body.

98, 01
The indexed file structure includes a count of the number of times the file is currently open for modification. The count should be zero whenever a file in a single-user environment is opened or a file in a shared environment is opened WITH LOCK. If the count is nonzero when the file is opened WITH LOCK, a 98, 01 error is returned.

98, 02
A fatal error occurred during a DELETE, REWRITE, or WRITE statement when the file was last open. The index structure is inconsistent and must be rebuilt.

98, nn
Invalid file structure. The nn subcode may be useful in determining which runtime procedure detected the error. For an indexed organization file, there appears to be an inconsistency in the file structure. If the error occurs when the file is being read, it may be a disk read error. If the error occurs during a DELETE, REWRITE, or WRITE statement, a later OPEN statement will probably receive a 98, 02 error. For a sequential or relative organization file, this error usually indicates the file description does not match the organization of the file, record type, record delimiting technique or record length.

99
A DELETE, READ, or REWRITE statement failed because the record is locked by another user.

```
C:\RMCOB> runcobol e1

RM/COBOL-85 Runtime - Version 5.24.00  or DOS 2.00+.
Configured for 001 user.
Educational Version - Restrict d U
Copyright (c) 1985, 1992 by Li        tware Corp.  All rights reserved.
Registration Number: GZ-0000-0    01

ST 16 E1 C? e
THIS IS DISPLAYED BY PROGRAM E1: COUNT= 0000001

COBOL procedure error 204 at line 21 in E1 (C:\RMCOB\E1.COB) compiled 93/10/09
18:26:32.

C:\RMCOB>
```

Figure E.4

Data and Reference Errors (Error Code >= 100)

Runtime error codes of 100 or greater indicate procedure or data reference errors. The 204 code shown here means that an object file for a program to be executed cannot be found. In this case it is not a main program that cannot be located; it is a subprogram that is being CALLed.

Runtime error codes greater than 100 indicate procedure or data reference errors. Figure E.4 is an example of a common error of this type, received if you try to execute a program that doesn't exist or can't be found.

101

No operand exists corresponding to the referenced Linkage Section item. There are more data items specified in the Procedure Division header than are specified in the USING phrase of the CALL statement in the calling program. The Procedure Division header in the first (or main) program in the run unit may incorrectly specify more than one data item.

102

A reference to a variable length group is illegal because the value in the DEPENDING data item (data-name-1) is less than the minimum value (integer-1) or greater than the maximum value (integer-2) in the OCCURS clause.

103

An identifier or literal referenced in an INSPECT CONVERTING statement is illegal. The sending field might be coded redundantly, or have a different length than the receiving field.

104

A reference to data item is illegal because the computed composite subscript value for a subscripted reference has a value that is negative, zero or exceeds the maximum value for the referenced item. There may be a reference to a Linkage Section data item whose description specifies more characters than are present in the corresponding operand in the USING phrase of the CALL statement.

105
A subscript calculation overflowed or underflowed.

106
An index-name values indicates more than 65535 occurrences.

107
A reference modification is illegal. The reference modification offset value is less than or equal to zero, or is greater than the length of the data item being reference modified. A reference modification length value is less than or equal to zero, or is greater than the remaining length of the data item being reference modified after application of the offset value.

201
A CANCEL statement has attempted to cancel a program that is still active; that is, a program that has called, directly or indirectly, the program attempting to cancel.

202
The program-name on a CALL statement has value that is equal to spaces.

203
The program-name on the Runtime Command or CALL statement does not match any of the PROGRAM-ID names in any library but does match a valid RM/COBOL-85 library object filename.

204
The program-name on the Runtime Command or CALL statement does not match any of the PROGRAM-ID names in any library searched and does not match a valid RM/COBOL-85 object filename or non-COBOL executable file. A mismatch between versions of the compiler and runtime environment can also cause this problem.

205
A CALL statement has attempted to call a program that is still active; in other words, a program that has called, directly or indirectly, the program attempting the call is in error.

206
The called filename is not an RM/COBOL-85 object file or valid non-COBOL executable file.

207
There is not enough memory to load the program from the Runtime Command or the CALL statement, or to build the in-memory library structures indicated in the Runtime Command, or to reserve memory for the ACCEPT and DISPLAY buffers. This may be caused by memory fragmentation resulting from the dynamics of CALL and CANCEL operations and file I-O, or it may mean the requested program is too large for the available memory. More memory can be made available during a

SORT statement by using the T Runtime Command Option to reduce the memory requested by sort.

208
The ALTER statement has an additional undefined section or paragraph name.

209
The GOTO statement was not altered before execution of the statement was attempted.

210
The PERFORM statement attempts to perform an undefined section or paragraph.

211
An "E" level compilation error has been encountered. (You tried to execute a flawed object file!)

213
The RM/COBOL-85 object library file specified in the Runtime Command cannot be found.

214
The RM/COBOL-85 object library file specified in the Runtime Command does not contain a valid object program.

215
A PERFORM statement in an independent segment has performed a section or paragraph in a fixed segment that invoked (performed) a section or paragraph in a different independent segment.

216
An external item with the same name and type (data record, file connector or index name) as an existing external in the run unit has a different description than the existing external. The length of the record being shared may be different, or, for an index name, the span of the table item associated with the index name is different, or the index-name is associated with a different external record. For a file connector, any of the file control clauses, file description clauses, or record description lengths are different. For a relative organization external file connector, this error is caused if the new external does not reference the same external data item for the relative key as is referenced by the existing external file connector.

217
An external file connector is invalid since it indicates a SAME AREA or MULTIPLE FILE TAPE association. Typically, the compiler prevents this error from occurring by diagnosing the problem at compile time.

218
There is not enough memory to allocate the data structures necessary to support an external item declared in the program currently being loaded.

219

There is not enough memory to allocate the data structures necessary to support entry into a USE GLOBAL procedure following the occurrence of an I-O error for which the USE GLOBAL procedure is applicable. The program will be terminated as if no applicable USE procedure was found.

299

An attempt to use Instrumentation on a run unit failed because a program in the run unit contains more than 65535 source lines or there was insufficient memory to allocate the data collection structure for a program in the run.

301

There was insufficient memory available to initiate a sort or merge process. The default or specified sort memory size was insufficient to hold ten records of the record length to be sorted, or the specified sort memory size is not available. Use the T Runtime Command Option to increase the memory requested by the SORT statement.

302

Fewer than three intermediate files were available to begin a SORT statement. The sort procedure cannot begin unless it is able to create at least three intermediate files.

303

A record read from a MERGE file or SORT USING file was not long enough to include all the keys.

304

Too many out-of-sequence records were passed to the sort process. Use the T Runtime Command Option to increase the memory available to sort; or, divide the records to be sorted into several files, sort the several files, and merge the resulting files.

305

A SORT or MERGE statement was attempted while a sort or merge process was already active.

306

A RELEASE or RETURN statement was attempted and no sort or merge was active.

307

A RELEASE or RETURN statement was attempted for a sort or merge description other than the one currently being sorted or merged.

308

A RELEASE statement was attempted in an OUTPUT PROCEDURE, or a RETURN statement was attempted in an INPUT PROCEDURE.

309

A RETURN statement was attempted in an OUTPUT PROCEDURE after the at end condition was returned on the sort or merge file.

310

An application I/O statement was attempted on a file currently opened as a sort or merge USING or GIVING file.

E.5   Normal Program Ending Messages

The RM/COBOL-85 runtime system (RUNCOBOL) interprets and executes the object code produced for a program by the compiler. The object code being executed may consist of one or more object files; more than one object file is involved when a program CALLs subprograms. The collection of object files involved in the execution of a program is called a "run unit." The runtime system can either end execution normally or detect a logic failure in the execution of a program. Both of these outcomes are reported by the runtime system.

If the runtime system ends normally, it does so when it encounters a STOP RUN statement or a GOBACK statement in the main program of a run unit:

```
COBOL STOP RUN at line number in programname.
```

You can suppress this message by using the K runtime command option when you execute the program. If you execute a program this way, you get back to the DOS prompt immediately when the program ends rather than seeing the "COBOL STOP RUN at" message:

```
C:> runcobol first1 k
```

In RM/COBOL-85 you can also code the STOP statement like this without the word RUN:

```
STOP 158.
```

or

```
STOP WS-VALUE
```

or

```
STOP "here is a message".
```

When you use a literal number, numeric (PIC 9) data name, character literal, or character (PIC X) data name in a STOP statement like this, the runtime system treats the stop as a pause. It provides the number or character string on the screen in a line that takes this format:

```
"literal or data item" at line number in ... Continue (Y/N)?
```

If you enter Y or y to this prompt, execution continues with the next executable statement. If you enter N or n, execution ends as if an ordinary STOP RUN statement had been encountered here.

Appendix F

Troubleshooting Common Problems

F.1   Hints and Helps

his appendix lists problems that you may encounter while attempting to use RM/COBOL-85. Browse through this appendix to become familiar with the advice listed here if you encounter situations that you cannot resolve in any other way.

F.2   Compiler or Program Run Fails; System Locks Up

Possible cause: This problem can result from use of incompatible versions of RM/COBOL-85.

Solution: If you already have the earlier version of RM/COBOL-85 installed on your computer, make sure you install the newer version in a different subdirectory, or completely replace your old RM/COBOL-85 software with the newer version.

Background: Some enhancements exist in the COBOL syntax supported by Version 5.24 of the RM/COBOL-85 compiler, which is supplied with this guide. All programs that compiled successfully under Version 4.10, which was supplied with the first edition of this guide, should work with this version of the compiler. But you can't, however, mix compiled programs or RM/COBOL-85 software components between versions. For example, you can't compile with the newer compiler and run a program under the old runtime environment, and you can't use the older compiler to prepare programs for use with the new version of the runtime software.

F.3   Compiler Cannot Process a Program

Possible cause: Program created using a word processor was saved as a word processed file instead of an ASCII ("DOS") file.

Solution: Read the program into the word processor that was used to create it, and save it as an ASCII file.

Background: Word processing files make unique use of the eighth bit of some bytes, and include nonprinting formatting characters. These characters have no place in COBOL program source code. Review Chapter 4 for additional background and a means to quickly test a program or file to see if it contains ASCII data or word processor codes.

F.4   Unresolvable Compiler Errors in Source Code

Possible cause: You may have coded beyond beyond column 72 on a line of source code in a program prepared with a text editor.

Solution: Examine all of the longest lines of your program using your text editor, and copy in the comment line housed in RULER.CBL on your RM/COBOL-85 diskette. Shorten or continue any lines that extend beyond column 72.

Background: As with mainframe IBM compilers (but not VAX COBOL) the RM/COBOL-85 compiler will ignore any characters in column 73 and beyond on any line of source code. Code in columns 73 and beyond is visible on your screen and printouts, but you may not realize that it is not "seen" by the compiler.

F.5 Runtime System Can't Locate Subprogram Modules

Possible cause: You may have placed all of your subprograms into one source code file, and compiled this to produce one object file. If you do this, you need to tell the runtime system the name and location of the single object file produced from compiling the subprograms.

Solution: Use the L option at runtime indicating the path and file name of the object file. This runtime option is described in detail in Appendix C. The general format of this command is:

```
C:> runcobol pgmname L=\subdir\filename
```

Background: You can organize your subprograms into one source code file, separating each program from the others with an END PROGRAM progname statement. This will allow you to compile all subprograms at once, and create one object file that RM/COBOL-85 regards as a "library."

F.6 Fields Out of Place in Data Read by a Program

Possible cause: You created the file using a word processor, establishing it as an ASCII file, but forgot to code the clause ORGANIZATION IS LINE SEQUENTIAL in the SELECT for it.

Solution: Code the clause ORGANIZATION IS LINE SEQUENTIAL in the SELECT statement, as illustrated in Chapter 5, section 5.2 of this guide. The general format of this statement is:

```
SELECT PHONE-CALL-FILE      ASSIGN TO DISK 'F1.DAT'
    ORGANIZATION IS LINE SEQUENTIAL.
```

Background: A line sequential file is an ASCII or "DOS" file. It has line feed/carriage return characters at the end of each line, where you pressed the *<Enter>* key (carriage return) when you created the data. If you omit the ORGANIZATION IS LINE SEQUENTIAL phrase, RM/COBOL-85 interprets your SELECT as indicating a pure data file, in which there is nothing at all between records. See the discussion in Chapter 4 for additional background.

You need to code ORGANIZATION IS LINE SEQUENTIAL when the data you are reading has been prepared as an ASCII file with a text editor or when it has been output as LINE SEQUENTIAL by a program. You normally output sequential data files and report files as LINE SEQUENTIAL. But not all files are written as LINE SEQUENTIAL. Indexed files cannot be output as LINE SEQUENTIAL, and files containing packed decimal data cannot be output this way. Indexed files and files with packed data fields contain bytes with bit patterns that conflict with the line feed/carriage return characters that delimit the end of LINE SEQUENTIAL records.

F.7   Data Read by Program Contains Spurious Characters

Possible cause: Data created using a word processor was saved as a word processed file instead of an ASCII ("DOS") file.

Solution: Read the file into the word processor that was used to create it, and save it as an ASCII file.

Background: Word processing files make unique use of the eighth bit of some bytes, and include nonprinting formatting characters. These characters have no place in data files processed by your COBOL programs. Review Chapter 4 for additional background and a means to quickly test a file to see if it contains ASCII data or word processor codes.

F.8   Subprograms Fail to Execute

Possible cause: You used too many levels of subprograms for the educational version of the compiler.

Solution: Do not have a subprogram attempt to CALL another subprogram. This may require a design change in your programming approach.

Background: The educational version of the RM/COBOL-85 compiler is set with certain limitations to preclude its use commercially. One of these limitations is the restriction of CALLs to one level deep. While you can use CALL to invoke a subprogram, a subprogram cannot invoke another subprogram. Review the complete list of educational version restrictions in section 1.2 of this guide.

F.9   Illegal Characters in LINE SEQUENTIAL File (97, 01)

Possible cause: You are trying to write a record that contains packed decimal (COMP-3 or PACKED-DECIMAL) data to a file defined as ORGANIZATION IS LINE SEQUENTIAL.

Solution: Either define all of the numeric fields in the record without a usage type of COMP-3 or PACKED-DECIMAL, or remove the ORGANIZATION IS LINE SEQUENTIAL clause from the SELECT statement for the file.

Background: LINE SEQUENTIAL files are ASCII files, which have line feed/carriage return characters at the end of every line. This type of file cannot contain packed decimal data because certain numeric values stored in packed decimal form create the same bit patterns as line feed and carriage return. You can write packed decimal data to BINARY SEQUENTIAL files, which is what you create if you do not specify LINE SEQUENTIAL. (See also the compiler B and V options in Appendix C.)

Index

Notes

Notes

Notes

Notes

Notes

Notes

Notes

Notes